Bollywood Babylon

Asian Cinema series

Edited by Anne Ciecko, *University of Massachusetts-Amherst*

Asia, the world's largest and most populous continent, is also the world's largest film producer. Much film history, theory and criticism reinforces Hollywood and European cinema as the dominant and exemplary paradigm, relegating Asian cinemas to the margins. The Asian Cinema series aims to re-position Asian cinema at the center of film studies and will cover national, regional and pan-Asian cinema as well as the global, transnational and diasporic flows of cinematic production, distribution and reception.

ISSN 1744-8719

Titles in the *Asian Cinema* series

Contemporary Asian Cinema: Popular Culture in a Global Frame
edited by Anne Ciecko

Bollywood Babylon

Interviews with Shyam Benegal

Edited by
William van der Heide

Oxford · New York

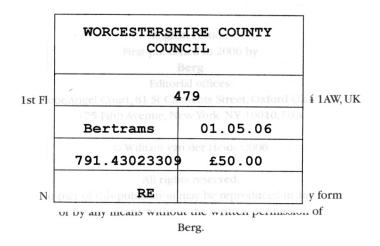

First published in 2006 by
Berg

Editorial offices:
1st Floor, Angel Court, 81 St Clements Street, Oxford OX4 1AW, UK
175 Fifth Avenue, New York, NY 10010, USA

Berg is the imprint of Oxford International Publishers Ltd.

Library of Congress Cataloging-in-Publication Data
Benegal, Shyam, 1934–
    Bollywood Babylon : interviews with Shyam Benegal / edited by William
van der Heide.—English ed.
        p. cm.—(Asian cinema series)
    Includes bibliographical references and index.
    ISBN-13: 978-1-84520-405-1 (pbk.)
    ISBN-10: 1-84520-405-0 (pbk.)
    ISBN-13:   978-1-84520-404-4 (hardback)
    ISBN-10: 1-84520-404-2 (hardback)
  1. Benegal, Shyam, 1934– 2. Motion picture producers and directors—
India—Interviews. I. Title. II. Series.

    PN1998.3.B467A3 2006
    791.4302'33092–dc22

                                                                    2005036265

British Library Cataloguing-in-Publication data
A catalogue record for this book is available from the British Library.

            ISBN-13   978 1 84520 404 4 (Cloth)
                      978 1 84520 405 1 (Paper)

            ISBN-10   1 84520 404 2 (Cloth)
                      1 84520 405 0 (Paper)

Typeset by JS Typesetting Ltd, Porthcawl, Mid Glamorgan
Printed in the United Kingdom by Biddles Ltd, King's Lynn

www.bergpublishers.com

To Julia and Balthazare

Contents

List of Illustrations

Front cover illustration: Publicity brochure of Mandira Devi (Rekha), Zubeidaa (Karisma Kapoor) and Victor (Manoj Bajpai) for *Zubeidaa* (2000). Courtesy of Shyam Benegal Sahyadri Films

Acknowledgements

This book is based on a number of lengthy taped interviews with Shyam Benegal that took place at his office and his home in Mumbai/Bombay in January 1999 and January 2003. The interviews are presented in full, although they have been edited for the reader, while attempting to retain their colloquial nature.

The interviews touch on all of Shyam Benegal's feature films (and some of the documentary films) completed or in production at the time, but the better-known films are given more attention than the others. Synopses are provided for all the films, although, for the same reason, some of the synopses are more detailed than others. Since I am not conversant with any Indian languages, my access to the films is limited to English subtitled editions, whether available on DVD (as an increasing number of the films are) or via television broadcasts. For this project, Shyam Benegal was my 'language guide' to the extent that that was necessary. Often it was more a matter of him explaining very specific cultural events (e.g. Chaumasa and Baramasa) or identifying particular historical figures (e.g. Alladiya Khan and Kesarbai Kerkar).

I wish to thank Shyam Benegal for the time he set aside for these interviews, especially those in January 2003, when he was extremely busy with the final stages of pre-production for the film then called *Netaji*, which was eventually released as *Bose: The Forgotten Hero*. I also thank his staff, especially Raj Pius, for their assistance in organizing the interviews and providing copies of publicity brochures. My appreciation also extends to Vanraj Bhatia and Shama Zaidi, who, at short notice, talked to me about their contributions to the films and their working relationships with Shyam Benegal.

I am grateful to the University of Newcastle (Australia), where I taught in the film studies programme from 1997 to 2003, for the two research grants that enabled me to undertake the trips to India.

The illustrations have been provided courtesy of Shyam Benegal Sahyadri Films, except for the photo in Interview 2, which was taken by Julia van der Heide, for which she is thanked.

Introduction: Shyam Benegal's Life and Films

I met Shyam Benegal in May 1997 at the Museum of Sydney, where he was introducing his latest film, *The Making of the Mahatma* (1996). I had seen many of his earlier films in the previous ten years on Australian television and was struck by their insistent social message (particularly class and caste issues), their emphasis on the plight of women (often expressed through their sexuality and in a more forthright manner than most other Indian films I had seen) and their stylistic and technical assurance. During this period, I had been teaching film studies at the University of Canberra and had gravitated towards Asian cinema, which had been undergoing exciting developments. I had always been interested in the films of Satyajit Ray, but in the 1990s popular Indian films (from the 1950s onwards) became available on videotape (often of poor quality and lacking English subtitles) through Indian food shops in Australia.[1] The resulting cinematic discovery also led me to see something of Bollywood in Shyam Benegal's films. I sought out Shyam Benegal at that screening in Sydney and suggested that I would like to interview him about his films and his approach to filmmaking, and that the interviews ought to be detailed and extensive with a view to them becoming the basis for a monograph about him. He agreed on the spot, but it took eighteen months before we were able to commence this project and it was not until five and a half years later that the interviews were completed.

BIOGRAPHY

While the ensuing interview chapters cover the relevant aspects of Benegal's life, the film industry in which he works and his films, it is useful to anticipate some of the major issues here. Shyam Benegal was born in 1934 in Hyderabad, the capital of the South Indian state of Andhra Pradesh. His father was a still photographer and, as a hobby, made 16 mm home movies. This led to the young Shyam Benegal making his own short films and developing a passion for filmmaking. He also watched a lot of American films at the local cinema but, perhaps more importantly, his father determined which Indian films the family would see on their monthly visit to the cinema. The films were chosen from only two studios: Prabhat (located in Pune, south of Bombay) and New Theatres

(Calcutta). These studios produced films that dealt with social and nationalist issues, subjects dear to the heart of his father, who was a committed Gandhian. It could well be argued that Shyam Benegal would eventually make films in the tradition of those studios – popular socially oriented Hindi-language films. He has never achieved the commercial success of those studios, but then Indian film audiences from the 1970s to the present day are very different from those of that earlier period. As a young man, Benegal founded the Hyderabad Film Society and chose Satyajit Ray's *Pather Panchali* (Song of the Road, 1955) as its first film; it was a harbinger of the central role that Ray would play in his conception of cinema. Benegal moved to Bombay in 1958 to pursue a career in cinema, although he had already decided against entering the Bollywood film industry, instead opting to learn the skills of filmmaking in the advertising industry. During the twelve years he worked in advertising, he made over 1,000 films. However, he never lost sight of his goal of making feature films and eventually quit the advertising business to develop the script for what became his first fiction film, *Ankur* (The Seedling, 1973).

INDIAN CINEMA

After the coming of sound, the Indian film industry expanded rapidly, partly because audiences could now hear the music of the songs and dances that were so central an aspect of traditional Indian culture. Films were made in many different Indian languages, but already in the early 1930s, Hindi-language films, made in Bombay, dominated (Maharashtra, the state in which Bombay is located, itself made films in the Marathi language). While, in time, the combined output of films in South Indian languages (Telugu, Tamil, Kannada and Malayalam) would exceed those made in Hindi, the Hindi cinema has remained the most commercially successful and most influential film industry in India.[2] The Indian film industry as a whole was to become the largest film industry in the world in 1971, overtaking Japan; its current output is around 800 films per year.[3] There is general agreement that the 1950s was the 'Golden Age' of Indian cinema, exemplified by Bollywood directors such as Raj Kapoor, Guru Dutt, Mehboob Khan and Bimal Roy, the last of whom actually started in New Theatres, although all of them were influenced by the Prabhat and New Theatres studios mentioned above. The first International Film Festival of India, organized by the Indian government, was held in 1952 and travelled to places such as Delhi, Bombay, Calcutta and Madras.[4] It exposed Indian filmmakers to Italian neorealism and led to directors like Bimal Roy incorporating some of its elements into his films. However, it was Satyajit Ray who adapted these European 'art cinema' strategies to Indian subject matter. His Bengali-language films, starting with *Pather Panchali*, did not initiate a new film movement, but did have a significant impact on young Indian filmmakers working in regional languages.

The 1960s saw the establishment of the Film Finance Corporation (FFC), which was originally charged with assisting and promoting the mainstream film industry, but became, through the direction of Indira Gandhi herself, a funding organization for 'modest but off-beat films of talented and promising people in the field'.[5] This set in motion the New Indian Cinema movement, also labelled the Parallel Cinema or the Alternative Cinema. Its first two films, Mrinal Sen's *Bhuvan Shome* and Mani Kaul's *Uski Roti* (A Day's Bread), were released in 1969 and were both in Hindi (the so-called 'language of Babylon' because it was the language of Bollywood), but most of the FFC-produced films were in regional languages. It was in this environment that Shyam Benegal completed his first feature film, *Ankur* (made in Hindi, as were most of his subsequent films), which was generally regarded as part of the same new cinema, despite the fact that it was privately funded. However, some filmmakers and critics at the time argued that its funding (from the advertising industry), its ideology (Nehruvian 'developmentalism'), its showy style (considered too close to Bollywood) and its commercial success placed it outside the parameters of the New Indian Cinema. *Ankur*, Benegal's later films and the films of directors like Govind Nihalani (Benegal's regular cinematographer till the early 1980s) were therefore defined as 'middle cinema', a term that Benegal himself rejects.[6] Nevertheless, it seems to me that Shyam Benegal has always engaged with Bollywood, particularly in the last ten years, but his films have remained quite distinct in their ideology, social agendas, narrative structures, engagement with spectacle (which includes the use of music, song and dance) and modes of address (through character analysis rather than character identification).

CRITICAL RESPONSES

Over the years Shyam Benegal and his films have been both praised and be-rated. He has been honoured in India on many occasions, most recently with the Indira Gandhi Award for National Integration that he received in 2004. It was presented to him by India's Prime Minister, Dr Manmohan Singh, who described Benegal as 'one of our most distinguished, innovative and socially conscious film makers' and noted that 'The empowerment of women has been an important underlying theme in almost all his films. In *Ankur*, in *Manthan*, in *Bhumika* and even in *Mandi*, Benegal's women are intelligent, powerful, purposeful, determined, yet humane and compassionate.'[7] The praise is fulsome, but what is most interesting is the particular films that are mentioned. *Mandi* (Market Place) was made in 1983 and the others in the 1970s. Like Satyajit Ray and, for that matter, Orson Welles, Shyam Benegal is cursed to being defined by his earliest films; the focus has always been on the films of the 1970s and particularly on *Ankur*.

Indian cinema has had little exposure in American and British film magazines and journals, but it is nevertheless striking how few times Benegal has been mentioned in them. For example, the British film magazine *Sight and Sound* has reviewed only one of his films, *Ankur*, and discussed two other films, *Manthan* (The Churning, 1976) and *Trikal* (Past, Present, Future, 1985) in two separate articles on Indian cinema.[8] The writers responded positively to the films and compared Benegal favourably to Satyajit Ray. Since then, not a word, not even when there were substantial retrospectives of his films at the National Film Theatre in London in 1988 and 2002. There has been a more active interest displayed in Benegal in recent years by non-Indian writers of monographs. Two books, one on the Indian cinema in general (Yves Thoraval's *The Cinemas of India*), the other on India's art cinema (John W. Hood's *The Essential Mystery: Major Filmmakers of Indian Art Cinema*) were published in 2000 in India and both included substantial sections on Benegal's films. Most impressive, however, is Sangeeta Datta's *Shyam Benegal*, published in 2002 by the British Film Institute as part of its World Directors Series; it discusses all of his films in some detail and provides a biographical and Indian cinema context. Once again, these authors regard Benegal's work highly, although there is a preference for the earlier films, and the comparison with Ray, where voiced, is not in Benegal's favour.

As far as Indian critics are concerned, there seem to be two quite different responses to Benegal's work. The first group, epitomized by Iqbal Masud, Chidananda Das Gupta, B. D. Garga and Aruna Vasudev, treat Benegal as a major director, confronting important social issues in films that are aesthetically pleasurable, but quite distinct from the commercial Hindi cinema.[9] The films are considered to have failings in structure, in their narrative elaboration and in their social critique, but their overall power and social concern are never questioned. A comparison with Satyajit Ray is also never far away, as in Das Gupta's comment on the differences between their films on the Indian Mutiny: 'Benegal's accent on confrontations and the apparent simplicity of his resolutions', referring to *Junoon* (Obsession, 1978), is set against Ray's *Shatranj Ke Khiladi* (The Chess Players, 1977) with its 'delicate and personal style, rich with nuance'.[10] Overall, Benegal's films are criticized for not fully observing the conventions of the well-crafted, protagonist-driven, psychologically motivated, realist narratives of the nineteenth-century novel and of the art cinema, especially that identified with Satyajit Ray. Benegal's so-called 'middle cinema' (sometimes caricatured as a middle-of-the-road one[11]) may not actually be a compromise between Babylon and art, but an 'in-between' place, a border position from which to explore the surrounding domains and formulate a heterogeneous rhetoric that encompasses both synthesis and difference.

The second group of Indian critics are the more academically oriented ones, such as Ashish Rajadhyaksha and M. Madhava Prasad, who argue that Benegal's blend of nationalist propagandizing narratives and advertising stylistics fatally compromises his work, denying the films the socio-cultural significance of the Bollywood cinema and the formal-cultural importance of filmmakers like Mani Kaul and Kumar Shahani.[12] Mani Kaul himself articulated this attitude in a documentary entitled *Cinema Wallahs* (Christopher Spencer, UK, 1998). He argues that around 1974 a split arose in the New Cinema movement with the arrival of a new kind of filmmaker from the advertising world, and that this cinema came to be called the middle cinema. This resulted in there being three kinds of cinema: 'the popular cinema [Bollywood], the populist cinema, if I may say so [middle cinema], and people who are struggling with cinematography [such as himself and Kumar Shahani]'. Ashish Rajadhyaksha describes the FFC as launching the New Cinema, resulting in avant-garde films by Kaul and Shahani 'as well as what came, with the work especially of Shyam Benegal, to define further an aesthetic of "state realism"'.[13] Apart from implying that Shyam Benegal's films were state-funded, which they were not until *Suraj Ka Satvan Ghoda* (The Seventh Horse of the Sun, 1992), the reference to 'state realism' has overtones of propaganda and ideological collusion. In another article Rajadhyaksha refers to Benegal's cinema as '"NFDC" realism' (the NFDC, the National Film Development Corporation, replaced the FFC in 1980), which 'purports to address fully formed members of civil society, functioning under the authority of their gaze, and usually constitutes an invitation to such audiences to, as it were, participate in and sit in judgement over whatever moral and ethical contradictions it presents to them in its presentation of "reality"'.[14] Such comments are very general and rather abstract, condemning Benegal as a ventriloquist, inexorably articulating the ideologies of the state and of the bourgeoisie.

On the other hand, M. Madhava Prasad analyses some of Benegal's films, specifically the 'rural trilogy' – *Ankur*, *Nishant* (The Night's End, 1975) and *Manthan* – in considerable detail in a chapter of his book *Ideology of the Hindi Film* entitled 'The Developmental Aesthetic'. Benegal's films are regarded in a more complex and contradictory way than Rajadhyaksha allowed, but the conclusion is much the same: Benegal's cinema 'was able to forge a new aesthetic of statist realism' through its combination of Satyajit Ray's realist approach, the exotic and sexualized feudal narratives of the regional cinemas and the homogenizing and nationalist adoption of Hindi.[15] Nevertheless, the commentaries on the three films are always stimulating, particularly in highlighting their relationship to the contemporary political and social concerns of 1970s India. In discussing *Ankur* and *Nishant*, Prasad argues that these 'narratives of feudalism' are and must be set in pre-Independence India, because Benegal's cinema cannot admit the existence of a 'still ongoing revolution ... [where] the nation-state is not yet governed by contract'.[16] However, his assertion that these two films are set in pre-1949 India is at odds with Shyam Benegal's comments in the fourth interview. Once again, the categorical nature of Prasad's argument needs to be approached with some caution.

It may be more productive to approach Benegal's work in a less conceptual manner, concentrating on specific tendencies, whether socio-political, cultural or aesthetic. This might take the form of an examination of the functions of the past and the present in his films. Most of the films deal with the past, but from *Bhumika* (The Role, 1976) on, the past and the present are strongly interconnected, with the present becoming a position from which to interrogate the past, rather than to indulge in it nostalgically. Similarly, the urban–rural interaction, so significant in a country like India, is constantly addressed in the films, even if only one of these locations is physically present, for example the urban background of the film crew in *Samar* (Conflict, 1999) or the urban migration dream of a couple in *Hari-Bhari* (Fertility, 2000). Other issues that could be productively tackled are the complex relationship between the spectator and the protagonists (with most of whom it is not easy to identify) and the changing role of music and song in the films – minimal in *Ankur* and idiosyncratically Bollywood-like in *Zubeidaa* (2000). Some of these matters are raised in the interviews in this book, which aims to contribute to an analysis of Benegal's films as well as to enable Shyam Benegal to comment on his own films.

THE INTERVIEWS

The interviews concentrate on Benegal's feature films and emphasize the social, cultural and aesthetic characteristics, although there is frequently some commentary on the production process. However, the first three interviews cover more general issues. The first interview is devoted to a documentary film, *Satyajit Ray*, which Benegal made in 1984 about that distinguished Indian film director. This film was chosen to open the discussion because it attests to the extent of Ray's influence on Benegal, from his decision to become a filmmaker to his approach to *mise-en-scène*, that is, the staging and shooting of shots and scenes. More significantly, the film largely consists of Ray talking to Benegal about his life and his films, and is an example of the 'interactive' documentary.[17] As such, the discussion of this film highlights the process of interviewing, which is as relevant to the methodologies adopted for this book as it is for the film *Satyajit Ray*, in particular the agendas that interviewers bring to such enterprises and the stories that interviewees want to tell. This discussion of the film's interviewing strategies may therefore also prompt the reader to become aware of the choices and procedures undertaken in the transformation of the recorded interviews into the present book. The same year, 1984, also saw the release of a documentary on Jawaharlal Nehru (*Nehru*); Benegal comments on the similar approach he took with that film and on the significance of both Ray and Nehru as Indian modernists.

The second interview addresses the formative influences on Benegal's career, familial as well as cinematic, by focusing on his 'life story' and its relationship to his work. Benegal discusses his father's home movie activities and his influence over the films he and his siblings watched. He mentions his relationship with his cousin Guru Dutt, whose films he admires, even though as a young man he already knew he wanted to make very different films. Benegal then describes his arrival in Bombay and his successful career as a director of advertising films, which taught him the basics of filmmaking. His years in the advertising industry in the 1950s and 1960s had a significant impact on his subsequent filmmaking – positively as far as Benegal is concerned. However, for many Indian film critics, this 'commercial' activity has tainted his feature films, even though Satyajit Ray's similar pre-*Pather Panchali* career has raised little adverse comment. Benegal argues that he remains committed to making documentary films, but that feature films represent a more effective way of reaching people. The interview also touches on the vexed question of authorship in the cinema and the complex impact of life experiences on creative work. Finally there is some discussion of how Benegal himself sees his development over the last thirty years.

The most ubiquitous of influences is generally considered to be the film culture within which one works and this is the thrust of the third interview, 'On Indian Cinema'. The interview ranges across the breadth (more than the depth) of Indian cinema and, to some extent, world cinema, covering industry practices, individual filmmakers, different movements and policy issues. Benegal acknowledges the appeal of the commercial Indian cinema, but emphasizes the much greater cultural specificity of filmmakers like Satyajit Ray. The discussion then covers the two other important Bengali directors, Ritwik Ghatak and Mrinal Sen, the avant-garde directors Mani Kaul and Kumar Shahani, the problematic term 'middle cinema', contemporaries like Govind Nihalani and Ketan Mehta, and diasporic filmmakers such as Shekhar Kapur and Mira Nair.

The next four interviews deal with all of the feature films and one television series. Some films are given less attention than others, either because the interviewer was not able to see the films – *Charandas Chor* (Charandas the Thief, 1975), *Aarohan* (The Ascent, 1982) – or they were viewed without English subtitles – *Kondura* (The Sage from the Sea, 1979), *Antarnaad* (Inner Voice, 1992), *Sardari Begum* (1996). The films are mostly discussed in chronological order and their division into four interviews is based on perceived commonalities. The fourth interview concentrates on the so-called 'rural trilogy'. These films are primarily concerned with contemporary social issues (gender, class and caste) and could thus be labelled as 'socials', a term that represents one of the major Bollywood film genres, especially in the pre-1970s period; it refers to films dealing with contemporary life (see note 3, Interview 5). Particular emphasis is given to *Ankur*, not only because it is Benegal's first feature film, but also because it remains his best-known film. Benegal mentions the story's origin in an event that occurred near where he lived as a teenager and the process by which it became *Ankur*. He describes how he established his production crew and found his actors, including Shabana Azmi and Anant Nag. The discussion then looks at the film in detail, in terms of its structure, style and themes. This approach is also brought to bear on the subsequent films of the trilogy, although specific aspects are pursued in each case, for example the significance of the *Ramayana* in *Nishant* and the Nehruvian development agenda in *Manthan*. The interview also mentions Benegal's second feature film, a comedy called *Charandas Chor*, an unusual genre choice and one to which Benegal has not returned, with the qualified exception of *Mandi*.

The fifth interview covers the period from the mid-1970s to the early 1980s. This group of films represent a broadening of Benegal's interests, stylistically and thematically. The films are more eclectic than the earlier films: a fictional re-creation of the autobiography of a well-known Bollywood actress that is also a homage to that film industry (*Bhumika*); an example of another unusual film genre for Benegal – a psychological drama – made in two separate languages, Telugu and Hindi (respectively titled *Anugraham* and *Kondura*); a historical romance set during the 1857 Indian Mutiny, which Indians call the First War of Independence (*Junoon*); a contemporary adaptation of the Indian epic the *Mahabharata*, making the film an example of the 'modern mythological' genre (*Kalyug* – The Machine Age, 1980); and a drama about land reform, commissioned by the Bengal government (*Aarohan*). *Bhumika* remains one of Benegal's most popular films, as does *Junoon*; the latter film, like *Kalyug*, was produced by (and starred) Shashi Kapoor, a major Bollywood star. These three films are given extensive treatment in this interview.

Interview six starts with a discussion of *Mandi*, a comedy-drama about a brothel. Like *Bhumika*, it could be described as a 'courtesan film', but it is also Benegal's first ensemble film and therefore somewhat in the vein of the Bollywood 'multi-starrer' phenomenon of the 1970s. Two other films of this period, *Trikal* and *Susman* (The Essence, 1986), could also be called ensemble films. The former is a historical drama about an extended Catholic Goan family on the eve of the forcible departure from that state of its Portuguese colonizer; the film is unusual because of its incorporation of magic realist elements, influenced by Benegal's reading of Latin American writers such as Gabriel García Márquez. The latter deals with the difficult working situation and personal conflicts within a weaving family and was financed by the Indian handloom co-operatives; the film is striking for its complex *mise-en-scène*, its concern with the craft of handloom in the face of industrial weaving practices and the functions of official Indian cultural programmes. The two major documentaries produced at this time, *Nehru* and *Satyajit Ray*, were discussed in the first interview. The last film covered in this interview is *Antarnaad*, a drama about a Ghandian movement that promotes personal and social self-esteem. As with *Manthan* and *Susman*, the funding was provided by the organization that became the subject of the film's narrative. Benegal's most ambitious production during this period was the fifty-three-hour television series, *Bharat Ek Khoj* (The Discovery of India, 1988), a history of India from the earliest times to the late 1940s, based on Jawaharlal Nehru's book, *The Discovery of India*. Benegal describes the importance of his (and Nehru's) version of the history of India in the face of increasing sectarianism.

The films of the 1990s are the concern of the seventh (and longest) interview. Like *Bhumika* and *Mandi*, the first film of this period represents a new direction for Benegal. *Suraj Ka Satvan Ghoda* is his most complex and self-conscious narrative, being about storytelling and the interpretation of stories; nevertheless it does not erase the social and interpersonal relationships so central to his earlier films. On the other hand, *The Making of the Mahatma*, an Indian/South African co-production, is one of his simplest films, narratively and stylistically; it concentrates on Gandhi's South African experience, which lasted twenty-one years and made him the nationalist leader he was to become in India, but it also touches upon the Indian diaspora in South Africa as a significant political and social force. *Samar* and *Hari-Bhari* were both financed by Indian government ministries. *Samar* deals with the contentious issue of untouchability, presented self-reflexively through the story of a film crew coming to a village to re-create a notorious event of some years earlier and finding that the issue affects them as much as it did the villagers. The subject matter of *Hari-Bhari* is women's reproductive rights and is set in a Muslim family of three generations. The film has some of the narrative complexity of *Suraj Ka Satvan Ghoda*, but uses songs in a manner approaching the pre-1990s Bollywood tradition. Finally, there is the 'Khalid Mohamed' trilogy, although the films, *Mammo* (1994), *Sardari Begum* and *Zubeidaa*, were not made consecutively. Khalid Mohamed is an Indian film critic whose life story attracted the attention of Shyam Benegal, resulting in Mohamed being invited to script the three films. Mammo was his grandmother's sister, Sardari Begum was a distant aunt and Zubeidaa was his mother. All three films are structured around an adult figure (the Mohamed character in the first and third film, and Sardari Begum's niece in the second) attempting to investigate and solve a puzzle arising from the past. The films become increasingly more complex and more spectacular, culminating in the most Bollywood-like film in Benegal's career, *Zubeidaa*. Benegal argues that in this film he set out to rejuvenate the relationship between songs and narrative that has become so mechanical in contemporary Bollywood cinema.

The last interview discusses the film that Benegal was working on at our last meeting. The film was then called *Netaji*, but it was released in 2005 as *Bose: The Forgotten Hero*. This is Benegal's most ambitious and expensive film and it deals with the last five years (basically the period of the Second World War) of Subhash Chandra Bose, India's most renowned freedom fighter, as he tried to convince the Russians, the Germans and the Japanese to help him eject the British from India. Benegal describes his interest in Bose in relation to other historical figures he has dealt with, especially Nehru and Gandhi. The interview concludes with some general comments on the changing nature of film distribution, including new technologies such as DVD and VCD, and on the demographics of Indian film audiences.

Notes

1. My discovery of and response to Indian cinema is discussed in more detail in van der Heide, 1996.
2. Rajadhyaksha and Willemen, 1999: 30.
3. Thoraval, 2000: 45-6.
4. Vasudev, 1986: 7.
5. Quoted in Rajadhyaksha and Willemen, 1999: 162.
6. The debates about the politics and aesthetics of the New Indian Cinema are complex, often confusing and certainly antagonistic. One particularly interesting, although strongly opinionated, account is M. Madhava Prasad's *Ideology of the Hindi Film* (1998), especially Chapter 5: 'The Moment of Disaggregation'.
7. *Times Foundation* (2004).
8. Gillett, 1976: 123; Milne, 1977: 95; Malcolm, 1986: 174.
9. Masud, 1985; Masud and Singh, 1989; Das Gupta, 1980: 38; Garga, 1996: 246-50; Vasudev, 1986: 40-1.
10. Das Gupta, 1980: 38.
11. Masud and Singh, 1989: 26.
12. Rajadhyaksha, 1996, 1998, 2000; Rajadhyaksha and Willemen, 1999; Prasad, 1998.
13. Rajadhyaksha, 1998: 537.
14. Rajadhyaksha, 2000: 278.
15. Prasad, 1998: 190-6.
16. Prasad, 1998: 196-7.
17. Nichols, 1991: 33.

Interview 1
On Satyajit Ray

Figure 1: Satyajit Ray interviewed by Shyam Benegal in *Satyajit Ray* (1984)

William van der Heide (WvdH): I'd like to start our conversation with the film that you made on Satyajit Ray in 1984: *Satyajit Ray*.[1] In the introduction to the published script of this documentary, Samik Bandyopadhyay suggests that Ray would have liked the film to be more Benegal than Ray – for it to be a response to his career.[2] Do you think that is the way it has turned out or is it more Ray than Benegal?

Shyam Benegal (SB): No, it was always meant to be a film on Ray, not on me. I was there to get to know as much as I could about him and his work and I wanted to remain as anonymous as possible in the process. After the film was done, Ray felt that he would have liked more Benegal and less Ray.

WvdH: More of Benegal than there was?

SB: But that was not the intention at all. The intention was the way I made it. The film was about him and I wanted as exhaustive an exploration both of his work and of the sources of his inspiration as possible. He probably felt that I should have been equally explored in the process – but that was never my intention.

WvdH: It was your intention to remain fairly much the invisible shaper of this particular documentary.

SB: Precisely.

WvdH: So Ray was the focus of attention and your main interest was in his work.

SB: That was the main thing. Ray was in many ways quite an extraordinary figure in Indian cinema because he broke with tradition in a manner that nobody else had done. He was a modernist in a very interesting sense. Unlike a lot of filmmakers who made films of social concern, Ray broke away from what one might call the normal definition of film entertainment in Indian terms. There is a very specific kind of form that Indian cinema uses which makes it different from any other cinema in the world. Our narratives are studded with songs and musical interludes, which can be traced back to the theatrical forms that we have developed. We have a text on the theatre called the *Natya Sastra* that goes back to the first or second century AD. Both classical as well as folk forms are based on a particular theory called the *nava rasa* theory. *Nava rasa* are the nine essences. There is typically a blend of nine *rasas* around one main *rasa*, which is usually love or heroism.[3]

WvdH: So Ray was a person who distinguished himself by being quite different in his approach to filmmaking.

SB: Yes, and I think that his approach had a great deal to do with his own background. You see, he belonged to a community that was part of the Bengal Renaissance. In nineteenth-century Bengal, there was a group of people called *Brahmos* – their meditative and religious practices were part of that reformation process and they placed a great deal of stress on rationalism and a universal kind of humanism. Ray was a product of that.

WvdH: As part of the Tagore tradition.[4]

SB: Yes, Tagore's father started it. Being part of that tradition, Ray's whole aesthetic development was obviously going to be a little different from what the mainstream was in India. So when he started making films it was clear that he didn't particularly care for the mainstream cinema entertainment. Being so different, it was therefore very interesting to explore his work. With a lot of other filmmakers you might explore their work in the context of Indian cinema, but here is suddenly someone who is starting a completely new kind of work. When *Pather Panchali* [Song of the Road, 1955] came out it resembled no other film made in India to that time. You knew it was completely different both in its structure, in its format, in the kind of characters he created – in everything. He was in many ways part of the literary developments in Bengal. So he was more connected with what had happened in literature rather than what was happening in the cinema.

WvdH: What attracted you to want to make the documentary at that particular time?

SB: Several things. Firstly, he was our foremost filmmaker. Secondly, the fact that I felt I had learnt a great deal about the cinema from his work. Thirdly, even more important than all this, I had been wanting to be a filmmaker for a long time but was always quite uncertain that I could make the kind of films I wanted to make, because I could never see anything in the world of cinema in India that resembled any of my ideas. It was when I saw *Pather Panchali* that I suddenly realized that it was possible to develop enough confidence in yourself to make the kind of film you wanted to make regardless of everything else. And *Pather Panchali* was that kind of a film. So it served as a tremendous source of inspiration. I was then absolutely certain that I could make the kind of films I wanted to make. For all of these reasons it became very important for me to make a film on him. I got to know Ray in the middle 1960s when he was making a film called *Nayak* [The Hero, 1966]. After that from time to time whenever I went to Calcutta I used to meet him and he used to keep a bit of time for me so we would spend an afternoon chatting about films. Not only about his work, but generally about film. Those were sessions that I found very satisfying. And he was certainly, as far as I was concerned, exceedingly accessible. I had no problems at all in meeting and discussing problems, even practical problems, in making films. So it seemed almost natural that I would want to make a film about him – at some stage.

WvdH: It wasn't something that he resisted? I had a feeling, having seen him in your film and also having read earlier interviews, that he was quite a reserved man.

SB: He was.

WvdH: And the idea of having a film made about him, where he was put in front of the camera, did not worry him?

SB: There had already been a film made about him and his work almost fifteen years earlier by Jim Beveridge, the Canadian filmmaker and film educationalist. Jim and Bhagwan Garga[5] had made a short documentary that was about fifteen or eighteen minutes long. When the Films Division broached the subject with me they were expecting to see a film that was twenty minutes long.[6] But I ended up by making a two hour, twelve minute film on him.

WvdH: You really wanted to explore his work in great depth?

SB: Yes. They gave me the money for a twenty-minute film, but I made a two hour, twelve-minute film instead. It was important to have a film biography of him and there were a lot of things that I discovered in the kind of realist/ naturalist genre of filmmaking he employed. For example, the environment that he created almost functioned as a character. It was an important aspect of his filmmaking, which also became very important for me when I was making films. I lay a fair amount of stress on the environment as part of the action. It's not just a background against which the action takes place. The environment plays an important part in the way characters develop and I wanted to explore that as far as his own work was concerned. And then there were other things. Before Ray, in terms of technique, most Indian filmmakers didn't pay too much attention to the kind of lenses they would use to place characters in relation to their environment or characters in relation to each other. Russian filmmakers like Eisenstein and Pudovkin used certain kinds of angles, certain kind of lenses, to show dominances – character dominances or ideology dominances. Satyajit Ray employed lenses to suit his needs, but a lot of people only used them to create sensational images, not as part of the interpretation. Ray's specific use of lenses was always in the context of his narrative and not simply to create an effect. Now these were the things that I felt were necessary to be shown in the film, particularly for those people who were keen cineastes or film students.

WvdH: I would like to talk about the structure of the documentary and how you approached it. It was interesting that you started with the production process, by showing Ray shooting *Ghare Baire* [The Home and the World, 1984], then moving on to some post-sync work on *Sadgati* [Deliverance, 1981] and finally showing an extract from *Sadgati*. You thereby introduced the viewer to film as a process and then as a product, and eventually presented Ray as the central creator of all of those things.

SB: Yes.

WvdH: In this way, you consciously brought the audience into the film. And then, it seems to me, you allowed Ray to take over the film. Basically he tells his own story; in fact the earlier part of the film is his autobiography. Were you content to have Ray tell his story to the camera?

SB: Yes. There are two ways of approaching biography. One is to allow the person to tell his own story from his own point of view, leaving it to the audience to have or create critical references. The other way of doing it is for those critical references to come into the film. Many biographical films are made where you have other people talking about that person. So the critical references are to be found in the film or it could be even in a book. But the approach here was not that. I wanted it to be as much as possible autobiographical – from Ray's point of view – and the audience then would bring or create for themselves the critical references. I didn't want to interview two dozen people about his work. I didn't want to do that because I felt that it was what most people did.

WvdH: The focus remained on him all the way through.

SB: It was then up to you to look at his work and note what he said about himself and then to work out a critique for yourself.

WvdH: During that earlier section in the film, you subtly use extracts from the films to represent Satyajit Ray's life. In other words, when he was talking about his upbringing and his going to school and university, the extracts from the films function as illustrations of his own life.

SB: Yes.

WvdH: Were you consciously presenting the films autobiographically?

SB: Yes to a large extent, particularly in relation to Bibhuti Bhushan Bandy-opadhyay's novel, *Pather Panchali*.[7] It was quite significant that Ray used that novel to make his first films – the trilogy – and it is also significant that he chose Soumitra Chatterjee to play the protagonist.[8] In many ways he functioned as Ray's alter ego in the films. Certainly in his interpretation of the book, Satyajit Ray saw himself as Apu.

WvdH: I have only read the first book. There are two books and three films, aren't there?

SB: That's right.

WvdH: So they overlap. The first book focuses on Apu as a young child and it is obvious that Ray developed a stronger narrative than was present in the novel.[9] The novel told little stories about the development of the young boy.

SB: It's a series of episodes loosely linked one with the other. Ray actually wanted to make some more films based on Bibhuti Bhushan's stories because I think he was very fascinated by him. There was one particular story, which is mentioned in my film – a film that he wanted to make about this old deranged uncle, who becomes a burden on the family. They decide to leave him some place, but the little boy suddenly develops a great sense of panic that he's never going to see this old man again, since he's been left at a crossroad far away from the village. The old man is very fond of smoking biris, so the boy's father leaves a packet of biris with him, and as the boy is being taken home by his father he turns to look if everything is all right with the old man. The road goes around a hill and all he can see is a thin spiral of smoke going up in the sky. He suddenly feels relieved that the old man is all right.

WvdH: Yes, it's a lovely image.

SB: Ray wanted to make a little film about that story, as he mentioned in the film.

WvdH: Yes, I do recall that. There is a certain point after the film extracts and Ray's story of his own life, where you come to the fore by providing, through voice-over, interpretations of some film extracts. It's in response to your question to Ray about the idea of control of images. I think the first example was from *Pather Panchali*, where Harihar returns home to find that Durga had died and his wife's wail is substituted on the soundtrack by the sound of a stringed musical instrument. You take control of the film for some time. Did you feel that it was necessary to be more overtly present at certain times in the film?

SB: Yes, because it was very important for there to be that response to his work – an interpretation of his work. Since I was making the film I felt that I had the right to do that. The main reason for doing that was to show how those films affected me personally. There are two, three such instances in the film.

WvdH: But most of the time your interviewing is very understated. Presumably you've cut your questions out of much of the final film.

SB: Yes.

WvdH: Did you feel that the film was an exchange between equals, or is it an exchange between a guru and a pupil?

SB: It was both actually. It shifted from one to the other. Since I have been an admirer of his work and I'd learnt a great deal from him about the cinema as a film practitioner, I felt the need to allow him to speak, because his ideas certainly were much more crystallized than mine. So we were moving from one relationship to the other.

WvdH: In interviews there are always issues of control, and sometimes people will use their power to control interviews, whether it be the interviewee or the interviewer. Was there any of that in your interviews?

SB: Not at all. I was also paying tribute to him, so there was no reference to power at all. When I make a film obviously I have control over the material, but I didn't wish to exercise it too much.

WvdH: Was he at all interested in how you might shape the film?

SB: No, I don't think so. When the Films Division decided that they wanted a film to be made on Ray, they asked me only after they had asked Ray whom he would prefer to make a film on him, and Ray, having thought about it a great deal, eventually suggested my name.

WvdH: I see.

SB: I didn't know this until I made the film. But he had actually said that, because strangely enough he didn't want anybody in Bengal to make a film about him.

WvdH: But that's in tune with the way in which he was both a Bengali and also a national and international figure. He was continually moving between these identities.

SB: When I later heard about him wanting me to make the film, I was a bit surprised.

WvdH: That he had asked for you so directly? In relation to something you mentioned earlier, the one time in the film that you voice Ray's influence on you is when you were talking about location shooting and camera placement.

SB: Yes.

WvdH: How had he taught you about that? It's often said that there is only one place to put the camera in relation to any particular shot in a film.

SB: One of the things that I learnt from him was how to set up the geography, so that when you come back to that scene again, you know your way about it. You may come to that same place in so many different ways, but you shouldn't lose your way about it.

WvdH: This is the mental image that a viewer has about where things are spatially located.

SB: Yes. And where anything is placed, even objects, anything. Because a lot of filmmakers often make the mistake of never setting out their geography. Ray had this wonderful sense of doing that with great economy. You immediately knew where you were located, either in a town, village or wherever, you knew the geography. It's like, let's say, if I'm shooting in Bombay the first aim is that the place has to be recognized as being Bombay, but you must also know how you get out of it and into it. These are things that he did exceedingly well and I learnt a great deal of that from him.

WvdH: I can think of that very powerful scene in *Charulata* [1964], where Charulata is in the house looking at the man walking along the street. You show that extract in the film. She moves from room to room to look at him from different places, so you get a very clear sense of where you are in relation to her and to him.

SB: It was a very important aspect for him and it is certainly a very important issue for me when I make films.

WvdH: I would like to come back to that later, when we might talk about some of your films and how the geography is actualized in particular cases. Towards the end of the film you started to use chapter headings, like 'On Form'. Were you intending to separate these issues from some of the earlier discussion, or were you wanting to be a bit more abstract?

SB: No, I wanted to look at all the facets of the man as well as his work, in slightly more specific terms. The point was to identify the kind of cinematic form that emerged with him. It was very important to know how he arrived at his editing style, his use of sound and his introduction of music. One of the things that Ray actually developed more than any other Indian filmmaker at that time was the use of non-synchronized effects, for instance birdcalls – different kinds of effects that were very much part of the interpretation. Sometimes they become a very important part of the narrative. Take for instance the film called *Aparajito* [The Unvanquished, 1956]. Do you remember that?

WvdH: Yes.

SB: In that film, the boy couldn't get a job in the city, but eventually finds work in some remote little village. As he goes to his lodgings, he hears a birdsong and he recollects his sister asking him about that same birdcall. That sound brings back his family situation. Ray used that sort of device quite frequently. I've used it too, in different ways, but without realizing that Ray had already done that. He gave meaning to every sound that emerged on the soundtrack and he orchestrated it as part of the interpretation, part of the narrative flow – to give it dimensions in memory and in geography. Perhaps he was the first Indian filmmaker to use sound in such ways.

WvdH: The soundtracks of some of your films also locate them very specifically. The sense of place is there through the sound as much as through the image.

SB: Sound not merely illustrates but functions as an equal complement to the visuals. Sound and picture together create your universe. Sound does not merely underline the visual.

WvdH: Similarly, the music does not merely underline the visuals, which is the traditional way, with the music telling you how to respond – whether to cry or to laugh.

SB: Yes.

WvdH: One thing that interests me about the film is the fact that it was shot in English.

SB: There are two reasons for that. One was because Ray didn't speak Hindi, the other that I didn't speak Bengali.

WvdH: I didn't realize that.

SB: In India you have this problem. I could speak Hindi, but he couldn't. He spoke Bengali, which I didn't. So it made sense to function in English.

WvdH: I know that English can serve as a sort of lingua franca in India. Yet Ray made a few films in Hindi, didn't he – *Sadgati* was made in Hindi?

SB: Two films, *Shatranj Ke Khiladi* [The Chess Players, 1977] and *Sadgati*.

WvdH: Yes, so I had presumed that he must have understood and be able to communicate in Hindi.

SB: He did understand the language, but he didn't use it.

WvdH: He wasn't confident enough in his use of Hindi?

SB: No.

WvdH: So the use of English didn't have anything to do with the film's international distribution?

SB: Not at all.

WvdH: I suppose that explains why the titles of the films were in Bengali, so that *Apur Sansar* [1959] was never translated as 'The World of Apu'. Was *Satyajit Ray* the only film that you made where you acted as the interviewer/documenter of an individual's life? I suppose your film about Nehru was very different.

SB: It was, but I used a very similar technique through Nehru's voice and his words. So it was also a first-person biography. I call it a first-person biography, not an autobiography. *Nehru* [1984] was a first-person biography because I used only his words – I didn't add anybody else's words. Because Nehru had written so much, it was easy to do that. I mean most people write diaries, he wrote books!

WvdH: It is amazing how Nehru, like Gandhi, was able to write so much while being engaged in a full public life.

SB: Exactly. So *Nehru* was done in a similar way to the Ray film, except that Nehru wasn't alive. But if he had been alive I would have probably followed a similar technique. Nehru was another figure I admire greatly because I think he provided us with a particular worldview and created in some ways a national consensus on the kind of worldview that India could possibly have. That was one of the reasons I chose to use this technique for that film.

WvdH: Both Ray and Nehru were modernists, weren't they?

SB: There is no question, they were modernists.

WvdH: Unlike Gandhi.

SB: Yes, unlike Gandhi, who was what one might call essentially a traditionalist who used modern methodology.

WvdH: Was the film on Nehru made a little later than the film on Ray?

SB: Actually both were more or less simultaneous. I'd started work on both these films in 1981 and they both came out in 1984.

WvdH: So these two figures represented for you the potential of Indian society and Indian culture.

SB: Absolutely. But this is an approach which of course today a lot of people are questioning, particularly in the present political atmosphere of this country. A lot of people are questioning these kinds of views, both the worldview that was created by Nehru, just as much as the view on the cinema advanced by Satyajit Ray.

WvdH: You mean the rationalist secularism that was implicit in those approaches?

SB: Yes. They are now being questioned by one section of the Indian political spectrum. Similarly one section of the cinema establishment is questioning Ray's work and even the kind of films I make.

WvdH: Indeed, even the kind of films that you make. In that encyclopaedia on Indian cinema that you have in your bookcase, your films are said to embody this ideology of Indian modernism.[10]

SB: Yes, it's a very peculiar kind of radical chic view, which I totally reject because I think it's not well thought out and that particular book has a lot of flaws. It's not as well researched as it should have been, and certainly it's not an encyclopaedia. It's polemical and you can't be polemical if you're producing an encyclopaedia.

Notes

1. *Satyajit Ray* is a 'talking head' documentary, in which Shyam Benegal interviews Satyajit Ray about his world and his work, accompanied by extracts from Ray's films, posters, stills and photographs of the Ray family and of Calcutta.

2. Samik Bandyopadyay in Benegal, 1998: v.

3. The *Natya Sastra* proposes eight basic emotions – love, humour, energy, anger, fear, grief, disgust and astonishment, which are experienced through eight corresponding flavours or *rasas* – sensitive/erotic, comic, heroic, furious, apprehensive, compassionate/tragic, horrific and marvellous (Warder, 1975: 172). Later a ninth *rasa* (serenity/peace) and even a tenth (devotion) were added (Mishra, 1992: 152). Most commentators apply the *nava rasa* theory to the Indian popular cinema, but it has recently been argued that 'the aesthetic mode of *rasa* informs the early films of Satyajit Ray' (Cooper, 2000: 15). Rachel Dwyer rejects Cooper's argument, but also criticizes the application of *rasa* theory to Indian cinema generally as a form of essentialist orientalism (Dwyer, 2002: 67–8).

4. Calcutta was the commercial centre for the British East India Company, and in the nineteenth century this led to a significant cultural interaction of Indian/Hindu and European/British values, which was labelled the Bengal Renaissance. The Bengalis most affected by this movement were the *Brahmos*, who rejected aspects of Hinduism such as idolatry, caste and *sati*, and who advocated sweeping social reform. It was eventually led by Devendranath Tagore, father of Rabindranath Tagore, who came to be its most illustrious son. A poet, dramatist, novelist, essayist, painter, song composer, philosopher and educationist, Rabindranath Tagore is acclaimed as Bengal's pre-eminent cultural figure. He befriended Ray's father, who was also a *Brahmo*, although Ray himself 'renounced' *Brahmoism* in his late teens (Robinson, 1989: 14–15, 33). Ray studied at Tagore's university and took 'his narrative and aesthetic inspiration from Tagore' (Dirks, 1995: 49).

5. Bhagwan Das Garga has written, directed and produced over fifty documentary films, including the film on Satyajit Ray. He has also published numerous articles and a book on Indian cinema (Garga, 1996). Andrew Robinson, in his book on Ray, lists two separate documentaries, one made by Garga in 1963 for the Films Division, the other by Jim Beveridge in 1968 for W-NET Educational TV (Robinson, 1989: 363).

6. The Films Division of the Ministry of Information and Broadcasting is the newsreel and documentary production and distribution organization of the Indian government. Every cinema in India has to show Films Division-approved documentaries and/or newsreels before the main feature film and pay for the privilege (Khandpur, 1985: 506–7). Jim Beveridge (National Film Board of Canada and Shell Film Unit) and Basil Wright were on loan to the Films Division from UNESCO in the 1960s (Rajadhyaksha and Willemen, 1999: 96). Shyam Benegal's *Nehru* was also made for the Films Division. Satyajit Ray made two documentaries for the Films Division: *Rabindranath Tagore* (1961), described by Andrew Robinson as 'very far from being propaganda of the type churned out by the Indian Government's Films Division or a film

like Shyam Benegal's lengthy portrait of Nehru' (Robinson, 1989: 277), and *The Inner Eye* (1972), about the painter Binode Bihari Mukherjee.

7. The author's family name can also be written as Banerji, which is the common anglicized version (Banerji, 1987: 9). Meenakshi Mukherjee argues that, 'Seen by the standards which are applied to the "well-made" realistic novel of the nineteenth-century western tradition, *Pather Panchali* lacks a cohesive structure, often meandering off in the manner of oral storytelling. Opu's [Apu's] imaginative response to the external world is the only loose thread connecting the whole' (Mukherjee, 1994: 128).

8. Soumitra Chatterjee plays the adult Apu in *Apur Sansar* and remained one of Ray's favourite and most frequently used actors. It has been suggested that Ray cast him so frequently because he looked like the young Tagore (Chidananda Das Gupta in Rajadhyaksha and Willemen, 1999: 75).

9. Ray, in adapting the novel, 'westernized' the narrative structure by bringing to it a 'tightness called for by the exigencies of the conventional feature film' (Ray, 1982: 271). The debate about Ray's 'Indianness' is examined in van der Heide, 1996. Interestingly, when the novel was translated into English, the ending was given a Western sense of climax and resolution; the translator justified his decision in the same way that Ray did (Clark in Banerji, 1987: 15).

10. Ashish Rajadhyaksha and Paul Willemen's *Encyclopaedia of Indian Cinema* (1999: 57-8 and individual film entries). Nevertheless, the book remains the most significant and authoritative source of information and commentary on Indian cinema in English.

Interview 2
On Shyam Benegal

Figure 2: Shyam Benegal interviewed by the author

WvdH: Our discussion of *Satyajit Ray* has revolved around issues of auto-biography, biography and their relationship to interpretation. I would now like to turn to *your* biography. I've read in a number of books the details of your upbringing but I want to raise rather more general questions about the significance of upbringing, of one's childhood and one's growing into adulthood, in terms of the historical moment in which one lives. You were born in 1934 and you grew up in the 1930s and the 1940s in Andhra Pradesh.[1] How significant was that in terms of what you've become?

SB: Well, it was very significant. You see it was a particular time. My father was part of the movement for home rule and so an Indian nationalist. Because there was a police warrant for some activity that he had been involved in, he moved to Hyderabad.[2] Hyderabad was then a princely state and not directly under the governance of the British and therefore the British warrants couldn't apply. So he escaped to Hyderabad and became a still photographer. He was also a painter and he had a very fine hand. His painting and photography had some kind of an influence on us children. I come from a very large family of ten children.

WvdH: I also come from a large family.

SB: My father was a very staunch follower of Gandhi, which meant that some of our values developed on account of the way he ran his household. We got very involved in wearing hand-spun clothes and he was very fond of reading Thoreau and Ruskin.

WvdH: These were the same writers that Gandhi was interested in.

SB: I read the books of Thoreau and Ruskin when I was very young – when I was about ten, eleven years of age. Not quite understanding much of it, but whatever I could understand must have had some kind of an effect.

WvdH: So you were educated in English?

SB: Yes, my education started with English in school. When I went to my first school at the age of five, I had learnt to read and write in Hindi at home, taught by my mother. But the main language of my formal education was English – as it was for a very large number of urban middle-class Indians, then as well as now. So it was easy to read the literature of the world from an early age.

WvdH: Is the danger of that, perhaps as with Satyajit Ray, that the literature of the world is more likely to be your reading focus than the literature of the culture in which you live?

SB: Yes that is true, but I had another kind of an influence, which was an uncle of mine who had escaped from Burma when the British surrendered Burma during the Second World War, and he had walked all the way from Rangoon. He came down with malaria and was seriously ill. So my father brought him to Hyderabad, where he recovered over several months at our home. He was the person who introduced me to Indian literature, whether it was Premchand[3] or Rabindranath Tagore or other writers as well as our epics like *Ramayana* and *Mahabharata* and the Puranic stories.[4] But I think that my father really transmitted to us his own aesthetic sensibility, which had a lasting effect on me certainly. We were living in an army cantonment area and five minutes away from the house was a garrison cinema, which used to run only foreign films, largely American films, but also a few British films – you know the old British Lion and later J. Arthur Rank films. But most of the films used to be American. It was much like in *Cinema Paradiso* [1988]. I had befriended the projectionist because I could never have the kind of money that would allow me to see more than one film in a month. But because of the projectionist, I used to end up by seeing ten or twelve films in a month. It was a large number of films for someone who was about six or seven years of age. By then I was absolutely and completely caught by the cinema.

WvdH: Was that your own doing, or were there relatives who introduced you to the cinema?

SB: No, except that my father had an old Bolex hand-cranked 16 mm camera and he used to make home movies of all his children. In his home movies he would trace the growth of a new child on film from birth until the next child came along, when he lost interest in the previous child.

WvdH: And with so many children he would have moved on quickly!

SB: Our home entertainment was usually when my father decided to show these films. He would edit them and then we would see these films when guests came to the house – it was the great after-dinner treat. We'd all set up the projector and he would show us these films, accompanied by a running commentary with everybody commenting on the happenings. He also used to make films of various things like army exercises, parades, drills and cavalry charges.

WvdH: But just for personal use?

SB: Yes. It was because he had this camera that he used to make these films. But those films became very important to me. Later he also would buy films – the Castle films.[5] He used to have these little Laurel and Hardy silent shorts, Charlie Chaplin, Buster Keaton and all that. So he used to have a collection of these films as well as something called *One Million BC* [1940], which was about Jurassic period animals and how the earth was born. These were all films made, I think, in the late 1930s and early 1940s, which used to be sold at Kodak outlets in India. Later for one of my birthdays he presented me with a magic lantern, and, having presented me with this magic lantern, I had to have films to show to my friends. Most of the films that I showed were cuttings off the projection room floor.

WvdH: Oh, I see.

SB: I put them together and then scratched them and drew on them as a kind of animation. So that's how I got interested in films.

WvdH: And already so actively at that early age.

SB: Yes, very actively. My oldest brother, now a commercial artist, was a student in Calcutta, and a great cineaste. He used to buy the *Penguin Film Review*s – this was before *Sight and Sound* – and after he had finished reading them he would send them to me. So my film education really started with all that. And then I decided to make a film of my own with my father's camera. We used to live in a fairly large house and our cousins from different parts of India used to come for summer vacations to our house. On one such vacation I decided I would make a film with everybody. And it was called *Chhutiyon Mein Maj Maza*, which means 'Fun during Holidays'.

WvdH: That was your first film.

SB: That was my first film.

WvdH: And how old would you have been then?

SB: I was twelve. I wrote the script and I shot it. It was kind of a 'who-dun-it' with one of the kids getting lost. It started off with a train coming into a railway station and everybody gets off. Then suddenly everybody gets back in and the train goes backwards. Those kinds of little tricks.

WvdH: Georges Meliès type of tricks.

SB: That was my very first film and then of course I got absolutely hooked on the cinema. Like most kids, I had wanted to be an engine driver before I wanted to be a filmmaker, but when I decided to be a filmmaker, I never changed my mind.

WvdH: But your education was more traditional. I suppose there was no other way at that time of pursuing your ambition to be a filmmaker.

SB: There was no way and certainly not where we were staying. If I was living in Bombay, it would have been a different matter, but Hyderabad was so far away. Whenever I told anybody I wanted to be a filmmaker, they used to respond with a laugh. Ultimately it was like having a hole in my head. Nobody ever thought it possible that I could become a filmmaker. They just thought that this was some kind of passing phase, which it was for a very long time. I went through school and college and did economics, and even toyed with the idea of teaching economics for a while. But cinema was much too strong and so, because there was no film institute, I came to Bombay.

WvdH: Before moving to Bombay, you had watched mainly American films?

SB: Mainly American films.

WvdH: No Hindi films at all?

SB: Yes, Hindi film watching was once a month with my parents.

WvdH: What sort of films?

SB: My father chose the films that we would see.

WvdH: Right. Was he very prescriptive in his choices?

SB: His choices would invariably be from films made by two studios. One was the Prabhat Film Studio at Poona[6] and the other was New Theatres in Calcutta.[7] New Theatres used to be well known for making films dealing largely with social issues of the time. Prabhat made films that were more nationalist. Whatever the subjects might be, the essential nature of those films was nationalist. So those were the Hindi films that we saw as children. Because he chose them.

WvdH: *Devdas* [1935] was made by New Theatres, wasn't it?[8]

SB: It was. Bimal Roy was one of the filmmakers who emerged from New Theatres.[9] New Theatres made a lot of very interesting films. And then there was Mehboob in Bombay who made films that were very left-oriented.[10]

WvdH: Like his earlier version of *Mother India* – *Aurat* [Woman, 1940]?

SB: *Aurat* and *Roti* [Bread, 1942], which had a class-struggle subject matter.

WvdH: Yes. He became a more spectacular filmmaker later in the 1950s, didn't he?

SB: Later, that's right.

WvdH: With *Mother India* [1957] and so forth. Therefore your father was concerned, I guess in line with his whole worldview, which you have described, that the films you watched had some serious purpose, whether it was in terms of nationalism or social concerns. So your only way of realistically getting into the film industry was to move to Bombay.

SB: Even then it was very difficult unless one became an assistant to somebody. But one very important thing happened when I was still in school. A cousin of mine used to be a dancer with Uday Shankar, who was Ravi Shankar's eldest brother and one of our great modernist dancers.[11] He had been touring Europe and America since the late 1920s and one of Diaghilev's dancers, Pavlova, went around the world with Uday Shankar. So, this cousin, Guru Dutt, who later became a famous filmmaker in Bombay, made his first film while I was still in school.[12] Then I knew that I could become a filmmaker.

WvdH: When one of your relations became a filmmaker.

SB: Yes. Guru Dutt became a dancer and actor in films and then became a film director at a very young age, directing his first film in Bombay when he was twenty-three. It was called *Baazi* [The Wager, 1951] and it was a big success. So when I finished college I came to Bombay. He offered me a job as his assistant. I didn't take it because by that time my ideas on films had changed quite dramatically and I didn't want to make the kind of films that he was making or the kind of films that were being made in Bombay. I wanted to make my own way.

WvdH: Even though his films had strong social concerns?

SB: Some of them had social concerns but they were very much within the format of the normal Bombay film.

WvdH: But I must say that some of his films are just wonderful.

SB: Yes, *Pyaasa* [Eternal Thirst, 1957], for instance, and *Sahib Bibi Aur Ghulam* [King, Queen, Knave, 1962] – they're wonderful pictures.

WvdH: They represent the peak of the Bollywood film.

SB: Yes, true.

WvdH: Did you actually know him?

SB: He used to come and spend time with us during vacations when he was still a dance director. He was as poor as a church mouse then, and for summer vacations he used to come to our place and his dance performances were our family entertainment. Yes, he was very close to us. His family was close to us and continues to be. Of course, he's dead now.[13]

WvdH: But he was brought up in a different part of India.

SB: He was brought up in Calcutta.

WvdH: How old would you have been when you came to Bombay?

SB: I came to Bombay in 1958. I was twenty-three at the time. I'd finished my Masters in economics, and had taught economics for about six months in Hyderabad. I then gave that up, came here and thought I could make my way into cinema through advertising. I did that because it was the beginning of advertising films and it was easier to make advertising films without going through a long period of apprenticeship. I joined an advertising agency as a copywriter, but within six months I was doing copy as well as making advertising films. And I think I learnt to make films seriously by making advertising films. I learnt everything actually – to use the camera, to do editing, to record sound. I already had my first script, which I'd written while I was still in college and which eventually became my first film *Ankur* [The Seedling, 1973].

WvdH: Right, so that idea had been with you for a long time before its fruition.

SB: For a very long time, and I'd written and re-written that script any number of times. I was also reading numerous serious books on the cinema. I'd read all of the Eisenstein and the Pudovkin that was available. Then that Karel Reisz book on film editing became my bible. It continues to remain a book that I recommend to any young filmmaker today.

WvdH: It was also one of the earliest film books that I read,[14] because I initially wanted to be involved in filmmaking, but it wasn't something I was meant to do. So you were happy to develop your filmmaking skills even though the form of expression was not something you were necessarily interested in – it was a preferable trade-off for you than being an assistant within the feature film industry.

SB: Yes, because that influence would have been much too strong.

WvdH: Were you already conscious of that at the time?

SB: I was very conscious of that from the very beginning. Once you became trapped in that, there was no way you could think independently. I would have lost all my other options.

WvdH: So this was the better alternative?

SB: Certainly for me, although it took twelve years in advertising and over 1,000 advertising films before I actually got down to making a feature.

WvdH: Did that ever seem like a never-ending period?

SB: Sometimes it used to make me very depressed because I was also becoming a great success in advertising.

WvdH: A dangerous situation!

SB: Yes, I was climbing the ladder. I'd become an accounts director; I was the head of the film department, head of the radio department and head of the copy department. I was number two in my agency. So by the time I was about thirty-three, I was going to take over an agency and that frightened me.

WvdH: Yes.

SB: And of course there was also another thing. Being an Indian from what one might call a lower middle-class family, your economic concerns are always very great. You want to be sure that you're going to get your next meal. And so those aspects were also worrying me. I was also married, but one day I decided that enough was enough. I had to make features and so I gave up advertising.

WvdH: So you cut yourself off from that?

SB: Yes, absolutely.

WvdH: Of course the certainty of you succeeding was not at all apparent.

SB: I wasn't sure even that there was a market for the kind of films I wanted to make. That was really the major problem then and it continues to be now.

WvdH: Some things don't change. Since you came here at that young age of twenty-three, do you feel that your cultural affiliation is that of Bombay and no longer Hyderabad?

SB: No, you see I'm very comfortable in Hyderabad; in fact I'm very comfortable in any part of India. However, Bombay is important, because it is much more alive. I have a lot more friends here; I find the atmosphere far more stimulating than any other place. I'm not one of those people who enjoy a solitary life. I need to have people around me. I feel much more relaxed when I'm in the middle of a lot of people than when I'm entirely by myself – I can take solitary life only for short spells. And certainly I need an environment that is stimulating, because Hyderabad was not terribly stimulating. It was as long as I was a student, but not afterwards. I must say that I have no difficulty in living in any part of India. I have no difficulty in living in any part of the world – in fact, one of the cities I enjoy most is New York, even though I haven't lived there for great lengths of time. Because after Bombay, I find the atmosphere in New York the most stimulating.

WvdH: It's a strange thing, because the impression that one might get of you from your films is not particularly urban. Your urban needs are strong as a person but they don't necessarily infuse their way into your films at all.

SB: No they don't, and in a sense what has always mattered to me is how people draw up their agendas. Take the economic agenda, the political agenda, the intellectual agenda of any community, of any group. Take India, for instance. In 1947 when we became free, the agenda of the government included the total community of India, but over time this has changed. The so-called 'liberalization' and 'globalization' in economics keeps 75 per cent of the population of this country on the outside. For me it has always been very important that everybody must be included. The idea of a certain kind of universalism, I might even add a certain kind of universal humanism, is very important for me. So even though I might personally prefer to remain in urban circumstances, I must bring everybody else within the ambit of my own thoughts.

WvdH: While it's always dangerous to be essentialist, it strikes me that one of the great lessons that India has taught the world in the past has been this sense of inclusiveness – of ideas, of cultures, of peoples, of religions, and so forth. And if there is something very worrying about India today, it is that these things seem to be fragmenting. There seems to be a greater focus on fundamentalism in all its forms.

SB: I would like to think it's a passing phase. These are things that happen from time to time. They have happened in the past. But I think today's world is perhaps slightly different from the way it was in the past. I mean there is a technology that brings with it a kind of arrogance, which automatically assumes that there is very little to learn from the past. And the effect of that I think is worrying. But I certainly value the essential Indian heritage, which is, as you say, inclusiveness – that there is no 'other', that we are all 'us'. That has been the bottom line for me as far as my own filmmaking is concerned.

WvdH: The documentary aspect of the advertising films that you worked on for such a long period of time has in some ways never left you.

SB: No, because I continue to enjoy making documentaries. Although I must say that I'm not fully satisfied with documentaries, because you only deal with observable phenomena. With fiction you can explore things much more deeply – you are interpreting, you are exploring, you are re-shaping material. With a documentary you can't really re-shape the material unless you wish to be non-factual. You have an obligation to factuality, as it were. But with fiction you can pursue what I call the truth – which is very subjective in any case.

WvdH: As you mentioned, making advertising films provided you with lots of skills. One of the most important of these must have been editing, because of the way in which you have to juxtapose material and tell a story in a very short period of time.

SB: But persuasion is also such an important aspect of it.

WvdH: Do you feel that persuasion is still there in your films?

SB: To some extent it might be, but I would like to think that it is not as manipulative as it is in advertising. But then, in any kind of work that you do, you are manipulating. In advertising that manipulation is exploitative. It has a very specific objective.

WvdH: To sell something, or to get people to do something. So for you the fiction film, the feature film, is the most satisfying and most important form of cinema?

SB: Yes, definitely, but also certain kinds of television, such as that massive fifty-three hour history of India I made called *Bharat Ek Khoj* [The Discovery of India, 1988], based on Nehru's *The Discovery of India*, which gave us our history, creating a picture we cannot only live with but grow with.[15] History as taught to us when I was in school, before we became independent, was Euro-centred, where we were looking at ourselves as the 'other'. It's an extraordinary situation. It's like Aboriginals having to look at their history through the eyes of the white man in Australia, and seeing themselves as the 'other'.

WvdH: That's right.

SB: So *Bharat Ek Khoj* set out to change that.

WvdH: So was that one of your agendas?

SB: Of course. For me it is certainly very important in my filmmaking – to draw a profile of ourselves whether it's historic or contemporary. To be able to see who we are.

WvdH: Rather than the way others might see you.

SB: Yes.

WvdH: Did Nehru himself have a similar objective in his book, *The Discovery of India*?

SB: It was one of the seminal works of Indian history. After it, Indian historians developed his ideas much further. Nehru enabled us to see ourselves both as a country and as a nation in ways that colonialism had made sure wouldn't happen.

WvdH: I want to return to the relationship between your life and your work and to the question of the shaping influences upon your work. Usually this is limited to what happens to one when one is young. Often when one talks about the relationship between work and life, it seems that once one becomes an adult it is no longer an issue. But there are always on-going influences, one is always interacting.

SB: There are always on-going influences all the time but I think there is a distinction. The difference is that until you find your own voice, every influence seems an influence, remains an influence, but those influences then get subsumed and emerge in your own voice. And that's the growing up process. When you look at a filmmaker's evolution or a writer's development, you'll find that early works always show traces of others, because there is mimicry at work there. It's like a child learning. The child learns by imitation and then eventually finds its own self, whether it's physical motor actions or speech. Having found one's own voice, influences carry on but in a subsumed manner.

WvdH: They are often much more diffuse. They're more complex in some ways.

SB: Much more complex.

WvdH: Because the whole cultural, political world that one lives in becomes part of all of those things.

SB: Absolutely.

WvdH: One responds to these things as an individual and that affects the way in which one might think about one's work, including the sorts of stories that one becomes interested in telling now as opposed to twenty years ago. Are you conscious of the way in which these things change?

SB: No, because that would've only made me self-conscious and would have then created a barrier. That should be left rightly to the critics.

WvdH: Yes, although you mentioned that around about the time of the making of *Mandi* [Market Place, 1983] there was a particular pivotal change.

SB: Yes, but that is when I look back now.

WvdH: It wasn't so obvious to you at the time?

SB: Not when I was actually involved in that process, but only when I look back.

WvdH: There's also a sense in which we usually look upon this as a one-way process that's going from one's life to one's work, but if one's work is meaningful, then that in turn is another influence on one's life. Is this 'reverse influence' equally important to you?

SB: Definitely, because it imperceptibly changes your whole view of things. Your material is probably very similar, but you're now looking at it from yet another point of view. That to me is the process of evolution. You get new perspectives and become aware of the multiple levels of different things that happen and their complexity. When you are looking at something for the first time you see it as a simple straight line, and then you realize that there are many, many other things to it. Then again the challenge lies in how all that can again be seen in the simplest form – not by simplifying it, but by encapsulating it in a simplicity.

WvdH: To be simple and profound at the same time.

SB: That becomes the continuing challenge.

WvdH: Presumably *Ankur* changed a great deal before you made it.

SB: It changed enormously because I had something like twelve years to work on it in the light of the kind of experiences I was going through myself.

WvdH: So they were interacting with each other.

SB: And working themselves into the script.

WvdH: In looking back at these films that you've made over so many years, do you see them differently now? Does your relationship to them change over time?

SB: The relationship changes very quickly. As soon as I've finished the film and after I've seen it with my unit – the first viewing is always for the unit – and once it is shown to the general public, it has its own life. I have no connection with it any more. In fact I don't go back to see my films for a long time afterwards. When I do see it again I never connect myself with it.

WvdH: You see it as a spectator?

SB: Yes. I think that's the best way to deal with it because I want to cut the umbilical cord the moment the film is done. You can't sit there and say I should have done this or I should have done that. It's an absolutely worthless activity.

Once it's done it's done, flaws and all. If it has any worth, it will carry on. If it doesn't, it'll sink like stone – and that's it.

WvdH: So it's both like but also quite different to one's children.

SB: Well it's more like children really. The fact is that you may have a relationship with your children but you have to allow them their life – so the film has its own life and there's nothing you can do about it afterwards and the recognition of that is a very important thing in the process of making films.

WvdH: So the relationship between intention and what you end up realizing is not necessarily that direct. It may not be so close. It may change.

SB: You may have intended it to go in a particular direction but it also gets its own life. It is realized slightly differently from the way you had intended, because there are so many factors in filmmaking – I don't particularly concern myself with that problem. To me what you have realized on film is much more important than what you intended, and to start to analyse it in those ways is quite fruitless. What the audience sees in a film need not necessarily be what you saw in it – they give it a certain kind of life and ultimately it is that which will live, not what you intended. It may be interesting in an academic sort of way but I have no serious intellectual or emotional concern about it.

WvdH: It's quite a different matter to talk about how you developed your ideas, and I'd like to do that when we talk about *Ankur*.

Notes

1. Andhra Pradesh, situated on the east coast of the subcontinent, is the largest and most populous of the southern Indian states. The main language is Telugu, and Telugu films constitute the largest single language bloc within the Indian film industry (21 per cent); in fact, films made in the four major Dravidian languages (the other three are Tamil, Malayalam and Kannada) represent over 60 per cent of all films produced in India (Rajadhyaksha and Willemen, 1999: 32). Four of Shyam Benegal's films are set (and shot) in Andhra Pradesh: *Ankur* (The Seedling, 1973), *Nishant* (The Night's End, 1975), *Anugraham* (The Boon, 1977) and *Susman* (The Essence, 1986), but only *Anugraham* is in Telugu – the Hindi version, made at the same time, is called *Kondura* (The Sage from the Sea).
2. Hyderabad is the capital of Andhra Pradesh and a centre of Islamic culture comparable to Delhi and Agra. It is not surprising, therefore, that the main language spoken there is Urdu.

3. Premchand is generally considered the finest of all Hindi fiction writers, although he initially wrote in Urdu. His short stories and novels focused on contemporary social situations and tended to be set in the villages of Uttar Pradesh. Two of his short stories, 'Shatranj Ke Khiladi' (1924) and 'Sadgati' (1931), were made into films by Satyajit Ray.

4. The *Ramayana* and the *Mahabharata* are India's most significant cultural texts. Originating as oral tales, they were written down in a number of different ways (Richman, 1991). The core story of the *Ramayana* revolves around Ram's wife, Sita, being captured by Ravana, the King of Lanka, leading to Ram destroying Lanka by fire, killing Ravana and having Sita undergo a trial by fire to confirm her chastity. The central conflict of the *Mahabharata* is between two groups of cousins, the Pandavas and the Kauravas, culminating in a cataclysmic battle at Kuruksetra. The Pandavas – Yudhisthira, Bhima, Arjuna, Nakula and Sahadeva – are aided by Krishna with advice (the famous *Bhagavad Gita*) and support (the demise of the Kauravas' supreme warrior, Karna, who turns out to be the Pandavas' brother). These two (very digressive) narratives remain at the heart of Indian social and cultural life and are the central 'anterior texts' of Indian cinema (especially, but not solely, the popular cinema). Shyam Benegal's *Nishant* is a revisionist version of the Ram/Sita/Ravana story, while *Kalyug* (The Machine Age, 1980) is a contemporary telling of the *Mahabharata*. The *Puranas* are collections of legends combined with religious information and have been labelled as 'the bibles of popular Hinduism', focusing on the various incarnations of God, such as Krishna (de Bary, 1958: 328).

5. For some historical information on Castle Films, see http://povonline.com/notes/Notes112905.htm (accessed 12 October 2005). I can recall seeing their 8 mm and 16 mm films in 'sell-through' catalogues in the 1960s; the films were typically the out-of-copyright or pirated comedy shorts of the American silent and early sound era.

6. The Prabhat Film Company's well-resourced studio in Pune/Poona was set up in 1933 and was an important production centre until it closed in 1953. It is best known for the saint films like *Sant Tukaram* (1936) and the socials by V. Shantaram, one of the studio's founders (Rajadhyaksha and Willemen, 1999: 178).

7. Together with Prabhat, New Theatres represented quality film production in pre-Independence India. The studio lasted from 1931 to 1955, although its peak period was the 1930s. Its top directors were P. C. Barua and Nitin Bose, who made films like *Devdas* (1935) and *Desher Mati* (The Motherland, 1938), respectively, both starring K. L. Saigal, the studio's most significant actor (Rajadhyaksha and Willemen, 1999: 166).

8. The character of Devdas, derived from Saratchandra Chattopadhyay's 1917 novel of the same name, has become one of the most enduring archetypes of

Indian cinema, first articulated in the 1935 film (even though the earliest film adaptation was made in 1928). Devdas 'came to signify romantic obsession and failure, having an almost morbid fascination with loss, the beloved, the mother, childhood and home' (van der Heide, 2002: 164).This 'renouncer-hero' was played by K. L. Saigal in the 1935 version, but in the 1940s and 1950s Dilip Kumar embodied him in films like *Deedar* (Vision, 1951) and the remake of *Devdas* (1955); Guru Dutt's *Pyaasa* (Eternal Thirst, 1957) and *Kaagaz Ke Phool* (Pale Flowers, 1959) reconfigured the archetype, as does Shyam Benegal's *Suraj Ka Satvan Ghoda* (The Seventh Horse of the Sun, 1992).

9. Bimal Roy was the cinematographer of the 1935 *Devdas* and directed his first films for New Theatres, before starting his own production company, Bimal Roy Productions, for which he made his best known films: *Do Bigha Zameen* (Two Acres of Land, 1953), *Devdas* (1955) and *Sujata* (The Well-Born, 1959).

10. Mehboob (or Mehboob Khan) is the third of 'The Great Four of the Golden Fifties' discussed so far (Masud, 1995), the other two being Bimal Roy and Guru Dutt; the fourth, Raj Kapoor, is not mentioned by Shyam Benegal. Mehboob set up Mehboob Productions in 1942, with the hammer and sickle as its emblem. Apart from the films already mentioned, his 1949 film, *Andaz* (A Matter of Style), starring Dilip Kumar (in a Devdas-like role), Nargis and Raj Kapoor, introduced the contemporary middle-class world to the Indian cinema, influencing its representation in many subsequent films, most significantly in Raj Kapoor's *Awara* (The Vagabond, 1951) (Rajadhyaksha and Willemen, 1999: 144).

11. Uday Shankar directed one film, *Kalpana* (Imagination, 1948), a dance spectacular that showcases his dance styles, choreographed 'with semi-expressionist angles and chiaroscuro effects', which influenced sub-sequent Indian films, especially the dream sequence in Raj Kapoor's *Awara* (Rajadhyaksha and Willemen, 1999: 311). Satyajit Ray was most impressed by the film: 'I never knew Indian music and dancing could have such an impact on me' (Robinson, 1989: 64). Ray engaged Ravi Shankar (the acclaimed sitar player and composer, who played with Yehudi Menuhin and George Harrison) to write the music for the Apu trilogy; Shankar also composed the musical scores for a number of early 'realist' socials, such as K. A. Abbas' *Dharti Ke Lal* (Children of the Earth, 1946), for Richard Attenborough's *Gandhi* (1982) and for Mrinal Sen's *Genesis* (1986).

12. Benegal is referring to *Baazi* (The Wager, 1951), which was Dutt's first film as a director. His debut film was *Lakhrani* (1945), made for the Prabhat Film Company; he was the assistant director and also performed in a minor role (Kabir, 1996: 17–18). His major films were *Pyaasa* (Eternal Thirst, 1957) and *Kaagaz Ke Phool* (Pale Flowers, 1959); two other films usually

attributed to him – *Chaudhvin Ka Chand* (Full Moon, 1960) and *Sahib Bibi Aur Ghulam* (King, Queen, Knave, 1962) – were credited to directors M. Sadiq and Abrar Alvi, respectively.

13. Guru Dutt died in 1964.

14. This Eisenstein–Pudovkin–Reisz trio would be very familiar to those who became interested in writings about cinema in the 1950s and 1960s. Theirs were certainly the first 'film theory' books that I purchased and read. While the translated writings of Eisenstein (e.g. *Film Form*, 1951) and Pudovkin (e.g. *Film Technique and Film Acting*, 1949) have remained central to classical film theory, Reisz's book, *The Technique of Film Editing* (Reisz and Millar, 1968; originally written in 1953), has rather fallen by the wayside – a recent book on the history of film theory doesn't even mention it (Stam, 2000). The fact that the book was published by a 'communication techniques' press (Focal Press) suggests that it might be considered more of a manual for filmmakers.

15. This book was written (in English), when Jawaharlal Nehru was imprisoned by the British in Ahmadnagar Fort prison in 1944 (Nehru, 1960).

Interview 3
On Indian Cinema

Figure 3: Shyam Benegal on location (*Bose: The Forgotten Hero*, 2005)

WvdH: I'm interested in the way you see your relationship to the Indian cinema and cinema more generally. How important is Indian cinema to you both as a spectator and as a maker of films?

SB: There's not one Indian cinema. There are many Indian cinemas. We have regional cinemas from different parts of India. There is a kind of pan-Indian film, which is the Hindi film. It's pan-Indian only in so far as Hindi films tend to travel much more than regional films – those made in Telugu, Tamil, Kannada, Malayalam, Marathi, Gujarati or Bengali, and so on.[1] When you talk about Indian cinema, most people tend to mean the Hindi cinema. My relationship with Hindi cinema is somewhat tenuous in so far as it's a kind of generalist cinema. Its common denominator has to be extremely wide and it has to appeal to a very large number of people. So the subject matter and the treatment of the subject matter in a Hindi film tend to be far more generalized. Until very recently, the characters in Hindi films never even had surnames.

WvdH: True, I hadn't thought of that.

SB: Characters only had first names. Surnames define a region, give it a geographical location. Hindi cinema never does that, and when it showed a city, whether it's called Bombay or whatever, it really didn't concern itself with that specific city or its specific character. So the films would be made in a never-never land. Hindi cinema has always functioned essentially as parable, and when you have something that functions as a parable, particularly a moral parable, you don't necessarily locate it geographically. Hindi cinema itself has a history and it follows from a certain form of theatrical entertainment in our country. Both the classical and the folk theatre always function as parable. All entertainment is supposed to have a certain moral at the end of it all. In that sense I am related to this tradition. But my relationship to Hindi cinema is tenuous because it doesn't concern itself with reality in any sense of the term.

WvdH: Or with that specificity of place and culture that you said it doesn't really want to deal with anyway.

SB: If you look at Tamil cinema or Telugu cinema or Malayalam cinema or Kannada cinema, you'll see that these South Indian regional cinemas had a very specific regional connection. There is a term that is used in South India when they talk about its connectedness to the soil. The term they use is nativity. It has nothing to do with the Nativity of Christ, but it refers to the character of the place. And those films have always had that character in terms of idiom, in terms of locating the people, in the manner in which they look, the manner in which they behave – there is a specific connectedness.[2]

WvdH: And that is attractive to you?

SB: Yes, that has always been much more attractive. Take, for instance, Bengali cinema, even excluding Satyajit Ray. You know that this is specifically set in Bengal, you can make out the kind of things that go on there and the very specific idiom of that region. The signs, the symbols, the signals, that emerge from those films belong specifically and recognizably to a place. This is certainly not the case in the average Hindi film. These regional films have been much more attractive to me and I feel more connected to that kind of cinema. I wouldn't make a distinction in terms of form, because the form of the film is more or less the same. The narratives still have a great deal of music and song and dance as has always been the case with cinema in India.

WvdH: So you've been talking about the popular cinema, whether it be this pan-Indian kind or the more regional kind. Of course, as you've already indicated, your relationship to another type of Indian cinema, that most obviously identified with Satyajit Ray, is very important to you and was probably the initial stimulus for your founding of the film society in Hyderabad.

SB: Oh definitely, because the film society aimed to look at the kind of cinema that was made in places other than Hollywood. Hollywood in many ways has been the inspiration for Hindi cinema, more than any other kind of cinema in India. Hollywood has this kind of international appeal particularly with its ability to create a cultural character that seems to be accepted internationally. Of course there have been different kinds of genres in American filmmaking like the western, which is culturally very American. Similarly there are the crime thrillers and detective movies, particularly of the 1930s and 1940s, which showed the underbelly of the American city. But these genres became very popular all over the world. Genres like the western were not necessarily connected with the United States alone, with the development of the spaghetti westerns in Italy and the curry western in India.

WvdH: Such as *Sholay* [Flames of the Sun, 1975].

SB: *Sholay* and films like that, including *China Gate* [1998] now.

WvdH: Is that a western as well?

SB: Very similar. It's of the same genre. Hollywood films have developed an international character – they've become culturally international or, if I might use another word, culturally neutral. So Hindi cinema has often taken these ideas and genres and its inspiration has always been Hollywood. When we started this little film society in Hyderabad, our intention was to go beyond that – to look at different kinds of cinemas of the world that did not necessarily take their inspiration directly from Hollywood, such as European cinema and Japanese cinema. Although I was brought up largely on American films and a few Indian films, I don't think I was that influenced in my own making of films by American cinema. Yet Hollywood cinema, which is the most successful in the world, uses cinematic language in a way that appeals to the largest number of people and this has been of continuing interest to me. The manner in which the *mise-en-scène* is worked out and the pacing of these films have been subjects of interest to me, even though I have not necessarily been influenced by this filmmaking in terms of subject matter.

WvdH: So the film society would've shown films from all over the world.

SB: There were Russian, Italian, early German, French, post-war French films, and films from the British Free Cinema and the post-war Japanese cinema.

WvdH: And the films of Satyajit Ray, were they important?

SB: Absolutely. His work was just beginning in India.

WvdH: This would have been about the time of the Apu trilogy.[3]

SB: Yes, the Apu trilogy, *Jalsaghar* [The Music Room, 1958], *Parash Pathar* [The Philosopher's Stone, 1957], and so forth.

WvdH: It has been said, I don't know if this is true, that the first film you showed was in fact *Pather Panchali*.

SB: Yes, that was the very first film and then after that came Mark Donskoi's Gorky trilogy[4] and other Russian films like Eisenstein's *Ivan the Terrible* [1944–5].

WvdH: Did you also write about film at that time – for programme notes or other publications?

SB: Programme notes were made, but nothing serious. But we used to conduct discussions on the films that we had seen. That was an important part of it.

WvdH: Commentators have noted the strong similarities between you and Satyajit Ray in that you studied the same sorts of things at university, both founded film societies, both worked in advertising, and both struggled to finance your first films, the scripts of which had been developed over a long time. In that sense there is a sort of parallelism between you and Ray. Do you feel that there is?

SB: Not in any serious way, only superficially. It is there in the sense that we both came from advertising, and struggled to make our first films, were involved in both the creation of film societies as well as conducting the film society movement, but this is really quite superficial because our backgrounds are quite different.

WvdH: And your films are quite different.

SB: Yes, our films are very different.

WvdH: At a conference I attended in Sydney at the end of 1998, Ashish Rajadhyaksha commented that the mantle of Indian cinema had passed from Satyajit Ray to you. He didn't necessarily mean that in a complimentary way. Do you accept that you have taken over the role that he had played in Indian cinema while he was alive?

SB: No. For a large number of filmmakers like myself, Girish Karnad and B.V. Karanth in Karnataka, Adoor Gopalakrishnan and Aravindan in Kerala – the generation that emerged in the 1970s – the path had been broken by Satyajit Ray.[5] Through his inspiration you could think in terms of making films that you would like to make rather than according to the patterns set by the film industry. It's very much like what American independents are doing, not walking the same path as Hollywood but creating their own ways of making films. In that sense Satyajit Ray continued to be that inspirational figure. But it did not necessarily mean that we were all totally in agreement with his ideas on the cinema. Ashish Rajadhyaksha probably meant that not only was he a source of inspiration but that we agreed with everything that Satyajit Ray said about the cinema. Not necessarily. Broadly speaking perhaps yes. The entire Film and Television Institute, of which Ashish was also a student, was based on the principle that you should be making films that were your own personal artistic expression, and that continues to be the bottom line for the teaching styles at the Institute.[6]

WvdH: How important for you are the other two Bengali directors – Mrinal Sen and Ritwik Ghatak?

SB: Ritwik Ghatak was inspirational in a very different way. If you study a Satyajit Ray film, you will see that the manner in which he used the cinematic language could be considered more internationally accessible because he employed a language of the cinema that was being used in different parts of the world.

WvdH: The European tradition.

SB: Largely the European traditions, I would imagine. Ritwik Ghatak's language was more rooted in the Indian tradition. I'm not sure he succeeded too well, but the fact is that he did try to do that. Therefore he's a very interesting figure in Indian cinema – some of his films are not realized too well, but others are very good films.[7] Then of course you have Mrinal Sen, whose filmmaking took a very political turn, in the sense of agit-prop.

WvdH: In the late 1960s, early 1970s.

SB: Yes, it was more like agit-prop film because he was strongly inspired by the Russian cinema of the 1920s and 1930s, specifically by people like Eisenstein.

WvdH: Did Mrinal Sen's political vehemence in his films at the time, which was about the time you started to make films, inspire you in any way by saying that one can include political comment in film?

SB: I've always found Mrinal's work very interesting, but I have never found it inspirational. His later films are the ones that I have found much more satisfying, not his early films.

WvdH: More the films of the 1980s like *Kharij* [The Case is Closed, 1982]?

SB: Yes, and *Akaler Sandhaney* [In Search of Famine, 1980]. Those I found much more satisfying as films. I found the earlier films interesting, but they actually left me somewhat cold.[8]

WvdH: I notice that Mrinal Sen has talked about now wanting to concentrate on the more personal ways people deal with social and political problems, rather than continue with the more strident engagement of the earlier films. Is there any relationship between what you're doing and what regional directors like Aravindan and Gopalakrishnan are doing?

SB: Not necessarily. If anything connected us, I think it was really the underlying humanism. Not anything else. You see that humanism connected us all to Satyajit Ray more than to Mrinal Sen or Ritwik Ghatak.

WvdH: What about some of the younger film directors like those who seem to have been inspired by Ghatak – Mani Kaul and Kumar Shahani?

SB: I don't see any connection between Ritwik Ghatak's films and films made by people who have seen him as their guru. I don't see any connection between a Kumar Shahani film and a Ritwik Ghatak film, nor do I see anything in common between a Mani Kaul film and a Ritwik Ghatak film. Mani Kaul has found his own voice and he's started to make his films in a particular manner, which is visually quite extraordinary. They are beautiful films with a deliberate slowing down of pace. His early films were quite minimalist in design, but very interesting. Mani found his own voice very quickly. Kumar, I think, took a little longer to find his own voice because you could see traces of a lot of things that seemed to have been derived.

WvdH: He worked in Europe for some time as well.

SB: With Bresson. Later on he found his own voice in films like *Khayal Gatha* [Khayal Saga, 1988], where you see him trying to extend the vocabulary of cinema. Kumar and Mani lost interest in narratives and audiences found it very difficult to connect with them.[9]

WvdH: I imagine particularly so in a country like India where a certain style of cinema had been so predominant.

SB: They were propounders of non-narrational cinema and, when you go into that area, then obviously you have to expect this kind of reaction.

WvdH: This also raises the whole question of funding, doesn't it?

SB: Yes, it does.

WvdH: Because these people depend on a state-based funding mechanism.

SB: There is no other way. They became entirely dependent on the states to fund their films.

WvdH: You've moved in and out of state funding at various times as well.

SB: I only moved into it very recently, because all my films until the early 1990s were made without any state funding.

WvdH: Some of the documentaries had been.

SB: Documentaries are different because in India nobody really funded documentaries – certainly not for the first forty-five years. Even now you are totally dependent on corporate or government funding to make documentaries. The exception is Anand Patwardhan, who has made films independently with support from little groups of people or under his own steam.[10] When it came to features, it was only in the 1990s that funding became difficult, with the growing crisis largely triggered off by the incredible exponential growth of television and the shrinking of the cinema market. People who were on the margins, like myself, suddenly found that all their sources of funding had dried up. Then of course to make our films, we needed a certain amount of support from the state.

WvdH: You were forced into a direction that you had avoided before?

SB: Yes, avoided because I always believed that we should be able to stand on our own two feet. I mean you don't create target audiences but you have to find your audience. This is very important, otherwise things will not live without constant subsidization.

WvdH: Is the trend towards state funding going to continue or is there a way out of this?

SB: Well no – it's slowing drying up. The policy of economic liberalization is based on the state slowly withdrawing from a large number of activities, and this is one of the activities from which the state is likely to withdraw. Not that it was terribly effective anyway, but it still was there. But I don't see any likelihood of it continuing in the same manner.

WvdH: Is that a real concern?

SB: It definitely is a concern. It means that a lot of people who are on the vanguard will have their opportunities sorely limited.

WvdH: Did you use NFDC funding for *Samar* [Conflict, 1999] as well?[11]

SB: I didn't use NFDC funding, but I'll tell you what I did which is an interesting thing. The Indian Ministry of Welfare has funds to help empowerment of the Dalit community.[12] They make documentaries and information type of films on that issue. I told them that I wanted to make a feature, not a propaganda film – I think I convinced them that it was not necessary to make propaganda films. You see a feature film can become part of the public discourse by not necessarily saying this is right and this is wrong. Whatever continues in the public discourse will be paid attention to. Social change cannot take place without it being part of public discourse, and therefore I said I would make a feature film. So I got funding from the Ministry of Welfare to make my film. It was routed through the NFDC largely because the government cannot deal with private individuals.

WvdH: This is a method that you've used before, haven't you?

SB: *Manthan* [The Churning, 1976], *Susman* [The Essence, 1986].

WvdH: Your approach to filmmaking has involved finding funds from particular state or private enterprise institutions, hasn't it?

SB: Right, or through a co-operative.

WvdH: I want to come back to this broader question of where Indian cinema is now. You have been placed in this category called 'middle cinema' since your first film. Do you feel that it's a valid way of talking about your cinema?

SB: I don't think so, because I don't know how it gets defined as middle cinema. Ultimately it's a question of you making a film according to your sensibility and your perception of things. Now the term 'middle cinema' stuck because *Ankur* was both commercially successful and a critical success. Some of the films that were made at that time were not commercially successful at all. So the term 'middle cinema' came to imply some kind of a compromise between the mainstream films that came out of the film industry and those that seemed like independent films of personal expression. But such a balancing act is an absurdity; nothing works like that.

WvdH: Some people also implied that it was a 'middle-of-the-road' cinema. A particular discourse about cinema in India finds an attraction in both the commercial cinema and the avant-garde but wants to deny the relevance of anything that is different to those.

SB: This was part of our discourse – it's no longer. It didn't make any sense at all because nobody ever thinks in those terms. You don't sit there and say I'm going to make an art movie with commercial ingredients in it.

WvdH: Finally in terms of some of the individual filmmakers, there are those who seem to me to be closer to you – people like Govind Nihalani, who of course came from your unit, but also people like Sathyu and even Ketan Mehta. These are directors who work in Hindi and make films that, would you agree, have a similar way of expressing themselves to your films?[13]

SB: No, each is an individual. They're working according to their own sensibilities and their own predilections. They're all making very different kinds of films, so it's not necessarily true to think or imagine that everybody is working as a team and wanting to make the same kind of films. That isn't happening.

WvdH: And you're not fighting over the same scripts?

SB: Certainly not.

WvdH: Your scripts are more individually developed anyway.

SB: Yes, absolutely.

WvdH: And what about some of the diasporic Indian directors, who have come into prominence, people like Shekhar Kapur.

SB: Shekhar is very much a product of Bombay cinema, but he was always interested in making films to which he could bring his sensibility. And when he got the opportunity to make *Bandit Queen* [1994] he made a film that was very successful everywhere. Of course he's gone into a completely different sphere now with *Elizabeth* [1998] and the films he's likely to be making. He will probably become part of the Hollywood mainstream.[14]

WvdH: Of an international sort of a cinema.

SB: Yes, it's possible because he's been the most successful Indian director in that sense.

SB: Both Mira Nair and Deepa Mehta are very much filmmakers in the American tradition. Although they have used Indian subject matter for their films, they are very popular internationally because the American cinema has a bigger market.[15]

WvdH: Is it a bit of a worry when Mira Nair comes here and makes a film about Bombay street children?

SB: It doesn't worry me.

WvdH: It's like an outsider coming in.

SB: No, she's not an outsider.

WvdH: But she's an insider outsider.

SB: Yes, she's an insider outsider. It's a very interesting thing. Actually I find Mira's films quite interesting. I liked her new film *My Own Country* [1998].

WvdH: It said in the paper this morning [19 January 1999] that it wasn't shown in Hyderabad [at the International Film Festival of India].

SB: Yes, I was trying to get it there, but it didn't happen.

WvdH: How important do you feel your role is in the development of a national film policy? I know that you've been involved in policy to some extent.

SB: Yes. Well I was part of two committees. One was a national film policy committee that was set up in the beginning of the 1980s. The main things then were the development of television and the complicated nature of film in India. Film is not a policy subject for government at the centre, while the state governments have completely different policies to cinema in their own regions. The entertainment tax is very high in some states and functions as a disincentive as far as cinema is concerned. So we wanted a kind of policy that would be fairly uniform for the whole country. We also wanted to look at cinema as an art form. We have different institutions like the Sangeet Natak Academy – the music and theatre academy – and we have an arts academy and an academy for painting and sculpture, and we wanted an academy for the cinema. The government hasn't taken any of these things seriously and different states continue to deal with film differently. We also were very keen that regional productions get some kind of support, particularly since they cannot compete easily with the pan-Indian Hindi cinema. The other committee was under Satyajit Ray in the late 1970s. I was a member of both those committees. We did bring out a very impressive document, very useful I thought, but very little has been done.

WvdH: Do you think that it is an important area to continue to be interested in?

SB: I think so. In India, cinema has always been part of the laissez-faire economy. Government support to the film industry in one way or another has been minimal, but what the government takes off the film industry is huge. In Maharashtra, 55 per cent of the price of the ticket is taken as entertainment tax. In Bihar it is 162 per cent of the price of the ticket.

WvdH: So it is a very important source of revenue for the state governments.

SB: The film business is therefore always trying to save itself from the government rather than get any kind of serious support from it. The politicians use film celebrities to garner support – the film industry has been used a great deal, but it hasn't received much attention from the government. Although recently it's been given the status of industry – for the first time.

WvdH: An official industry?

SB: Official, yes.

WvdH: That may well have some benefits.

SB: It will take time because the film industry functions like a cottage industry. Financing has always been through private sources. There has been no corporate financing of films by banks, insurance companies or financial institutions. So by getting the status of industry there will be some move towards working out a set of disciplines for the film industry.

WvdH: What about the difficulty of getting your films shown in cinemas? As you mentioned, you hoped to have *Samar* shown soon.[16]

SB: I have found a distributor for Maharashtra – what we call the Bombay territory – but I have to find distributors in other regions.

WvdH: So that's a very long process.

SB: It is – but I'm hoping that it won't be so difficult with this one.

WvdH: It raises the question of how people can get to see your films. They are distributed in cinemas, but do all of your films also end up being shown on television?

SB: They do. We get nation-wide television coverage. In fact my later films have been seen by a much larger audience than my earlier films. The earlier, very commercially successful films were never seen by as many people, because my later films were given television premieres.

WvdH: Is that way of showing the films financially viable?

SB: Not yet. You do need a combination of cinema screenings as well as television showings to recover the cost of the film.

WvdH: What about video as a distribution mechanism? I know that commercial Hindi films are widely distributed throughout all Indian communities in the world usually as pirated videos. Is video of any significance for you as a way of distributing your films?

SB: In India, not seriously now because there's so much video piracy and because there are so many television channels. Before television grew to the extent that it has in India, video was a fairly important means of getting a reasonable amount of revenue, but it no longer is so. Outside India, it is still fairly important.

WvdH: You have an interested audience outside of India as well. How important is the film festival circuit for you as a means of getting your films known and therefore seen?

SB: Not very effective, because for that you really require a fair amount of promotion. We haven't created the mechanism necessary to promote our films well at film festivals. We do appear at film festivals, but we've never really succeeded in marketing the films. It's always been some accidental something that happened. One of the best examples is Satyajit Ray's films. If it wasn't for John Huston, who saw *Pather Panchali* when Satyajit Ray showed it to him in Calcutta and decided to have it shown at the Museum of Modern Art in New York, it would have never reached the United States. And if it hadn't won the award at the Cannes Film Festival, it wouldn't have received any kind of attention in Europe. As a matter of fact it didn't for a very long period of time. It was only because of a small-time British film distributor [Contemporary Films], who also promoted my earlier films, that it got to be seen widely in Britain. And if it wasn't for Madame Kawakita, who saw *Pather Panchali* and just fell in love with it, it wouldn't have been known in Japan. This wasn't part of any kind of strategy, unlike what happened with Australian cinema, where a lot of money was spent to promote films and filmmakers like Peter Weir at Cannes, Venice and Berlin. There was this great push by the South Australian Film Corporation to promote Australian cinema and they went into it in a very big way, like China did with a filmmaker like Zhang Yimou. We've never done that, and we've never thought it necessary, nor have we had the necessary infrastructure to do that for Indian films.

WvdH: Does that mean that your international audience is really not only financially fairly insignificant but maybe also culturally insignificant?

SB: Well I wouldn't say that, but it's become less significant now than it used to be in the 1970s and 1980s. For the first fifteen or sixteen years, there was a great following for these films amongst our expatriate community, because at that time the big Bombay films hardly got any kind of distribution outside India. But now it's that kind of film that gets around more quickly than our kind of film.

WvdH: It's interesting that some of these big movies are being shown in cinemas in America.

SB: Yes, and in Britain.

WvdH: Even SBS television is showing some of the blockbusters like *Sholay*, which is very surprising because I would have thought that those films were not likely to be of great interest to the general audience.[17] It may be that the Indian communities in Australia are requesting such films.

SB: They have supported these films very strongly.

WvdH: Even the middle classes.

SB: Yes.

WvdH: Many Indian people still feel that the Bombay cinema is where their heart lies, even if their mind isn't necessarily in accord with it.

SB: There's a certain familiarity, there's a certain feeling of comfort.

WvdH: Maybe of home as well.

SB: Absolutely.

WvdH: They've been brought up with these films. Maybe like we've been brought up with Hollywood films of the 1940s and 1950s – there's comfortableness about that too.

SB: Yes, that's what it is largely.

Notes

1. These are the dominant languages of Andra Pradesh, Tamil Nadu, Karnataka, Kerala, Maharashtra, Gujarat and West Bengal, respectively. As mentioned in the previous interview, the first four states make over 60 per cent of all Indian films, whereas films made in Hindi (the 'all-Indian' films) represent just 20 per cent of total production (Rajadhyaksha and Willemen, 1999: 32). These Hindi films, however, have much larger budgets and their box-office takings far exceed those of the regional cinemas combined. Traditionally, Bombay (now Mumbai) was the production centre for Hindi films (hence Bollywood), but the situation is much more complex now, with Hindi films also being produced in other centres and successful regional films being dubbed into or re-made in Hindi for all-Indian distribution.

2. Sundar Kaali analyses the Tamil nativity film genre as an instance of the containment of modernity through the 'phallic affirmation of the rustic', with the rustic hero imposing his authority on the urban educated heroine (Kaali, 2000: 173).

3. This refers to the three films Satyajit Ray made from two novels by Bibhuti Bhushan Banerji, about the coming into adulthood of Apu: *Pather Panchali*, *Aparajito* and *Apur Sansar*.

4. Somewhat like the Apu trilogy, the Gorky trilogy depicted the early life of the Russian writer, Maxim Gorky: *The Childhood of Maxim Gorky* (1938), *My Apprenticeship* (1939) and *My Universities* (1940). The films were also favourites of the Australian film society movement in the 1960s, but they have largely disappeared from contemporary discussion of Soviet cinema.

5. Girish Karnad is a major Indian playwright, whose first film as scriptwriter and co-director (with B. V. Karanth) was the Kannada language *Vamsha Vriksha* (1971). He scripted a number of Shyam Benegal's films (*Nishant*, *Manthan* and *Kalyug*), also starring in the first two. His big budget Hindi film *Utsav* (The Festival, 1984) was produced by Shashi Kapoor (as *Kalyug* had been). B. V. Karanth continued to make films in Karnataka, usually with Girish Karnad. Adoor Gopalakrishnan and Govindan Aravindan are directors based in Kerala, who both work outside the commercial regional cinema tradition. Beginning their feature film career in the early 1970s (like Karnad, Karanth and Benegal), each has produced a series of striking, distinctive films, such as Gopalakrishnan's *Elippathayam* (The Rat Trap, 1981) and Aravindan's *Thampu* (The Circus Tent, 1978). Aravindan died in 1991.

6. The Film and Television Institute of India was set up in the former Prabhat Film Company Studio in Pune in 1960 as a training institution for aspiring filmmakers. Girish Karnad was its Director in 1974/5 and Adoor Gopalakrishan graduated from there in 1965 (Rajadhyaksha and Willemen, 1999: 95, 122, 102). Shyam Benegal was Chairman of the Institute for the 1980 to 1983 and the 1989 to 1992 trienniums (Datta, 2002: 58).

7. Writers like Ashish Rajadhyaksha consider Ritwik Ghatak as the most significant and innovative of all Indian filmmakers, developing an epic style that combines realism, myth and melodrama in films like *Meghe Dhaka Tara* (The Cloud-Capped Star, 1960). He was a Professor of Film Direction at the Film and Television Institute in 1966/7, where he taught future directors like Mani Kaul and Kumar Shahani (Rajadhyaksha and Willemen, 1999: 100, 365).

8. Mrinal Sen is the third of the Bengali 'triumvirate' (the other two being Satyajit Ray and Ritwik Ghatak), who all started film directing in the early to mid-1950s; only Sen is still alive and still making films. Influenced by European modernist film and 'third world' political cinema (e.g. Jean-Luc Godard and Glauber Rocha), Sen made a number of formally and politically radical films in the 1970s, when Calcutta was the centre of much social and political unrest. His 1969 Hindi-language film *Bhuvan Shome* is regarded as one of the founding works of the New Indian Cinema. In his 1980s films, he employed stars like Smita Patil, Shabana Azmi, Naseeruddin Shah and Om Puri (the last three together in the 1986 film, *Genesis*), all of whom had worked with Shyam Benegal in the 1970s.

9. Mani Kaul and Kumar Shahani represent the more experimental wing of Indian cinema. Both were taught by Ritwik Ghatak at the Film and Television Institute; while both drew upon European modernist cinema (e.g. Robert Bresson), they have shaped their aesthetic practices with reference to Indian performance, musical and painting traditions. Mani Kaul's *Uski Roti* (A Day's Bread, 1969) was, together with Mrinal Sen's *Bhuvan Shome*, one of the pioneering films of the New Indian Cinema, defining much of its 'formal vocabulary' (Rajadhyaksha and Willemen, 1999: 124). Kumar Shahani's *Tarang* (Wages and Profit, 1984) is, like Shyam Benegal's *Kalyug*, a contemporary adaptation of the *Mahabharata*, but Shahani rejects a dramatic approach in favour of an epic one (Chakravarty, 1993: 255).

10. Anand Patwardhan is regarded as India's most accomplished documentary filmmaker. While the films avoid didacticism, they also reject the 'objectivity' often considered crucial to documentary practice. Patwardhan instead adopts a strong position in relation to the socio-political issues he examines, whether in the feature-length films about Hindu fundamentalism, e.g. *Ram Ke Naam* (In the Name of God, 1992), or the very short but powerful presentation of the Dalit perspective in *The Other Story* (1994). His most recent film, *War and Peace* (2001), examines the India–Pakistan nuclear arms race.

11. The National Film Development Corporation (NFDC) is the central agency in India promoting 'quality' cinema. It produces and finances feature films; co-productions have included Richard Attenborough's *Gandhi* (1982), Mira Nair's *Salaam Bombay!* (1988) and Shyam Benegal's *The Making of the*

Mahatma (1996). It also exports Indian films and imports and distributes foreign films in India. 'Under the direct influence of Prime Minister Indira Gandhi, the FFC [The Film Finance Corporation, which became the NFDC in 1980] initiated the New Indian Cinema with Mrinal Sen's *Bhuvan Shome* and Mani Kaul's *Uski Roti*' (Rajadhyaksha and Willemen, 1999: 162).

12. The Dalits (meaning 'the oppressed') were originally called the Untouchables. Gandhi proposed that they be named the Harijans ('children of God'), but the community itself insists on Dalits. All three terms are used in this book.

13. Govind Nihalani was Shyam Benegal's cinematographer up to and including *Kalyug*, after which he turned to direction himself. His best-known film is *Ardh Satya* (The Half-Truth, 1983), a hard-hitting exposé of police corruption; the television serial *Tamas* (The Darkness, 1986) was a confronting and controversial study of the impact of Partition on ordinary people. M. S. Sathyu's *Garam Hawa* (Hot Winds, 1973) also dealt with the Partition, through a Muslim family's dilemma between staying in Agra or leaving for Pakistan; the film is considered the first Indian film to deal with this catastrophic event (Chakravarty, 1993: 248). It was co-scripted by Sathyu's wife, Shama Zaidi, who has worked on almost all of Shyam Benegal's films as scriptwriter and/or art director. Ketan Mehta graduated from the Film and Television Institute in 1975 and made a remarkable directing debut with *Bhavni Bhavai* (A Folk Tale, 1980), which mixes traditional folk performance with Brechtian distanciation. Some of these bold juxtapostionings are also evident in *Mirch Masala* (A Touch of Spice, 1985), starring Smita Patil as a woman who refuses to submit to patriarchal oppression – Patil's role has been directly compared with (and contrasted to) the character she played in Shyam Benegal's *Bhumika* (The Role, 1976) (Mazumdar, 1991). In 1992, Ketan Mehta released *Maya Memsaab* (The Enchanting Illusion), which continued his interest in hybridity, adapting Gustave Flaubert's *Madame Bovary* to an Indian context through the employment of Hindi cinema stylistic characteristics.

14. Shekhar Kapur's most successful Bollywood film was *Mr India* (1987), labelled by a character in one of Salman Rushdie's novels as 'Just a made-in-India runty-bodied imitation Bond' (Rushdie, 1995: 168), but Sridevi's spectacular water-drenched-sari dance routine epitomizes the strategy by mainstream Indian filmmakers to confine sexuality and eroticism to the song and dance numbers. While his filmmaking activities increasingly take place outside of India (*Bandit Queen* was made for Britain's Channel Four) Kapur defines his work in relation to India and Indian cinema, arguing that *Elizabeth* is influenced by Bombay cinema (melodrama and music) and that the issue of communalism and the rise to power of a powerful woman is as applicable to contemporary India as it was to Elizabethan England (Kazmi, 1999: 20).

15. Mira Nair began as a documentary filmmaker in the USA in the Leacock–Pennebaker tradition, and the documentary style remains a significant aspect of the portrayal of Bombay street children in her film *Salaam Bombay!*, which was highly praised by Western critics, but less enthusiastically received in India – Rustom Bharucha calls it the paradigmatic NRI (non-resident Indian) film (Bharucha, 1989: 1279). The same description could be applied to her recent film *Monsoon Wedding* (2001). Deepa Mehta also started in documentaries in Canada and made feature films in Canada and the USA before embarking on her ambitious and controversial 'elements' trilogy, of which the first two have been released: *Fire* (1996) about a lesbian love affair between two sisters-in-law (set in a middle-class urban Indian family, but shot in English) and *Earth* (1998), a story of a Parsi family in the city of Lahore on the eve of Partition (this time shot in Hindi). The third film, *Water*, premiered at the Toronto International Film Festival in September 2005. There are very few women film directors working in Indian cinema; examples include Aparna Sen, who works in the alternative/middle cinema terrain, e.g. *36 Chowringhee Lane* (1981), and Kalpana Lajmi, who was Shyam Benegal's assistant before moving to direction at the more mainstream end of the spectrum, e.g. *Rudaali* (The Mourner, 1992).

16. *Samar* was released in India in the second half of 1999.

17. SBS (Special Broadcasting Service) is Australia's multicultural radio and television service. Its television channel's film broadcasts are primarily non-English-language prestige and cult productions from around the world. While it has concentrated on Indian alternative and middle cinema films, in recent years a number of mainstream Hindi and Tamil films have also been shown.

Interview 4
From *Ankur* (1973) to *Manthian* (1976)

Figure 4: Lakshmi (Shabana Azmi) in *Ankur* (1973)

WvdH: On the plane from Hong Kong to Bombay I sat next to a businessman from Pune and I told him why I was coming to Bombay. He had heard of you and after a while he said that he remembered *Ankur* [The Seedling] very well. I was rather surprised, but I wonder if that film has perhaps resonated most with your audiences of all your films?

SB: Yes. Mainly because it was the very first film. It was also commercially very successful. Even today after twenty-six years, a large number of people continue to remember that film and some people remember it very vividly, but I attribute that largely to the fact that it was perhaps the first one of its kind, particularly in the Indian cinema. Although there were other films like it made, this was the most widely distributed of all the films made during that period.

WvdH: So it is in a sense your *Pather Panchali*.

SB: In that sense.

WvdH: Anyone thinking about Satyajit Ray or his films always thinks of that film.

SB: Well, that's what they do with me too. They think of *Ankur* before they think of anything else.

WvdH: Is that a bit frustrating for you?

SB: Well, I wouldn't say frustrating; it's a historical thing, that's how it happens. There's nothing you can do about it.

WvdH: No.

SB: Although it's a less fully realized film in many ways compared to several of my later films, but then it caught people's imagination in a way that the others haven't done. There are three other films of course that people do often refer to – *Manthan*, *Bhumika* [The Role, 1976] and *Junoon* [Obsession, 1978]. These films sometimes come up in a similar way – but it's always been *Ankur* before that.

WvdH: You mentioned that you had the idea for this film twelve years or so before it was actually made. How has the film changed over this period and why did you, coming from the background that you've described, decide to make a film about this particular subject?

SB: Well there were two reasons. It was based on an actual incident, which occurred when I was sixteen or so. There was this little farmhouse not far from where we lived and it was the story of one of the chaps who was a friend of mine. He was sent off by his father to look after the farm with a certain amount of city education. And so I saw it as a very interesting situation, with the father very feudal, while this boy is more part of the middle class – the attitudes were very interesting to study. I had written a short story based on that incident for my college magazine. Later I decided that I was going to make a script of it. But my first attempts at scripting it turned it into a very melodramatic kind of story, which I wasn't very happy with. I was very enthusiastic about it but later when I read it again I felt that it was much too melodramatic. I then reworked it many times before I eventually made it into a film, because then one could see the social dimensions of it much more clearly.

WvdH: By the time you made the film in 1973, the context of the story would have altered, because of the political changes that occurred in the 1960s and 1970s.

SB: Yes, absolutely. The 1950s and 1960s were the crucial period as far as India was concerned with land reform programmes in some states. The whole feudal structure was breaking down and new structures were being formed. So in the context of that, the script also tended to change.

WvdH: Then there was the difficulty of finding someone to fund your film.

SB: That took a very long time.

WvdH: And this is where your agency work came in.

SB: While I was working in an advertising agency, I used to take the script and meet producers. I met a very large number of producers and they were all concerned about the film having a heroine who sleeps with and bears a child with a man other than her husband and yet the audience is expected to have sympathy for her. I would come against this kind of reaction, because the Indian film stories are usually very traditional and very conservative.

WvdH: And this wasn't an acceptable story?

SB: Certainly not acceptable as a film story. Until finally I talked with a distributor of advertising films, which in those days used to be shown in cinemas all over the country. He was a friend of mine and I asked him one day why he didn't think of producing a film. He said if it didn't cost very much money he might think of doing that. I said it's going to cost practically nothing. I wanted only a very small sum of money to make the film and he agreed. Fortunately for me, not merely did he become a producer but he was also my distributor.

WvdH: Because he was already into distribution anyway – a very fortuitous arrangement!

SB: Yes.

WvdH: Was that company, which was Blaze Enterprises, set up or was it already in existence?

SB: There was a company called Blaze Advertising Services, which was in existence. Blaze Film Enterprises was formed by these people in order to produce films.

WvdH: Did they only ever produce your films?

SB: They produced five of my films, one film for Govind Nihalani and one film for Shekhar Kapur – *Masoom* [Innocent, 1982].[1]

WvdH: That arrangement obviously worked very well for you and continued for some time.

SB: It continued until both the partners died.

WvdH: Those were the ones you dedicated *Bhumika* to.

SB: Yes.

WvdH: Basically there were two families involved.

SB: That's right. Once the original people died, their children couldn't get along with each other, so they split and that was the end of Blaze Film Enterprises as a company. If they had continued I should imagine that to this day I would never have needed another producer.

WvdH: Yes, because it was such a good arrangement.

SB: It was a very good arrangement. They had very good distribution and I could carry on making films one after the other every year without any problems. They broke the whole distribution system. Distribution of Hindi films functions like a cartel, with everyone tending to distribute the same kind of films. They're very afraid of trying to distribute a film that doesn't fall into the general pattern of Hindi films. If you don't have so many songs or dances, they get very anxious and they're not sure they want to release pictures like this. But these people had no such inhibitions.

WvdH: So I suppose the next thing was getting a crew to make a film like this and also the cast - these people don't come out of thin air.

SB: No.

WvdH: How did you set up the production unit?

SB: The unit was easily constructed because I had been in filmmaking for some time and so that wasn't too difficult. Govind Nihalani had already been my cameraman on a fairly large number of documentaries and even advertising commercials. I had my editor - the same editor I've had for most of my films until very recently - Bhanudas [Divkar]. The difficult part was casting the film. Originally I thought I might take a couple of stars for the film, but none of them agreed to be in the film. They were unwilling for the same reasons that producers didn't want to pick up this film - expecting the audience to identify with a heroine who sleeps with a man who is not her husband. So everybody in that film was new. Shabana Azmi had just come out of the Film and Television Institute of India.[2] Somebody had asked her to come and see me because I was casting for a film. I'd chosen an actor to play the role of the young man, but this boy fell sick with jaundice just before I was going off to location. The dialogue writer for this film, Satyadev Dubey, who was a playwright and theatre producer, sent me one of his young actors thinking that I might use him as the young man in my film. He needed some moral support so he brought another young man with him. As it turned out I took the young man who'd come as the moral support.[3]

WvdH: That's the danger of taking someone with you to an audition.

SB: Yes, he became a fairly well-known actor and later on a big star in Kannada cinema – Anant Nag, who's now [January 1999] a Minister in the Kannada state government.[4]

WvdH: People like Shabana Azmi and Anant Nag as well as the technical crew have now become mainstays of Indian cinema. Why do you think you have been so successful in finding the casts that you've had and in predicting the abilities of the actors over so many years?

SB: Very difficult to tell. But one thing is certain. The people who have worked with me are very talented and have a great deal of commitment. Commitment is very important. If you have somebody with a great deal of commitment, then it follows that even if they don't have that much talent, their willingness to give their all is something that commends them. There are a very large number of actors in the Bombay film industry today who started their careers with me. But after a while you develop a reputation as being a person who can spot talent. So a lot of talented people come to see me.

WvdH: It becomes a self-fulfilling prophecy.

SB: Yes, it's a self-fulfilling prophecy in that sense, which is what has happened in the last twenty-five, twenty-six years. So a large number of the most talented people in the film business today started off with me.

WvdH: And they continue to work at various times with you as well.

SB: They do.

WvdH: Obviously, the production unit that you have is a very important unit in the literal sense of the word, having that unity, and that commitment.

SB: Yes.

WvdH: You made the film on location in Andhra Pradesh. Did you make a conscious decision to shoot it in Hindi?

SB: Yes. Originally I had planned to do it in Telugu. It was really at the suggestion of my producer, who said that if you make the film in Telugu we will never be able to release it anywhere else. I was making the film near Hyderabad – a multi-lingual place – and they speak a kind of Hindustani there called Dakhni, which is the language I eventually used for the film.

WvdH: Right, so it's an accented Hindi?

SB: Yes, it's an accented Hindi and it could be understood everywhere that Hindi is spoken. I'm glad that I didn't make it in Telugu because then I would have remained a regional filmmaker.

WvdH: But in a sense, by becoming a Bombay filmmaker, you had embraced a Hindi film perspective of wanting to communicate with the broader community.

SB: But I believe that the more culturally specific you are, the more universal you will be.

WvdH: Because of that specificity.

SB: Yes. This is why I feel that I don't have to work in that culturally generalized context, taking a completely homogeneous view of life.

WvdH: If we come to the film itself, what's striking is that the opening sequence has a strong ethnographic feel to it, in that the credit sequence sets up a particular local ritual in an almost documentary way. We meet the central couple in the film taking part in this ritual because they want a child.[5]

SB: It's a fertility ritual.

WvdH: That's very striking because there is very little of that sense of the anthropological in the rest of the film.

SB: It does come and go throughout the film. It is there. For people who live an agrarian life, the seasons are very important. There are always rites for different seasons. There are also rites of passage and that keeps coming through the film. We have a traditional form, which is called Chaumasa and Baramasa. Chaumasa refers to the four seasons and Baramasa are the twelve months of the year. There are rites for every month, and rites for seasons, which also closely resemble rites of passage in life. In some ways, the film is one of the rites of passage of that young man.

WvdH: Even though you've presented it as a very critical one.

SB: Yes.

WvdH: But woven into that are the other rituals that have to do with the way in which the people live on the land.

SB: During the month of winter solstice, dawn excursions take place with groups of people singing hymns going around the village; this ends on the Sankranti day, which occurs on the 14th of January and signifies change – from the cold season to the warm season. There are many such things throughout the film.

WvdH: There is also that group of singing men who wander behind the back of the hut in the film.

SB: There's also the other rite of passage – the funeral. These different things are very much part of agrarian life in India. Into that you have this kind of intervention.

WvdH: There is quite a radical shift after that opening ritual sequence, when we suddenly move to the urban environment, where we meet the young man, Surya, and learn about him and his family.

SB: And about his relationship with his father.

WvdH: And importantly about his father's relationship with his mistress.

SB: That's it.

WvdH: We then go with him to the village. Interestingly, we're not in the village watching him coming. Was that an important strategy for you?

SB: It was important because he had not lived in a village. He was different from his father in that sense. He had not grown up in the village, he was being sent there. So it is his discovery of rural life.

WvdH: Initially he comes across as a very positive figure. He's a man who rejects the feudal aspects of caste, for example. He doesn't want anything to do with the priest. And so he becomes a positive identification figure for the viewer, but gradually, as the film goes on, that relationship changes and we become more and more critical of the way in which he deals with life. And maybe, towards the end, he is a lesser man than his father.

SB: He is.

WvdH: Because at least his father is honest about his relationship with these people and is not duplicitous. Why did you feel the need to present such a very critical perspective of the educated middle classes?

SB: The middle classes continue to remain in transition. It's a class that hasn't created its own values. The whole feudal system had very specific values. They were oppressive, they were terrible but they had a set of values. But here is a situation in which that old value system has not been replaced by a new value system. It's a transitional phase in which there is actually a breakdown in values. To me the film was in some ways a reflection of the processes taking place in India.

WvdH: The character of Lakshmi is someone attempting to negotiate a place in relation to this middle class – she has to make the best of it.

SB: Yes, absolutely.

WvdH: Her sleeping with Surya – a situation that was considered unacceptable for an Indian film – is never seen in moralistic terms.

SB: It's not, but it is seen in moral terms in that she too has a right as a human being. She has the right to a full life.

WvdH: Lakshmi has a right to a life even though she was married to her husband against her will. He had provided for her family and she accepted that they would become husband and wife.

SB: Yes.

WvdH: I feel that she is the dominant figure in her relationship with her husband. She controls their world but she can't control the world of the landlord's son. She is trapped in that world. Is that the sort of dichotomy that exists for women like her?

SB: I wouldn't over-generalize, but to some extent, it is true. She certainly can't be in control of the situation she is in. She is a victim as far as the landlord is concerned. She's a victim of so many factors because she's a dependent, she's a serf of the land and so she has very few choices. When it comes to a personal relationship with her husband, she does have control. It's a feudal situation in which she lives on the landlord's land and remains entirely at his mercy.

WvdH: Yes, that's right.

SB: This is part of the socio-economic condition, which people remain in throughout large parts of India.

WvdH: Surya's wife is equally a victim. She is also trapped in a particular role that she has to play, which is to reject the servant girl.

SB: Yes, she is. It would be automatic for her to do that even as a human being, as a person, as a wife. She wouldn't and she cannot accept a situation like this for herself where another woman is involved with her husband. So she tries in her own way to separate that relationship, but she's also very human and she can see the problems of her husband – that essentially he's a very weak human being.

WvdH: This becomes apparent at the end of the film.

SB: She loses respect for her husband.

WvdH: We see him whimpering at the door at the end, unable to face what's happened. There's been some criticism, including from Satyajit Ray, of the melodramatic ending of the film.[6]

SB: I don't think that it's melodramatic at all; I think it's very true. But what I think Ray had said was that he felt that I had tipped things against Surya.

WvdH: Demonized him in a way.

SB: I had tipped the story against him. I don't think I did. Ray also mentioned something else. He said I'd created a quadrangle and that creating a quadrangle wasn't the best way to deal with a story. He said stick with the old triangle. This is what he told me – personally I mean – he didn't write about it. I disagreed with him because in this case my concern is not just about Surya, but also about a certain generation that was coming into adulthood at that time. I was looking at the transition, where old values no longer held and new values had yet to emerge. So this young man had no real values, even though he thinks he has.

WvdH: Lakshmi does get what she wants in the film. She has the child who she desired so greatly even though it was in this very unfortunate circumstance. But she does actually gain what she prayed for at the beginning of the film.

SB: She's not a helpless victim. It goes against my grain to portray people as helpless because if I have any kind of agenda it's to show that people can empower themselves. That is one of the aspects that you might find in all my films.

WvdH: As far as the *mise-en-scène* of the film goes and the way that you constructed the shots particularly around the house of the landlord's son, it seems to me that you've organized the scenes so that they're often set up from the perspective of Surya rather than from the perspective of Lakshmi. Was there a particular way that you thought about visualizing those scenes between the two of them?

SB: Yes. You may have noticed that even in the beginning when he goes to the village, it's his response to the farmhouse and the fields that is accentuated, not the other way around. I've maintained that all the way through the film, so that for much of the time you do see the film from his point of view – you are taken into the narrative from his position. Where it really changes is when the little boy at the end of the film throws the stone at the house.

WvdH: The shot before that is of Surya crying inside the house, standing against the door.

SB: Yes. We move away from him towards an objective view without any subjective rhythms or viewpoints.

WvdH: Was he the little boy who we saw a number of times throughout the film?

SB: Yes, he had seen the deaf mute steal toddy from the tree and he was witness to several things that happened in the village during the film. It is his response to the happenings that are represented by that stone throwing.

WvdH: And it was important that it was a little boy rather than an adult.

SB: Right, it was important to me because he's not carrying any baggage of the past; he's not carrying any kind of views, other than what he has seen. It's what one might call an uncluttered straightforward response.

WvdH: What did the screen going red indicate?

SB: There's a historical context there. Telangana, where I shot the film, was an area of quite considerable upheaval during the period in which the film was set. There was a peasant revolt against feudalism and it became very militant. It eventually had to be put down by the Indian army. The film shows that there is an awareness growing among people of their own rights – it's the beginning of what is going to become a full-blown revolt against this whole system.

WvdH: This historical context is most interesting. Even though the film doesn't provide an overt indication of when it's set, Lakshmi referred to a Telugu film which was made in the 1940s.

SB: That's it.

WvdH: So the film is actually set in the late 1940s?

SB: Early 1950s.

WvdH: There are also references to the playback singer Lata Mangeshkar and the actress Nimmi.[7]

SB: The film Lakshmi refers to is called *Balanagamma* [1942], which was a very well-known Telugu film that went on for ever. It used to be the favourite film during that time for a religious festival called Shiva Ratri, which occurs in February, and you're supposed to keep awake all night. This was a favourite film to get people to remain awake because it ran all night.

WvdH: So it was a useful film to name in your film.

SB: Yes, because it was very popular in that region.

WvdH: This first film of yours also focuses on woman as the basis of a critique of society, not only through Lakshmi but also through two other women in the film – one of whom is gambled away like Draupadi in the *Mahabharata*, while the other is tried in the village for leaving her husband for another man. Did you intend to provide a broad perspective of the ways women are treated in the society?

SB: Yes. Woman as commodity, woman as serf, woman at the mercy of man. All these concepts are fairly traditional to Indian society, but also occur in all societies of the world.

WvdH: It's often suggested that the modernization of women is the modernization of a society.

SB: Yes, because gender equality automatically represents massive social change. It also represents a massive change in the entire socio-economic structures of the country – even the politics of the country.

WvdH: Gender equality and sexuality in relation to gender are issues that seem to recur throughout your work.

SB: Social change is constantly focused on these things. You'll notice that in the politics of this country it's a constant theme that enters the mainstream discourse. We're now talking about reservations [of seats] for women in Parliament and in various legislative assemblies. In the political and economic life of the country, the establishment of women's rights is a necessary part of social egalitarianism.

WvdH: Right from the beginning you indicated your interest and concern with that theme and, as you say, it comes through again and again. You mentioned that the film was somewhat unsatisfactory. What would you say were the things that in retrospect disappointed you about the film?

SB: Well there are a couple of things – they were mainly technical. It wasn't in terms of performances or character development, which worked out quite well in the film. But in terms of its pacing and rhythm, sometimes I felt it was a little too slack. It was lack of experience, lack of understanding of how long narratives work. After a while you learn through experience when to cut. You don't allow your information to dissipate entirely within a shot. These are things that you tend to learn.

WvdH: I remember a scene where Lakshmi is at the market buying provisions and she turns around to see her husband drunk and asleep on the cart and she walks past him into the distance. The shot goes on for quite a while and I think it is in fact useful that it does. There you wouldn't want to cut it any earlier.

SB: No, not there.

WvdH: It's a wonderful moment – expressing her concern and ultimately her frustration with him.

SB: The problem is not in moments like that; it's in other situations. There are moments where there's no necessary information and the shot just remains, it becomes decorative.

WvdH: Your aim would be to chop away at those sorts of things?

SB: You don't want them to go on where nothing more is going to emerge from them.

WvdH: No, except time.

SB: Yes.

WvdH: And some filmmakers do want to deal with time.

SB: That depends on the kind of film you're making. There are certain concepts in the cinema where there's a deliberate holding on to shots so that you're forced to go along with that rhythm – the filmmaker has some other design in mind, sometimes like minimalist music. There are different ways of approaching a film, but this particular film was not that kind of a film, it was a fairly straight narrative.

WvdH: *Charandas Chor* [Charandas the Thief, 1975], which I haven't seen, is, I believe, made for children. This is quite a different direction after the first one, isn't it?

SB: Yes.

WvdH: Was there a particular impetus that drove you to make that film?

SB: Well yes. I got very interested in certain folk stories. There's a wonderful folklorist in Rajasthan called Vijay Dan Detha, who collected a lot of folk stories from there. One of them was this story of an honest thief. The story was marvellous because it has this wonderful sense of discovery for children, particularly when they relate themselves to moral questions – to right and wrong, honesty and dishonesty. It was a beautiful story, which I changed and set in Chhatisgarh, which is in Madhya Pradesh.[8] The only urban actress was Smita Patil – it was her first film with me – and the rest of them were all folk actors belonging to folk theatrical companies.[9] There is a very fine theatre producer we have in India called Habib Tanvir and he has specialized in that form of folk theatre, which is known as Nautanki, and these are all Nautanki actors.[10] Habib himself played a small part in the film as a lawyer. The reason for doing this film was largely because I was impressed with these actors, whom I had worked with earlier on a series of television extramural educational programmes for small children. I'd done a series of twenty-nine programmes for a satellite television experiment in 1974. The programmes were educational modules, which could be set up in different ways for children, using learning methods from non-literate oral societies. I made them with these actors and I felt that it would be a wonderful idea to make a children's feature with them, and that's how I chose this story of *Charandas Chor*. It had a lot of slapstick humour and it was done as a slapstick comedy, using acting styles ranging from Buster Keaton and Chaplin to Laurel and Hardy.

WvdH: It's the only one that you've done in that slapstick mode?

SB: I haven't done any more like that. I didn't have an opportunity and my own interests started to move in other directions. But it was a very satisfying film to make.

WvdH: With *Nishant* [The Night's End, 1975] you returned to many of the same issues that you had dealt with in *Ankur*.

Figure 5: Poster for *Nishant* (1975)

SB: Right, and there we returned to the beginnings of that massive revolt in Telangana that I mentioned.

WvdH: So the ending of *Nishant* is the beginning of that revolt, that rebellion against the *zamindar* [landlord] regime.

SB: Exactly.

WvdH: You don't locate the film. The opening title states 'In a feudal state … the year 1945'.

SB: No, I had located it. What had happened was, in 1975, when I made this film, Emergency had been declared by Mrs Gandhi and censorship was very strong. Now it so happened that soon after the Emergency was declared, the film was ready and it was in competition at Cannes. It had gone to various important festivals and had won several awards. When the film had to be censored, the censors banned the film. I, Satyajit Ray, Mrinal Sen and a whole lot of filmmakers wrote a letter to the Prime Minister, Mrs Gandhi. She was very upset that the film was banned like that because she felt that it was going to rebound. She asked to see the film. She had loved *Ankur* and was very curious why her government had banned this film. She liked the film very much and she was very upset with the Minister of Information and Broadcasting for banning the film. But he couldn't completely retract from his position so he said that I would have to make some ridiculous cuts in the film. Since they were not at all significant, I agreed to cut it down. Then I was told that you couldn't say that this happened in independent India. So he insisted that we should have a placard at the beginning of the film and at the end of the film that these events had taken place before India became independent. I was very happy to put that in, because I knew that as far as the audiences were concerned they would be drawn to the statement that it had happened before Independence and there would be this big laugh by the audience as soon as this placard came up. It really was ridiculous. So the reference to a feudal state was really imposed by the censors. At that time you had no civil liberties at all, so you had to subvert the process.[11]

WvdH: I don't know whether this is related, but there's a little dialogue scene later on in the film between Sushila, the Shabana Azmi character, and the servant in the house where there is no sound on the soundtrack.

SB: There is sound.

WvdH: But for a short while, maybe about thirty seconds, the dialogue continues visually, but there's no sound.

SB: But there are effects. That was purposefully done, because there was nothing more to say. It was used as a technique for the film.

WvdH: As in the first film, you set up a social structure – here you take about twenty minutes to set out the workings of the village and of the *zamindar* family.

SB: It's laid out in great detail because it was important to do that.

WvdH: And you used the theft of the jewels from the temple as a sort of mechanism for the viewer to get to know the various characters.

SB: To know the power structures of the village.

WvdH: Then after about twenty minutes, like in the first film, we have the outsider come into the village. Here the teacher brings his wife and child and they become a trigger for the conflicts that occur.[12]

SB: Yes.

WvdH: Even before the teacher's wife, Sushila, is abducted, it appears to me as if you are paralleling the teacher and his wife with Vishwam and his wife. You cut between them on visual symbols, like water being poured, already linking those two couples. Did you want to stress that there was some similarity between the two marriages?

SB: There was a certain kind of similarity. There was also a certain degree of indifference and neglect, in both cases. There is also the restlessness of the schoolteacher's wife, Sushila. She has hardly any social communion with anyone and her husband is so indifferent to her own sexuality.

WvdH: She wants to keep attracting him, even asking him to buy a mirror for her. So, despite the fact that she is abducted and raped, the film is also about her sexual awakening and the development of her own individuality, isn't it?

SB: Yes, that is the main thing.

WvdH: It's very interesting because she is being degraded, while at the same time an awakening is occurring as well. The husband, the teacher, doesn't come out of this terribly well.

SB: He comes out as a wimp.

WvdH: Is he a bit like Surya in *Ankur* then?

SB: Yes he is, in the sense that he has not found his own values. He is forced into action, eventually. Then there is the fact that the wife really doesn't want to go back to him.

WvdH: So is he another ineffective middle-class intellectual?

SB: He is.

WvdH: Some people have suggested that the film is related to *Straw Dogs* [1971], but I'm not sure that I see that as being very important.

SB: No, I don't think it is.

WvdH: The expectation that he might fight for her is quite contrary to his nature.

SB: He couldn't have done that – he's a schoolmaster. What his wife resents is his inability to recognize her as an individual with her own feelings. He does want to fight against injustice and various other things, but he can't see his own injustice to his wife.

WvdH: While he doesn't ever say it himself, he probably would refuse to have his wife back. Others say that he doesn't need to take her back, because she has been used by another man.

SB: But he has to redeem himself, he must become whole again.

WvdH: But do you think he does in the film?

SB: Well he attempts to, certainly.

WvdH: He tries to do it through bureaucracies initially.

SB: It doesn't work. None of the instrumentalities of the government and the state come to his aid at all. Finally the village itself rises up and he becomes part of that.

WvdH: But he can no longer save his wife because she is really no longer his wife.

SB: She doesn't want to come back to him.

WvdH: At that moment when she meets him in the temple she has already decided and then she proceeds to demand her own rights in the new household.

SB: That's it.

WvdH: She's seen that she's no longer part of her husband's world.

SB: No, exactly.

WvdH: The flashpoint that occurs at the end of the film is brought about by the religious procession coming past the house of the *zamindar*.

SB: Yes.

WvdH: Is it important that it is a religious event that causes the trigger for the violence?

SB: Yes, because it's religious events that get people together. There have been folk performances of the epic *Ramayana* at the temple leading up to this festival. This epic is the story of good prevailing over evil and it is a model, with the village being used as a parallel. Typically, the entire village takes part in the procession and the temple car or chariot is taken to the most prominent person in the village and he would do the *arati*, which is a kind of *puja* of the God.[13]

WvdH: The worship of the God.

SB: In the film that becomes the occasion when the village people revenge themselves on the landlord and his family.

WvdH: There has been some debate as to whether it's actually a revolution or just a violent devastation, in other words whether it has a purpose or whether it is purely revenge.

SB: There's no question it is revenge. But historically speaking, events like this became the beginnings of a far-reaching revolt that took place in that region, Telangana. This Telangana movement was an anti-feudal militant movement that got rid of quite a number of these big feudal landlords and attempted to create a kind of a commune. This took place around the late 1940s and early 1950s in that part of India. The film itself was based on an event that became the beginning of that revolt and that incident did take place very close to where I shot the film.

WvdH: As you mentioned, the *Ramayana* references are very strong in the film, and in a sense what happens is that Sita escapes with Ravana, rather than Ram rejecting Sita because of her supposed unfaithfulness. It really turns the traditional story on its head.

SB: Yes. In the last part of the *Ramayana* a washerman actually accuses Ram of taking Sita back after she's been abducted by Ravana. Now Ram is considered India's most just king and Ram Raj is the ideal state. Ram decides that with one of the least members of the populace accusing him, he cannot have her as a stigma on his rule. So Sita finds herself rejected. That's one of the concepts we've turned on its head – she leaves with the abductor rather than stay with her husband, who has in fact fought to get her back. But it deals also with the fact that she recognizes her own sexuality. That's one of the main points about the story.

WvdH: There is also her sense of her independence, which stands in contrast to Sita, who was willing to go through fire to prove her devotion to Ram and he eventually took her back on that basis. Traditional stories like the *Ramayana* and the *Mahabharata*, which you use in *Kalyug* [The Machine Age, 1980], are also central to the Hindi popular cinema, but your use of them is often much more ironic and much more critical. Is that an important distinction for you?

SB: Yes, but there is also a keener understanding of the epics themselves because the epics have a complexity that a lot of us would like not to see. There are social views and attitudes that exist in the epics that are quite extraordinary, apart from the many interpretations and interpolations that have come into those epics. One has to look at them in so many different ways, whether it is for an ironic perspective or to use them as parallels. Whichever way you look at them, they play a very important part in Indian life.

WvdH: You wouldn't want to reject their importance in any way?

SB: Not at all, because they are the essential lifeblood of Indian civilization.

WvdH: The final scene, which is abstract like the final scene of *Ankur*, has the camera tracking into the children in the temple. Are they still listening to the performance of the *Ramayana*?

SB: No, well actually, yes. It's this new version.

WvdH: The new version of the *Ramayana*?

SB: Yes.

WvdH: The one that the film has told?

SB: Yes. That's what they've been witness to.

WvdH: Like the little boy in *Ankur* who's been witness to all the events in the film?

SB: Yes, because that's the way things move into the future.

WvdH: Was the film based on a play by Vijay Tendulkar?[14]

SB: No. It was based on an incident that was one of the seminal events of the Telangana movement.

WvdH: Yes, as you mentioned.

SB: Utpal Dutt, one of our great theatre producers of Bengal, had asked Vijay Tendulkar to write a play based on that incident.[15]

WvdH: Oh I see.

SB: When Tendulkar mentioned this to me, I suggested he write a film script instead.

WvdH: Instead?[16]

SB: Yes. So he wrote a film story rather than a play. I sent him off to the places where this particular incident had taken place, and after considerable research, he wrote the script.

WvdH: You worked with him again in *Manthan* [The Churning]. Was that a play that he had already written?

SB: No, that was an original script again, based on research of how the milk co-operatives were developing. It all started when I was doing a couple of documentaries about the co-operative movement, particularly milk co-operatives, which have been the most successful in India – they've made India the second largest milk producer in the world. By next year [2000] we should be the largest milk producer in the world. It's a miracle that has taken place. While I was making a film called *The Quiet Revolution* [1975] about this process, I came across many different kinds of incidents and spoke to the man who was behind it all, Dr Kurien. I told him that if one really wants to understand this thing it requires a fiction feature, rather than a documentary. Documentaries don't have the kind of emotional strength and charge that you need. You have to get to see the motivation of people themselves and how they work, what their relationships are, what the politics of the village is, what the social characteristics of villages are, what the economic problems are and then how they relate to one another in different ways. Dr Kurien thought of a wonderful idea because the milk producers, the farmers, would give milk twice a day, in the morning and the evening, at the milk collection centres all over the state, and they get paid in the evening for the milk that they gave in the morning and in the morning for the previous evening's milk. So he asked these people if they would like to be producers of a film about their experience – it wouldn't cost them very much money, so they just got two rupees less on a particular day.[17]

WvdH: That's wonderful, isn't it?

SB: They not only earned back their investment, they also made a profit. And they also became the primary audience for the film in the first instance.

WvdH: Did they come to Bombay to watch the film?

SB: No, they saw it in Ahmedabad and in different places where they actually lived. They would hire lorries and buses and whole villages would come to the cinema and see their film.

WvdH: So they were in fact making their own film successful.

SB: Yes, although the film was very successful all over the country. It was among the most widely seen films in this country, through 16 mm prints, through super 8 and eventually through videocassettes. It probably has been seen by more people than the most successful commercial film in India.

WvdH: Because it worked on that grass-roots level.

SB: And then UNDP [the United Nations Development Program] used it. It was shown in China, in Russia. It has been used in their co-operative movements. In Latin America. In Africa. It's had an enormous use all over the world. It's one of those extraordinary things that happened with that film.

WvdH: The fact that it was a fiction film was only to its advantage in that respect?

SB: Yes.

WvdH: Even though the audiences were so diverse in terms of their own cultural experience.

SB: Yes, because it was a fiction film, it could cross cultural boundaries.

WvdH: More easily than a documentary.

SB: More easily than a documentary would.

WvdH: Just before leaving *Nishant*, there was one last question that I had about the use of the song as commentary, which you introduce in that film and which becomes an ongoing means in your films of commenting on the action. Here you use a sixteenth-century poem for that purpose.

Figure 6: Poster for *Manthan* (1976)

SB: But in *Nishant*, it's more a commentary on Sushila and her feelings. The poet, Quli Qutb Shah, was one of the most famous kings of a medieval kingdom of that region called the Qutb Shahi kingdom. He was one of the first poets of the Urdu language in the country, when that language had not yet fully developed. It's a very beautiful poem about love and longing.[18]

WvdH: The scoring of the poem by Vanraj Bhatia is lovely too. For *Manthan*, you used an original poem as commentary.

SB: Yes.

WvdH: Vanraj Bhatia told me how it was composed and that there were problems with the timing, because the opening shot of the train coming into the station wasn't long enough.[19] I felt that the song in *Manthan* functioned as Bindu's voice.[20]

SB: Yes.

WvdH: Because she doesn't have much of a voice in the film.

SB: No. She also belongs to an Untouchable community, which is kept voiceless – a totally marginalized community.

WvdH: The song articulates her longing and her desire for love, but there's also an irony in the poem describing the 'ideal village'. There's nothing ideal about that village.

SB: No.

WvdH: But it's a wonderful song that comes in at various times throughout the film. What does it do that could not have been presented through the plot? Do you think it adds something in particular?

SB: It does. Vanraj Bhatia wrote the song in the form of Gujarati folk music. That gave it a great deal of the character of the region, so that you knew where you were. The lyrics were an invitation to come to that village, where milk flows.

WvdH: Yes, an ideal sense of life.

SB: It is also a kind of desire for life to be like that – the whole film is moving towards that objective anyway.

WvdH: Towards the resolution of the power conflicts within this community. What's so interesting for me is that you start, as in the previous films, with a stranger coming into town and finish with him leaving, but the film remains with the Untouchable trying to determine how he should take responsibility for his own life.

SB: This involves both the gaining of self-esteem and developing the ability to do things for themselves, which was taken away from them over a long period of time.

WvdH: Do you think that this needs to be done, as it does in the film, by this urban intellectual outsider?

SB: Not necessarily, but it does require some kind of a catalyst. It does not necessarily have to be an outsider. For anything to start to change within the community requires an infusion of a new idea. Otherwise everything remains static. So it always requires some kind of an intervention.

WvdH: And that's the role of Dr Rao in the film. But as with some of these figures in earlier films, the teacher in *Nishant* or the landlord's son in *Ankur*, Dr Rao is not altogether a knight in shining armour. This is an important approach, so as not to construct the heroic figure typical of some liberally inclined Hollywood films. Dr Rao's character is complicated by his own desires and fallibilities.

SB: Right. By his own unhappy marriage – he neglects his wife; he feels that she doesn't understand him. All sorts of other complexities enter into the picture.

WvdH: His wife with her passion for Hindi film music is obviously not interested in what he's doing. And he's attracted to the Untouchable woman Bindu, but he doesn't want to take it too far. There are practical reasons for that, but his desire for Bindu becomes representative of his relations with the farmers. He can't go too far, he can't be part of them. Do you think that's so?

SB: Yes, he can't be. He has to maintain a certain kind of discipline because that discipline breaks down with one of the members of the team having an affair with a village girl, which causes all kinds of social upheavals. So he has a problem because he really cannot express how he feels about Bindu. If he did, what he came there for would actually be destroyed.

WvdH: On the other hand she feels that he has looked at her and that he is not willing to proceed with what that implied.

SB: That's right.

WvdH: She becomes extremely confused. Later on, she tries to voice that, but she's not allowed to speak. Others insist on speaking on her behalf. Such things stop the film from becoming a propaganda film, which I suppose is always the danger with this sort of film.

SB: Yes, the danger is there. I didn't want to make a propaganda film. It had to remain with its human dimensions.

WvdH: Were you pressured into being more propagandist than you were?

SB: No.

WvdH: You had total freedom?

SB: Total.

WvdH: Is the documentary in the film in fact *The Quiet Revolution*?

SB: Yes.

WvdH: We know very little of Dr Rao's cultural background. He is a blank figure in some ways.

SB: Well, of course he is urban middle class, but I never really felt the need to show that too much because it's understood. In India certainly it's understood. I mean he's the kind of person who has a degree of idealism and wants things to change. He's of a generation that came into adulthood soon after Independence and who believed that this country needed to change.

WvdH: This is the Nehru legacy.

SB: Yes, the Nehruvian legacy. I didn't need to detail that much more because it's easily understood.

WvdH: The sort of idealism that he holds and tries to activate perhaps didn't persist in the following generations.

SB: Now, in the 1990s, the influence of so-called 'liberalization' has made people feel that it's very important that they do well for themselves. Being successful today means also making a lot of money. For that earlier generation it wasn't quite like that.

WvdH: It strikes me as being one of your most optimistic films, suggesting the possibility of change from within the individual or within the community.

SB: True.

WvdH: I noticed that some or all of the dialogue was done by Kaifi Azmi.[21]

SB: Yes.

WvdH: He worked with Guru Dutt in the 1950s and he's Shabana Azmi's father. Why did you engage him?

SB: Because he belonged to a generation that understood these ideals. He is a person whose value system was very close to this.

WvdH: What did he do that Vijay Tendulkar couldn't have done?

SB: Vijay Tendulkar wrote the script in English. Kaifi Azmi wrote the dialogues.

WvdH: Was it spoken in Gujarati or with a Hindi-Gujarati accent?

SB: It was spoken in Hindi, but we actually invented a language which was not quite Gujarati and which was not quite Hindi because people in that region don't really speak Hindi. They speak Gujarati. But people outside of Gujarat could understand what was being said; yet you knew that it related to a specific region. So what was done was to invent a language, which was understandable all over the country.

Notes

1. Blaze Film Enterprises produced *Ankur*, *Nishant*, *Bhumika*, *Mandi* and *Trikal* (Past, Present, Future, 1985) for Shyam Benegal and the television serial *Tamas* (The Darkness, 1986) for Govind Nihalani. The original partners were Mohan J. Bijlani and Fali M. Variava. *Bhumika*, dedicated to their memory, was produced by their children, as were *Masoom*, *Mandi*, *Trikal* and *Tamas*, after which internal conflict led to the demise of the company.
2. Shabana Azmi has become the most visible emblem of the New Indian Cinema, although she has also acted in commercial films, e.g. *Amar Akbar*

Anthony (1977) and *Masoom* (1982). While she has worked with most of the major directors of the alternative cinema movement, including Satyajit Ray (*Shatranj Ke Khiladi*) and Mrinal Sen (*Genesis*), she is most identified with Shyam Benegal. Apart from *Ankur* (giving a remarkable performance in what was only her second feature film), she had major roles in *Nishant*, *Junoon*, *Mandi*, *Susman*, *Antarnaad* (Inner Voice, 1992) and *Hari-Bhari* (Fertility, 2000).

3. Satyadev Dubey wrote the dialogues for *Ankur*, *Nishant* (also acted), *Bhumika* (also co-scripted), *Kondura* (also acted), *Junoon*, *Kalyug* and *Mandi* (also co-scripted). Dialogue writing has always been a separate, distinct and credited activity within Indian cinema; M. Madhava Prasad argues that within the Hindi cinema it is quite an autonomous practice 'with its own minor star system' (Prasad, 1998: 70).

4. Anant Nag performed in *Ankur*, *Nishant*, *Manthan*, *Bhumika*, *Kondura* and *Kalyug* for Shyam Benegal. He and his brother, Shankar Nag, became major stars in the commercial Kannada cinema, often playing brothers in family dramas (Rajadhyaksha and Willemen, 1999: 156–7).

5. *Ankur* starts with a group of villagers walking and dancing through rugged terrain towards a temple, where Lakshmi (Shabana Azmi) and her husband, Kishtaya (Sadhu Meher), undertake rituals that will aid them to have a child. The film then cuts to an urban environment, where Surya (Anant Nag) has just completed his college examinations and marries, but his new bride is still too young to live with him. He pleads with his father to allow him to continue his studies, but is told he is lazy and is sent off to look after the family farm. Surya arrives at the farmhouse, where he meets Lakshmi and Kishtaya, who live in a thatched hut some distance from the house, which she looks after, while her husband, who is deaf and dumb, does odd jobs on the farm. Lakshmi is surprised that Surya wants her to prepare and serve him meals as she is of a lower caste, but Surya says he doesn't believe in the caste system. Kishtaya is a heavy drinker (of palm wine) and one morning Lakshmi awakes to find him gone. Surya tells her that her husband has left her and that he will look after her; she now lives in the house with him and they sleep together. Eventually, Surya's wife, Saru (Priya Tendulkar), arrives and is suspicious of Lakshmi's presence, demanding Surya tell Lakshmi to leave because of her caste status. In time, Surya discovers that Lakshmi is pregnant and insists she have an abortion, but she refuses. Kishtaya returns and is delighted that his wife is pregnant and takes her to the temple to give thanks. Kishtaya seeks work from Surya, who assumes Kishtaya has come to confront him about Lakshmi's pregnancy and whips him brutally. Lakshmi intervenes and curses Surya, who runs into his house, closes the door and weeps convulsively, watched by Saru. A young boy throws a rock through Surya's window and runs away as the screen turns to red.

6. In an article written in 1974, Ray discusses *Ankur* as well as *Garam Hawa* (1973), *Maya Darpan* (1972) and *Duvidha* (1973). He suggests that in Benegal's film, melodrama is particularly evident in the film's denouement, in which the hero's 'monstrosity' is out of keeping with his earlier characterization. He also advises Benegal 'to keep away from quadrangles in the future' (Ray, 1976: 102–3).

7. The playback singer, who actually sings the songs mimed by a film's actors, is a relatively unknown figure in most of the world's film industries. However, in India, playback singers constitute a star system as popular and significant as that of the actors themselves. Lata Mangeshkar is the most popular and prolific playback singer in Indian cinema. She started singing in the late 1940s and continues to dominate film songs in Hindi and other Indian languages to this day, allegedly having recorded over 25,000 songs (Rajadhyaksha and Willemen, 1999: 144). Her cultural impact is such that Sunil Sethi can rhapsodize as follows: '[Her] voice, like Mahatma Gandhi's loin cloth and Rabindranath Tagore's beard, has become a part of India's collective unconscious' (quoted in Garga, 1996: 192). Shyam Benegal engaged her to sing two of Karisma Kapoor's songs in *Zubeidaa* (2000). Nimmi was a well-known actress of the 1940s and 1950s, starring in films such as *Barsaat* (Rain, 1949) and *Deedar* (1951); in the former film Lata Mangeshkar sings Nimmi's songs.

8. *Charandas Chor* is 'about petty thieves in a village who keep eluding the bumbling police until the central character, Charandas (Lalu Ram), is executed for being honest rather than for being a criminal' (Rajadhyaksha and Willemen, 1999: 422). The film was produced by the Children's Film Society, which was under the control of the Ministry of Information and Broadcasting; these films were then made available to educational organizations for a nominal fee (Rajadhyaksha and Willemen, 1999: 76). Chhatisgarh became a separate state in 2000.

9. Until her untimely death at the age of thirty-one in 1986, Smita Patil was considered the only Hindi actress able to match Shabana Azmi. *Charandas Chor* was her first film and she remained one of Benegal's favourite actors, starring in his next four films (*Nishant, Manthan, Bhumika, Kondura*) as well as in *Mandi*. She also worked with many of the other major directors of the New Indian Cinema, including Satyajit Ray (*Sadgati*), Mrinal Sen (*Akaler Sandhaney*), Ketan Mehta (*Bhavni Bhavai, Mirch Masala*), Govind Nihalani (*Aakrosh*, Cry of the Wounded, 1980; *Ardh Satya*) and Kumar Shahani (*Tarang*). She moved into the popular Hindi cinema in the 1980s, e.g. *Shakti* (The Strength, 1982) and *Ghulami* (1985), but without a great deal of success; her roles lacked the vitality and sensuality that marked her earlier films (Gandhy and Thomas, 1991: 127).

10. Nautanki has been 'one of the most beloved and popular forms of theatre in the heavily populated central Indo-Gangetic plain of north India, primarily Uttar Pradesh, Punjab, Rajastan, Hariyana and Bihar states' (Brandon, 1993: 99). In *Teesri Kasam* (The Third Vow, 1966), Waheeda Rehman gives a wonderful performance as an actress in a Nautanki troupe.

11. In a fascinating chapter on censorship during the Emergency, Aruna Vasudev documents the film's fate after the Cannes screening. It was invited to the Chicago Film Festival in November 1976, but now the Ministry of Information and Broadcasting insisted that further texts be inserted at the beginning and the end: 'This film is a fictionalized recreation of a story of the past when the feudal system was prevalent in British India. It has no bearing with the present day India where feudalism has been abolished and no section of the people suffer from any oppression from another section' and 'The scenes depicted in this film relate to a period when India was not independent. Citizens of India today enjoy equal rights and status, and working together, are moving ever forward', respectively. (These two texts are absent from the 1996 SBS broadcast of the film and the 2000 Videosound DVD.) Then the Ministry barred the film from the festival altogether, only to permit its showing a week later, by when it was too late to have the film subtitled for the festival (Vasudev, 1978: 176–7). This paranoia and incompetence might be seen as amusing in retrospect were it not for the film remaining burdened by those government edicts. Even as well researched a book as M. Madhava Prasad's *Ideology of the Hindi Film* accepts that the film is set in British India and goes on to label *Nishant* (and *Ankur*) as 'narratives of feudalism ... distanced from the present by the rupture of independence' (Prasad, 1998: 196).

12. *Nishant* opens with a priest (Satyadev Dubey) noticing that the temple has been robbed of its jewels. The youngest brother of the *zamindar* family, Vishwam (Naseeruddin Shah), is responsible; his eldest brother, Anna (Amrish Puri), is annoyed about it, but tells the priest the jewellery will be replaced. Their two other brothers, Prasad (Mohan Agashe) and Anjaya (Anant Nag), regularly sexually abuse the local women and encourage Vishwam to join in, despite the disapproval of Vishwam's wife, Rukmani (Smita Patil). This is the world into which a new teacher (Girish Karnad), his wife, Sushila (Shabana Azmi), and their son come. They notice the brutal behaviour of the *zamindar* brothers and are not happy with their accommodation. Sushila is also critical of her husband and continually asks him for a new mirror and a sari. Sushila wanders around the village and is noticed by Vishwam, who, with the help of Prasad and Anjaya, abducts her from her house. The teacher tries to engage the help of the police, the regional newspaper and a magistrate to have her returned, but they display little interest, even wondering why he would want a 'used woman'

back. Sushila is raped by Prasad and Anjaya and even Rukmani shows little sympathy for her. Sushila demands to be taken to the temple, where she finds her husband. She accuses him of not trying to save her and calls him a coward; she returns to the *zamindar* house, where she demands her rights in the household, after no longer refusing Vishwam's advances. The teacher and the priest encourage the villagers to stand up to the *zamindar* at a number of local events, including a theatrical performance of the *Ramayana* at the temple. A procession leaves the temple, and when it arrives at the *zamindar*'s house, the villagers attack the family and kill most of them. Vishwam and Sushila flee the house, but are beaten to death by the villagers, before the teacher can intervene. In the final shot, a group of children are sitting in the temple doorway looking out.

13. *Arati* involves the 'burning and rotation of incense sticks and oil lamps before the deity' (Kapur, 1990: 243).
14. Vijay Tendulkar is, like Girish Karnad (who plays the teacher in the film), one of India's foremost realist playwrights.
15. Utpal Dutt is considered 'India's best-known exponent of theatre for political and social purposes' (Brandon, 1993: 110). His theatre directing was influenced by the activities of the Indian Peoples' Theatre Association (IPTA), which was associated with the Communist Party of India. In the 1940s and early 1950s, the IPTA was considered 'the only instance of a cultural avant-garde in contemporary Indian history' (Rajadhyaksha and Willemen, 1999: 109). Utpal Dutt directed a number of films, but he was better known in the film industry as an actor, primarily in Hindi films, but also in films directed by the Bengali 'triumvirate', Mrinal Sen, e.g. *Bhuvan Shome* (1969), Ritwik Ghatak, e.g. *Jukti Takko Aar Gappo* (Reason, Debate and a Story, 1974), and Satyajit Ray, e.g. *Agantuk* (The Stranger, 1991).
16. This question and the one a few lines earlier were based on the rather different version of the script's origin in Rajadhyaksha and Willemen (1999: 425).
17. Rajadhyaksha and Willemen claim that the funding was actually provided by the National Dairy Development Board in order to 'enhance [its] image' in the face of economic mismanagement and questionable financial practices (1999: 428).
18. Without my beloved, I cannot exist a moment.
    Those who have not experienced love,
    do not understand the depth of love.
    If you ever meet my love,
    you cannot make him understand.
    Without my beloved, I cannot exist a moment in life.
    (from the subtitles of the SBS broadcast of the film)

19. I interviewed Vanraj Bhatia in Bombay on 21 January 1999. He feels that he has done his best work with Shyam Benegal, even though they disagree about almost everything, including politics (if he had realized what *Nishant* was about, he would not have agreed to write the music). He composes very quickly and intuitively. He studied with Nadia Boulanger at the Paris Conservatoire in the late 1950s and his music combines Western and Indian musical traditions. His first feature film was *Ankur* and he has written the music for all of Shyam Benegal's other feature films, except *Charandas Chor*, *Aarohan* (The Ascent, 1982) and *Zubeidaa*. He has also worked with Kumar Shahani, Ketan Mehta and Govind Nihalani, as well as writing the background music for a number of commercial films, e.g. *Damini* (1993).

20. *Manthan* opens with the song, welcoming the stranger to the village, accompanying the arrival of Dr Manohar Rao (Girish Karnad) at the railway station. He is a veterinarian sent by the Dairy Board to set up a milk co-operative society, but is treated with great suspicion by the local people, including the Harijans (previously called Untouchables and now referred to as the Dalits) Bindu (Smita Patil) and Bhola (Naseeruddin Shah), who sell their milk to the local milk factory owner, Mishra (Amrish Puri). The village headman (Kulbhushan Kharbanda) assumes he will head the co-operative, but Dr Rao affirms the equal rights of all prospective members. The villagers are gradually convinced to sell their milk to the co-operative. One of Dr Rao's team members, Chandavarkar (Anant Nag), has sex with one of the village women; Bindu, meanwhile, senses that Dr Rao is attracted to her. Dr Rao's wife, Shanta, reluctantly joins her husband, being unsympathetic to his task and to his involvement with the Harijans. Dr Rao once again tries to convince Bhola to join the co-operative, but Bhola complains that one of the team members is having an affair with a Harijan woman. Chandavarkar is expelled from the village. Bhola joins the co-operative and helps elect another Harijan as chairman of the co-operative, much to the disgust of the headman. Bindu's husband beats her because he believes she's having an affair with Dr Rao. However, although she is indeed attracted to Dr Rao, and he to her, he suppresses his feelings and appears to ignore her. Mishra helps her, but has her sign a letter (which she is unable to read) accusing Dr Rao of raping her. A lawyer tells Dr Rao of this and he becomes despondent. Meanwhile Mishra tries to have Dr Rao recalled to the city and cajoles and bribes the villagers to return to his milk factory. Dr Rao is ordered to return to the head office. He tries to say goodbye to Bindu, but her husband warns him off. As Dr Rao and his wife board the train, the song returns and Bhola runs through the village to catch up with Dr Rao. He is too late, but he encourages his fellow villagers, including Bindu, to return to *their* co-operative.

21. Kaifi Azmi (who died in 2002) was an Urdu poet of considerable standing and, like many such poets, he gravitated to writing lyrics for songs in films such as Guru Dutt's *Kaagaz Ke Phool*, M. S. Sathyu's *Garam Hawa* and Kamal Amrohi's *Pakeezah* (Pure Heart, 1971). He was also a scriptwriter and dialogue writer, combining the two in *Garam Hawa*, but functioning only as the latter in *Manthan*.

Interview 5
From *Bhumika* (1976) to *Aarohan* (1982)

Figure 7: Usha (Smita Patil) in *Bhumika* (1976)

WvdH: Your next film was *Bhumika* [The Role], which in the light of the ones that we've discussed so far seems like a strange direction for you to take. This fictional re-creation of an autobiography of an actress is a thematic departure. What interested you in this sort of a story?

SB: Well, two things. One was that Hansa Wadkar's autobiography was interesting because it was very frank.[1] She held nothing back and she spoke her mind absolutely freely, which is rare for people writing their autobiographies. She had to create space for herself in an area that was totally male-dominated. So she was, what one might call, an early feminist in the Indian context. Secondly, I was very interested in how the film industry itself developed in the country, through the 1930s, the 1940s and the 1950s. I felt that it would be a marvellous film to make and I was also fascinated with the form, with how images evoke periods, through colour, black and white and different tonal qualities. That had a lot to do with the technology of the time. In India in the 1930s and early 1940s, there used to be a particular kind of film stock that came from America, which created a certain kind of texture. That film stock was very slow and therefore you had to light objects in a particular way to get a certain kind of depth. In the 1940s, Kodak stock was introduced and resulted in different textures – the lighting also changed because the film stock was faster. This was followed by the first monopak colour stock, which created different image characteristics. And later there was the regular Eastman colour. So in the film we used different kinds of stock that relate to the different periods. This was part of the whole scheme of this film.

WvdH: Was that the reason why you decided to use a flashback structure?[2]

SB: Right. I used that so you could see the difference. It was also determined by a certain limitation, because in the mid-1970s we went through a very severe shortage of raw stock as a result of our foreign exchange resources. Consequently, we couldn't get as much stock of the same kind as would be necessary to do a whole film.

WvdH: You make the best of these limitations. In one of the earliest flashbacks, where Usha is still a little girl, there is great depth of field in the scene in the house where she moves between the father's bed, the grandmother's bed and the mother's bed. Was that meant to suggest the qualities of the 1930s film stock?

SB: Yes, the qualities of that stock were wonderful. The film was also the story of how films were made in India in the 1930s, the 1940s and the 1950s, what the prevailing thinking was and how people related different kinds of films to different regions of India. Bengali films had a certain pace and a certain dramatic character and chose certain kinds of themes, while films made in Bombay had a different character.

WvdH: At one stage, someone says that the film they watched was almost as good as a Bengali film.

SB: Yes.

WvdH: Were you trying to comment on particular films of the 1930s and the 1940s?

SB: Particular kinds of films rather than specific films. In the 1930s and early 1940s we used to have several genres of filmmaking. There were mythologicals and there were stunt films like the Wadia films.[3] So the film was a kind of a history of Indian cinema over that period.

WvdH: Sometimes you had fun with it because one of the film posters you see in the film credited the music to Vanraj Bhatia [*Bhumika*'s composer]. The protagonist's name, Urvashi, is a mythological name, isn't it?

SB: Yes, one of the great courtesans of the gods.[4]

WvdH: So she was not only a woman who became a commodity in this industry, but also a mythological temptress figure, resulting in a sort of dichotomy, with her being used and also using others at the same time. Did you want to present that complexity in her character?

SB: Yes. I may not have been terribly conscious of doing that, but the choice of the name automatically assumed that relationship.

WvdH: It struck me that here was this woman, Usha, who was trying to find herself and find a way that she could be independent. And yet she couldn't be independent, in that her ultimate desire was to be a housewife.

SB: That's it.

WvdH: She was punished terribly when she did eventually become a housewife. Was she ever able to survive the male-dominated world that she was attempting to negotiate?

SB: Well, the key to that is the end of the film because she has to recognize that if she wants to be independent, she would have to be alone.

WvdH: Which she accepts at the end of the film, doesn't she?

SB: When the actor wants to renew his connections with her, she doesn't answer.

WvdH: Her adult daughter had earlier told her to stop acting and to stop quoting lines from the movies. For me this implied that she might still have been acting right up to the end of the film.

SB: The fact is that there is that ambiguity in her personality. You can't have everything. You can't have your cake and eat it. She had to choose. Wadkar of course eventually gave up films.

WvdH: She did. Well before she had to.

SB: Yes, and she went back to her husband, who was a dreadful man.

WvdH: Like Keshav Dalvi in this film. While she has an ambiguity and complexity about her, the men have none at all – they're almost two-dimensional.

SB: I'm not sure that they're two-dimensional. They're very much part of the patriarchal society where the world never asks them to prove themselves, whereas a woman needs to prove her credentials in every situation. So that's why they look so ridiculous in the process.

WvdH: Her husband is the most complex of the males because he keeps on changing his position. He is almost her pimp, getting her work even though she might be having affairs. Yet he also wants her. He doesn't quite know what he wants from her.

SB: He does care for her, because with her by his side he becomes whole. He becomes whole only because of her.

WvdH: Yet he almost forces her to recommence her affair with the actor Rajan. I very much like the scene where her husband tells her that she has to come to the party that Harilal the producer organized. She dances with Rajan, and this is seen from the perspective of her husband, as he watches this relationship starting to take off again. He hates it but he also needs it.

SB: He is also a victim in that sense.

WvdH: Rajan is a victim of his own self-absorption.

SB: Absolutely.

WvdH: He's always looking in a mirror. The film director, Sunil Verma, is also a narcissistic figure, isn't he?

SB: Yes.

WvdH: The most worrying figure is probably Vinayak Kale, who resembles characters from some of your earlier films, doesn't he?

SB: Yes. He is in many ways the kind of archetypal macho male character that feudalism produces. In that sense he's a very traditional figure.

WvdH: That part of the film is set in Goa, a traditional world far removed from the metropolitan and urban environment.

SB: Absolutely.

WvdH: It seems to me that while all of these people fail Usha, her daughter is the only one who doesn't. Her daughter even rises above her mother.

SB: Even though Usha wasn't a particularly good mother, she created a space for her daughter. Her own attempts to create a space for herself allowed the daughter to have her own space.

WvdH: It's a space that Usha's mother, Shanta, doesn't allow her daughter to have. There is also the suggestion of an affair between Shanta and Usha's husband. It's her grandmother, the courtesan, who does provide some space for Usha herself.

SB: That's right. She's a model for the granddaughter.

WvdH: Are film actresses the new courtesans of Indian culture?

SB: They were considered to be, but are no longer.

WvdH: But they were at that time?

SB: At that time, because they suddenly lost their place in traditional society. They were not necessarily welcome in what one might call decent households.

WvdH: Actresses were considered to be a bit like the female characters in *Mandi*, having very little social worth.

SB: All this has changed, because actors and actresses today are considered to be part of the elite of Indian society.

WvdH: Smita Patil's performance in the film is quite remarkable. She shows a range there that wasn't obvious in the earlier films.

SB: I felt that she did have that range when I first discovered her. This film gave her an opportunity, but both she and I had to work very hard to get her to do that, because when I was in pre-production, I wasn't sure that she had the commitment or the grit to go through with this. But I discovered later that she did, because she really worked very hard on this film.

WvdH: I can imagine. She obviously dominates the film.

SB: She had to; otherwise the film would have been a failure.

WvdH: Her character is embodied in the title of the film, isn't it?

SB: Yes.

WvdH: The roles that everyone has to play and that she has to play too, especially the role of the female in this society and the Hindi film stereotype of a woman. The musical composition of the film would have been much more extensive than for most of your films.

SB: Much more, although I use no background score in the film. There were only songs. The song format of the film was in many ways like the song format in a normal commercial Bombay film, but musically it had the character of the music in 1930s, 1940s and 1950s films, including the lyrics that used to be written for these songs. So Vanraj Bhatia worked very extensively on creating the film music character of those two and a half decades. Apart from that, there was also the classical music. We chose a particular *gharana*, a particular school of music – *gharana* literally means household. The school of music that we chose was the Jaipur Gharana. It was the most recent of the schools of music. The finest singers of the Jaipur Gharana have come from around Goa. The musical structure of a particular piece of music has three basic sections: the first section is known as an *alap*, the exposition of the mood, which is without rhythm; the second part introduces the rhythm; and in the third part the tempo increases. Even within the three sections there are several divisions. In the Jaipur Gharana the first part is almost eliminated, so there is only a very short *alap*. Everything is rendered in the middle section, with the tempo never going beyond a certain level. This kind of rhythm gives a great deal of warmth to the music. This structure was worked out by Ustad Alladiya Khan and became known as Jaipur Gharana. This style of singing is heard on the radio in certain sections of the film. One of its great exponents was a singer called Kesarbai Kerkar, according to me the finest of the twentieth-century classical singers of India. For the grandmother's voice I used a Kirana Gharana singer. But the *raga* she sings is a popular *raga* with the Jaipur Gharana singers. This music conveys the sort of security a child feels in the embrace of the mother. Jaipur Gharana singing has a great deal of that warmth which I wanted for this film. This was important because this woman is completely insecure. She's seeking that kind of giving warmth, where there is no taking, the sort of warmth she never finds in any of her relationships. So musically it was very important to have that character.

WvdH: That music is then contrasted to the Hindi film music.

SB: To the film music of different periods.

WvdH: The most prominent of those is Usha's dance number in the beginning of the film, which recurs a couple of times in the film. Was that done using that monopak Technicolor, with its very bright, very gaudy colours?

SB: Yes – very strong colours and over-saturated.

WvdH: Were you attempting to create a picturization that was like the Hindi film?

SB: Yes, absolutely.

WvdH: You wanted to acknowledge it, rather than send it up?

SB: I was just acknowledging it. The main thing was really to tip one's hat to this tradition of the cinema.

WvdH: That scene where Sunil Verma has Usha do a song in the rain in the park is clearly an acknowledgement of that very traditional setting of a song.

SB: Yes.

WvdH: When he says that he would have liked her to have got wetter, he is engaging in that typical Hindi film strategy of eroticizing the female body, like in *Mr India* [1987], where Sridevi dances in the rain.

SB: Yes, absolutely.

WvdH: The construction of the *mise-en-scène* is particularly complex in the film. This applies not only to the early scenes but also to the final Goa scenes, in which you set up the camera in relation to the characters in that big house so as to define place in a very emphatic way.

SB: She feels so put upon that she seems to shrink in that house.

WvdH: She always looks out the windows as well, but she can't get out. She's trapped in and by the environment. The film is also a continuation of your involvement with Girish Karnad – this time not on the screen but as the scriptwriter.

SB: One of the scriptwriters.

WvdH: What did he contribute to the script?

SB: Girish is very good at working out dramatic structures. Vijay Tendulkar has a great sense of drama and he can create wonderful dramatic situations. But when it comes to structures, Girish has almost a mathematical mind. It was very important for me to get him to work on this film, because it has a very complex structure. Both of them are essentially playwrights. Girish has won the highest literary award this year in our country.

WvdH: I noticed that in the newspaper.[5]

SB: Tendulkar and he are the foremost playwrights in our country.

WvdH: Still today?

SB: To a large extent, yes. They are the ones who have been acknowledged. There are younger playwrights emerging who are very interesting, but one will have to see a certain amount of work before one can make a judgement about them.

WvdH: I found it interesting that with Girish Karnad and Shabana Azmi receiving awards, the names of your films crop up all the time.[6] Your involvement with these figures that are so central to Indian dramatic and film culture is obviously crucial as well.

SB: It happened at a certain historical time really, when it all came together.

WvdH: After *Bhumika*, you returned to Andhra Pradesh to make a film in Telugu.

SB: Yes, *Anugraham* [1977], which means 'the boon', was based on a novel written by a very brilliant Marathi novelist, C.T. Khanolkar, who died very young. The novel was an examination of the Brahmin psyche. It was a very interesting story and I wanted to make it in Marathi but unfortunately I couldn't, so I found a producer who was willing to produce it in Telugu. I made the film on the east coast – on the Andhra Pradesh coast. We also made a second version in Hindi concurrently. That was called *Kondura* [The Sage from the Sea]. The Telugu version has been seen a great deal in Andhra Pradesh; the Hindi version hardly got any release, but it was shown on television. For me it was an interesting project because I've never dealt so much with the psychology of people. This is really a psychological film, not the kind of social film that I normally do.[7]

WvdH: There followed two films that you made with Shashi Kapoor as producer and actor. How did your relationship with him and his film company, Film Valas, come about?

SB: At the time, Shashi was very keen to produce films. He didn't want to produce the kind of films that were normally made in the Bombay film industry, which actually were the type of films in which he was performing. He was a very successful actor and a big star.[8] He wanted to produce films, which he felt would have rational and logical kinds of stories, while still remaining popular – not over-intellectualized or experimental films. He wanted films that would be considered entertaining but not ones that played to the gallery. One day when I met him he asked whether I would like to direct a film for him. I had recently read a short story by an Anglo-Indian writer called Ruskin Bond who writes a lot of stories relating to the Raj – being an Anglo-Indian he has a certain feeling for the Raj. This short story was called *A Flight of Pigeons* and dealt with a little incident that took place in 1857 during what we call the First War of Independence and the British called the Mutiny. It was set in a small cantonment town called Shahjahanpur in central Uttar Pradesh. In the story, the local British and the Anglo-Indian community were attacked in church one Sunday morning and most of them were massacred. Among the people in the church was a girl called Ruth Labadoor and her father, who was killed in that attack. The person who led the group that massacred these people was a Pathan from that region. There are a lot of Pathans there, Rohilla Pathans, who had settled in regional India, having come from Afghanistan.

WvdH: They're considered a warrior people, aren't they?

SB: Not necessarily. They're very much assimilated now and are land-owning agricultural people with orchards, particularly mango orchards. The short story was about another Pathan called Javed Khan, who was smitten by this girl Ruth and eventually manages to abduct her as well as her mother and grandmother. He then wants to get married to her but he doesn't quite succeed in doing so. It was a true story. I conceived of it as a romantic period drama – the love of a Pathan for an Anglo-Indian girl. I wanted to make a period film, because I enjoy such films myself and love creating historical periods. I showed the story to Shashi and he was very interested, as was Jennifer, his wife. So he asked me to work out a script, which he liked, and we made the film, which we called *Junoon*.

WvdH: Do you think he was partially interested because he was married to Jennifer Kendal? While theirs was an English–Indian relationship, rather than an Anglo-Indian one, the subject must have been of interest to them as a couple.

SB: Yes, it was, and Jennifer played the mother in the film, as it happened. The daughter was played by Nafisa Ali, whose first film it was. Nafisa Ali herself had an Indian father and an Anglo-Indian mother. She was at that time a national swimming champion and a wonderful rider. I had to do a lot of research for the film, because that story was very slim; it was just a short story. I went to the National Archives in Delhi and studied the period to trace out the story of the Labadoor family and of Javed Khan.

WvdH: Yes, because, as you said, they were actual figures.

SB: In the meantime I went to Shahjahanpur and also found the graves of some of these people, including the father's grave, which is there in the Christian cemetery.

WvdH: So the end title of the film, about Javed eventually dying in battle and Ruth going back to England as a spinster, describes what actually happened.

SB: Yes, Ruth went to Calcutta, where she ran a boarding house for a while, and from there eventually went back to England, where she died. We got all those details from the archives.

WvdH: Was this originally to be your only film with Shashi Kapoor?

SB: No. Shashi was very happy with the film – although it didn't do all that well, it covered his costs. It became successful later, but when we actually made the film, it wasn't a huge success.

WvdH: Even though it was a very romantic story.

SB: It was more successful in Britain, where it opened in very good cinemas. The British press went absolutely gaga over it.

WvdH: I read that Shashi Kapoor started the company Film Valas to distribute *Bombay Talkie* [1970] made by the Merchant–Ivory team, which had already produced a number of films on the Indian–British relationship, starting with *Shakespeare Wallah* [1965].[9] So the British film-going public would have been interested in the story of your film, even though you offer a different perspective.

SB: Yes, a completely different perspective.

WvdH: *Shakespeare Wallah* is particularly interesting in that it starred Shashi Kapoor and Geoffrey Kendal. Shashi Kapoor had become involved with Geoffrey Kendal's Shakespeareana theatrical group in the 1950s.

SB: Geoffrey was Jennifer Kendal's father. Geoffrey Kendal had first come to India in 1946. He would come annually and perform in colleges and schools all over the country. In fact all of us grew up on his renditions of Shakespeare. He came to my own college too. Jennifer was there, as was the other sister who became a big star in London.[10]

WvdH: After *Junoon* had been completed, was there any interest on Shashi Kapoor's part to make another film with you?

SB: Yes, he decided that he would like to produce another film with me. I'd been working on a project of developing a contemporary perspective on our two major epics, the *Mahabharata* and the *Ramayana*, which are a part of our consciousness, in a manner that during the Renaissance *The Odyssey* and *The Iliad* probably occupied the minds of Europeans because they saw that as their heritage. But of course the *Ramayana* and the *Mahabharata* are much more directly connected with the lives of our people than *The Iliad* and *The Odyssey* were for the Europeans, because they adopted it rather than it being naturally the fountain of their culture and wisdom. On the other hand, the *Mahabharata* and the *Ramayana* are very much part of the soil of India. I always felt that the characters of the *Mahabharata* were the archetypes of the entire human experience and I wanted to take those archetypes and place them in contemporary situations. I wanted to have a similar plot line to the *Mahabharata*, but based on an industrial family. One of the things about Indian industry has been that they've all been family concerns, and by the time the second and third generations come along, they've always led to splits and battles within the family. This was particularly so in the 1970s, when some major industries in India collapsed as a result of family splits. This was old capitalism moving towards a new kind of corporate capitalism. So I started to work on a script that took the *Mahabharata* as the essential framework and the characters were based on the archetypes drawn from the *Mahabharata*. This became the script of *Kalyug*. I produced the film's structure and a very well-known industrialist, Vinod Doshi, who had some interest in the theatre, wrote the first draft of the script. He also played Kubchand, the Dritarashtra character, in the film. Vinod Doshi's family had the misfortune of splitting in the same way twenty years later. It was almost as though he could foresee what was going to happen in his own family. Then Girish Karnad worked on it, as did Vijay Tendulkar, Satyadev Dubey and my other collaborators. Shashi produced the film and it was a little more successful in the marketplace than *Junoon*. Later on, in the first half of the 1990s, it became a staple for our television soap operas. They were clones of *Kalyug*.

WvdH: You mean that these were all modern versions of the *Mahabharata*.

SB: Yes, modern versions. They just took material from *Kalyug*. The film worked out quite well, but then Shashi over-extended himself in the sense that he produced two more films that didn't do all that well – one was Govind Nihalani's *Vijeta* [Victory, 1982] and the other was Girish Karnad's *Utsav* [The Festival, 1984], which was even more ambitious. Then Jennifer died and that really shattered Shashi and he withdrew generally from a lot of things, including the amount of work he was doing in film, and he concentrated his attention on the theatre, which was really her inspiration. He is now semi-retired, enjoying the company of his grandchildren.

WvdH: Was there any sense, because Shashi Kapoor was involved and because these were more expensive films than those you'd made before, that you had to be conscious of a popular response to the films?

SB: I don't think I was conscious of any of those things, but people used to say that. These were subjects that were larger in scope. When I started, my films were really almost like little microcosms of social situations and they were small-scale productions. We didn't commercialize these two projects in the sense that they were not designed for the market. They were made the same way I've made all my films – I've always believed that if you make a film that you yourself can be completely absorbed in and enjoy, then surely there must be other people like you who would enjoy the film. What other test can you have? Unless of course you design it as a product, and I doubt very much, given my sensibility, I'd be able to do that. Not that I think there's anything wrong in people doing that. But I don't think I'm capable of doing it.

WvdH: Shashi Kapoor is also the first commercial Hindi actor you worked with, followed by Rekha in *Kalyug*. Their performance mode would have been somewhat different to that which you had developed over the years.

SB: Yes, but you mustn't forget that Shashi Kapoor's essential training was in the theatre. He acted for his father, Prithviraj Kapoor, who used to run a theatre company and was himself a theatre actor and also a very big cinema star. Shashi had not only been acting in commercial Bombay films. He had also acted in films for British directors and in the Jim Ivory and Ismail Merchant films. So he had worked in different film cultures and had a good overview of what was happening. He and his wife had very good taste in the cinema, in terms of the kinds of films they would like to go and see and enjoy, because they were interested in films from Britain, France, Italy, America and everywhere else.

WvdH: But Rekha would have been a somewhat different case, wouldn't she?

SB: Rekha was very much a mainstream actress. *Kalyug* was the first time she had acted in a film that was outside the commercial cinema. Since then she has been in different types of films. She's worked for Mira Nair, she worked for me again in *Zubeidaa* [2000] and she worked for Muzaffar Ali in *Umrao Jaan* [1981]. She's a very good actress, apart from being a star.[11]

WvdH: What sort of a producer was Shashi Kapoor?

SB: He was very involved as a producer. He would never interfere in the creative aspect of a film, but he was an excellent producer. He was very sympathetic to the director's needs, which is very rare. It's almost a cliché to say that the producer/director relationship is always confrontational. He was very sympathetic to the director and he always wanted to be very helpful, even if it went over budget. Nothing went really over budget in our projects, but they did in his other two films. The fact was that he was very sympathetic. He wanted the director to have the best.

WvdH: Yes. But he had two hats on too, didn't he? He was also your main actor and that would have been a very different relationship.

SB: Yes.

WvdH: In *Junoon* [Obsession], the historical context is very interesting in itself and in its relationship to the characters. What did you want to suggest by taking a story which was set in that particular moment of Indian history?[12]

SB: The main thing for me was the ambiguity, which has always been there, of our relationship with the British. It showed itself historically in so many different ways, including when the Nationalist Movement was active, because the British–Indian relationship is a very strange kind of love/hate relationship. It isn't a simple straightforward thing like the anti-colonial movements in places like Indonesia or African countries that wanted the Dutch or the British to leave and didn't ever want anything to do with them again. The British–Indian relationship has never been like that. It has always been a very strange one where you hate them one moment and you like them another moment. There has been a certain amount of give and take. In truth, British colonialism was as bad as any other kind of colonialism and in fact it was more take than give. But there was always a sneaking kind of respect for each other, like Gandhi's relationship with the British or Nehru's relationship with the British. From 1885 onwards we fought to make India free, and in 1947 when India becomes free we also opted to be part of the Commonwealth. It's an extraordinary situation.

Figure 8: Poster for *Junoon* (1978)

So I wanted to look at that relationship, and *Junoon* gave me a wonderful opportunity.

WvdH: In the light of this sense of ambiguity, the film seems to not want to tip the scales in one direction or other as to which side was the more violent.

SB: You couldn't actually tip it in any one direction. The cruelty of the British in quelling the revolt was incredible, while the violence of the sepoys when they revolted was also incredible. So there was very little to choose.

WvdH: Were there any comments when the film was released that you were being too ambiguous or too even-handed in your treatment of the British and the sepoys?

SB: Not in India. In Britain, some people did. What was more, the British censors were very upset with the church massacre scene and demanded cuts.

WvdH: It is interesting that the film focuses on Muslim Indians and their attitudes to the Labadoors and to the British more generally. This in turn is contrasted with the attitudes and the allegiances of the Hindu family, Ramjimal's family. This immediately sets up a communal distinction. Were you interested in exploring that in any detail?

SB: To some extent. It was also a question of who was gaining from the British at the time. Ramjimal was somebody who dealt with them on a business level, while the Pathans had nothing to do with them. But it wasn't really a communal issue, although it showed itself as such later. After the revolt was quelled, the British decided that they were going to change the whole social scheme of things so that this would never happen again. They actively encouraged the Hindu community to get themselves a British education. In response certain Muslims, despite opposition from within the Muslim community, argued that Muslims should also accept an English education, in order to stop the Hindus from taking over. The British always played one side against the other. As there are so many social fault-lines in India because of its vast diversity, it has not been too difficult for people to play on those fault-lines, and the British always used them. In the 1880s the balance changed again, and in the period leading up to the 1930s there was a much more active interaction between the Muslims and the British; those Muslims who worked against independence bought themselves a country.

WvdH: In that respect, the contrast between the Muslim families and the Hindu family in the film was to be prescient of where things ended up in the twentieth century.

SB: Yes.

WvdH: The holy man at the beginning of the film, the fakir, becomes a commentator on the events in the film, a sort of a Shakespearean fool.

SB: To some extent, yes. He's a commentator/seer. There were such people at that time. One particular fakir from South India went round saying that the British would not rule for more than ninety years.

WvdH: The opening sequence is really very powerful, displaying the sense of chaos and of dread that saturates the film. This is particularly evident in the music and the singing and in the trance-like movements of the fakir.

SB: The song was a very famous *rang* in Qawwali, which is a form of Muslim devotional singing. A *rang* is a series of revelations in praise of the Sufi masters.[13] This *rang* was written by Amir Khusro, one of the great renaissance figures of India, who lived in the thirteenth century. He was a central Asian, who wrote both in Persian and in Braj, a precursor language of Hindi. He was one of the great synthesizers of Hindu–Muslim cultures in India. He was also a great musicologist and invented seven instruments, including the tabla and the sitar. He is credited with many *ragas* and some wonderful seasonal and festival songs, which are sung in northern Indian villages to this day.

WvdH: You seem to be really interested in and have a great knowledge of Indian classical music. Is that a particular passion of yours?

SB: Yes it is, but only as a listener. I don't play an instrument, but I like music generally. I like Western classical music too, especially opera, and also jazz. Now I enjoy world music as well.

WvdH: That opening sequence really sets the mood for the rest of the film. But it also sets the mood for the way you use songs in the film, like the songs the women sing while on the swing in the mango orchard, especially the one sung by the daughter-in-law.

SB: That is a song that is always sung at Shravan, which is the second month of the monsoon. Then Ruth's mother sings a little song from Shakespeare. The scene shows the meeting points of different cultures. It was an opportunity to look at different cultures and also to look at the essential plurality of Indian culture. We're not a mono-cultural people.

WvdH: The songs seem to be more overtly picturized than they were in the films made before this time. Vanraj Bhatia told me that, unlike Guru Dutt, you can't create really effective song picturizations. He said he has talked to you about this, but to no avail. But it seems to me that song picturization does start to become a significant element with this film. Apart from that opening sequence, which is a real virtuoso piece of camera work, there is the 'voice-over' song about Javed's desire, as he walks to the room of the Labadoor women and looks at Ruth, who is clasped in her mother's arms. Then Firdus, Javed's wife, walks up behind him and looks at him watching Ruth. These tensions then spill over into the events of the next morning when all these characters are standing on the internally facing balconies looking at each other and at the pigeons. Did you set out to actively musicalize the camera work and the editing in a scene like that?

SB: The music becomes the emotional link to the scenes and suggests what's happening in their minds as well.

WvdH: As well as the implications it has for the other characters there. But like in the earlier films, such as *Nishant*, you've used music here very much as a commentary. Only in your more recent films do the songs become more distinctive segments.

SB: Yes.

WvdH: Still, in this film there was a more significant attempt on your part to put together a song picturization.

SB: You know there is a certain tradition in Indian cinema in relation to song picturization. One of its great exponents was Guru Dutt, who picturized songs within the situation of the story.[14] Most Indian films take the song out of the situation. They become what we call items. They are interludes, and if they're interludes, then you can do whatever you want with them. But in *Junoon*, they have a thematic connection and a narrative connection. The context is constantly kept in mind. This is one particular tradition in popular Indian cinema. I used that tradition because it's easier to do that for me.

WvdH: This is in contrast to a Tamil film called *Indian* [1996], which touches on the Subhash Chandra Bose story.[15] There's a sequence there where the main characters are talking to each other in Chennai and suddenly the film cuts to a song and dance number set in Sydney. It is a radical rupture in narrative continuity.

SB: That of course is also very much the style of popular Indian cinema. I find it very difficult to do that.

WvdH: The other song sequence, which we've already mentioned, is that idyllic scene of the women on the swing in the mango orchard. It reminded me of the swing sequence in *Charulata*, which is also a beautiful moment. Here the tensions that underlie the relationships between these women are dissolved. It focuses on the women sharing their cultures with each other. Swing scenes seem to occur quite frequently in Indian films, representing a significant cultural activity.

SB: It provides a certain sense of freedom. It's essentially what one might call 'taking the air'. It typically takes place in the break between the rains when the air starts to cool and the dust settles. It's a very wonderful time of the year and people, women particularly, take to swings – at least traditionally in village India. There is a sense of them coming out into the world. It has a great sense of liberation.

WvdH: I've seen such events depicted in miniature paintings as well.

SB: This period between the rains is the month of Shravan, equivalent to the period from mid-July to mid-August.

WvdH: Javed's desire for Ruth seems to be incredibly intense and maybe even unexplainable.

SB: It's totally obsessive. It's also linked to the historical situation. Ruth's mother tells him that if the British capture Delhi then he can't have Ruth. So him getting Ruth would be equal to the sepoys beating the British.

WvdH: Thus linking the historical and the personal.

SB: In olden times, when battles were won, the prize catch was the women of the other side, who became part of your harem, or whatever. In fact many of the kings married the wives or widows of the person they defeated.

WvdH: Ultimately he does realize that to pursue his desire, he would be destroying the relationships around him. But he also says that he wants Ruth because he wants a son.

SB: He's only offering a rationale.

WvdH: What about the other way around – Ruth's attraction or non-attraction to him?

SB: Eventually she is attracted to him.

WvdH: She is. It seems to me that she becomes more and more attracted to him as he becomes more and more of an archetypal Indian warrior. Whereas earlier, when he vacillates about being involved in fighting the British, she doesn't seem to respond to him at all. Her states of mind in this regard are visualized in a number of dream or fantasy scenes throughout the film. However, I believe that the major relationship in the film is that between Javed and Mariam, Ruth's mother.[16]

SB: Yes. There is a battle of wills between those two.

WvdH: But it is also a sort of love story.

SB: It is. They epitomize the British–Indian relationship.

WvdH: There is a great deal of tension in their relationship as one gains control over the other. They bare their personalities to each other. It's almost like a love relationship. Viewers at the time must have been conscious that Shashi Kapoor and Jennifer Kendal were married to each other.

SB: Yes.

WvdH: Was this extra-filmic aspect of any interest to you when making the film?

SB: Only in terms of them representing two cultures.

WvdH: Their characters were much more interesting than that of Ruth. As you said, it was Nafisa Ali's first film. I didn't really think that she carried it off too well.

SB: She was not a very good actress.

WvdH: It was sometimes hard to read what her character was up to. Whereas with the other two there was never any doubt about the way they related to each other. The film is also concerned with looking and listening. Characters seem to be constantly looking at and upon each other and this is brought about partly by the verticality of your *mise-en-scène*, with balconies above and below each other around the internal courtyard.

SB: Yes.

WvdH: They were also constantly listening to each other, either noticed or unnoticed by the other party.

SB: This had to do with dominances, with how the dominance shifts from one person to another.

WvdH: It was done without employing the typical voyeuristic techniques. While much of the film was about Javed's desire for Ruth, there were very few point of view shots of him actively looking at her as a sexual object. Were you interested in exploring looking as an aspect of desire without it becoming one of sexual exploitation by the character of Javed or by the audience?

SB: I didn't want to reduce everything to only sex, because obsessive love has very little to do with sex. It's a different kind of thing. It's a sense of losing yourself.

WvdH: One of the other major relationships is that between Javed and his brother-in-law Sarfraz, and this is exemplified through their relationships to the pigeons. While Javed owns them, Sarfraz seems to be linked to them, particularly to the dead pigeons.

SB: Yes, but you have to understand that there's a certain culture in Uttar Pradesh of being pigeon fanciers. And Javed is a pigeon fancier. It's also seen as a decadent aspect of life. It may be culturally very sophisticated but it's also very decadent. Sarfraz sees that as an aspect of Javed's decadence, of his unwillingness to make the kind of commitment that Sarfraz sees as necessary.

WvdH: There are times when Ruth seems to make no distinction between Javed and Sarfraz. In Ruth's fantasies, which you visualize at various times in the film, she does not really make any distinction as to which of them is the threatening figure. Sometimes it is Sarfraz, sometimes it is Javed. They became an abstract 'other' for her – the Indian as the 'other'. Mr Labadoor comes across as a typical English colonial fool. He presumes that the Indians will never rise up against the British.

SB: That's because he's never had to have a serious relationship with any Indians. The British in India during colonial times could live totally encapsulated in their own world that had no connection whatsoever with the local people. That was a Victorian phenomenon. It wasn't like that until the 1820s or 1830s. But then it increasingly became like that, particularly after the Mutiny, when the separation became absolute. There wasn't any kind of serious social intercourse. There was not the slightest interest in each other's life style.

WvdH: Consequently, his death in the church, while part of the carnage that is going on, doesn't affect the viewer very much.

SB: It doesn't mean anything to anyone.

WvdH: Except to the British censors.

SB: Except to them.

WvdH: The battles in the background of the story are not directly shown, but rather are alluded to by the comings and goings of Sarfraz's people, as he and his men left the town for war and then returned. We hear about what happened. The fighting itself is left to our imagination. Why did you feel that the final battle couldn't be left to our imagination?

SB: You had to have it. If you didn't have it then you wouldn't have felt the eventual seriousness of it, because the loss was a real one. With the refugees leaving the town, it was a point of no return.

WvdH: The battle was very violent. The departure of the refugees made me think of Partition. Did it for you as well?

SB: Yes, of course. This was a point of no return. Everything changed and will remain changed.

WvdH: So this was the seed that in some respects was going to end up in Partition.

SB: Yes.

WvdH: The story that Ramjimal's wife tells the Labadoors in her house was rather strange. It drew upon the *Ramayana* and it immediately made me wonder who Ram was in the film, who Sita was and who Ravana was. Ramjimal might be Ram and Javed is a sort of Ravana figure. But who is Sita? Ruth or her mother, Mariam?

SB: Ruth.

WvdH: I had some difficulty in understanding why Ramjimal's wife then started to talk about Sita blessing the English as the rulers of India. What was the significance of that?

SB: The significance relates to the fact that the British could only rule India with the acceptance of the majority of Indians. Otherwise, how was it possible for 60,000 people to take over a country of 350 million people. It wasn't as though India was like the Americas, because in India there were already settled communities, a very sophisticated system of administration and a long history of the judiciary. So how was it possible, if they didn't actually allow them.

WvdH: Is that a criticism of India at that time?

SB: Yes, it is a criticism. The Indian temperament is one of enormous trust and tremendous confidence that everybody who comes here will eventually get assimilated.

WvdH: But is that necessarily a criticism?

SB: I wouldn't think it's seriously a criticism. It's just that the British never got assimilated. Everybody else did. The Central Asians got assimilated, but the French and the British remained apart. If the British actually had assimilated, the situation would have been very different, because they would have been part of India. They never were part of India as the Arabs and the Pathans were. The British were the only people in the history of South Asia who did not get assimilated.

WvdH: What made you decide to change the title from *A Flight of Pigeons* to *Junoon*?

SB: The film concentrates on Javed's obsession and *Junoon* means obsession. When we released it in England, we called it *A Flight of Pigeons*.

WvdH: This was because the short story would have been well known there, I suppose. I saw an audiocassette of the music from the film in a music shop in Bombay, but when I went back for it I realized that it was actually a band called Junoon.

SB: Yes, it's a Pakistani band. The name is based on my film.[17]

WvdH: *Junoon* was made at about the same time as Satyajit Ray made *Shatranj Ke Khiladi*.

SB: *Shatranj Ke Khiladi* was made about a year before *Junoon*, although there was no connection because I was making *Junoon* anyway. I knew that Ray was making *Shatranj Ke Khiladi*. But neither he nor I were really conscious that we were both doing a film relating to the 1857 Mutiny.

WvdH: So it was pure chance. But it was no accident that he chose to use Shabana Azmi. That came from his awareness of her work with you.

SB: Yes, particularly in *Ankur*. He had written a piece about her performance.[18] He had also written to her about how much he liked her performance and was looking forward to working with her when the opportunity arose. That opportunity did arise when he was making *Shatranj Ke Khiladi*.

WvdH: Shama Zaidi told me that she worked on that film as well.

SB: She wrote some parts of the dialogue and she also designed the costumes for that film.

WvdH: Whereas you had to flesh out *A Flight of Pigeons* a lot in order to make a film out of it, the opposite would have been the case with the *Mahabharata*, wouldn't it?

SB: Yes, quite the opposite.

WvdH: The title of your version of the *Mahabharata* is *Kalyug,* which means, I think, the age of discord or the age of chaos.

SB: The age of discord is called Kaliyug. But our title was not Kaliyug; it was *Kalyug* [The Machine Age], which means the age of iron, the age of steel, the age of industry. It's a play on the word. After all, it was the industrial age that brought greater chaos to the world than anything else before it. There's been a lot of progress but not all of it is positive.

WvdH: It is not necessarily to the advantage of the population. This idea of modernization is a very two-edged sword for a country like India. The ruthlessness of the characters, while locatable within the *Mahabharata*, is also identifiable in Indian industrial society of the 1970s. I would have thought non-Indian audiences would find *Kalyug* more difficult than most of your other films.

SB: They didn't actually find it more difficult. After all, industrialization was an experience that the West had been through maybe a hundred years earlier. Of course, they couldn't pick up the references to the *Mahabharata* that would have added depth to their understanding. They simply saw it as a family going to pieces.

WvdH: I heard somebody describe the film as a thriller about someone being killed. In that context, I thought that the *Mahabharata* references were important to suggest that this situation is not just about the 1970s, but also indicative of the human condition.

SB: That's difficult to do unless people are familiar with the *Mahabharata*. It's similar to showing Theo Angelopoulos' *Ulysses' Gaze* [1995] here – the audience would only pick up the surface meaning.[19] Some subjects may have universal application, but can then be limited by one's own cultural understanding. Certain films can go beyond all that because they're on a much simpler level. Films like *Bicycle Thieves* [1948], for instance, or old Chaplin comedies would be universally loved because they only touch upon common features in all the cultures. But not all stories are like that.

WvdH: No, but that is no reason not to do them.

SB: Exactly.

WvdH: Ashis Nandy, in writing about *Kalyug*, says that it takes the perspective of Karna.[20]

SB: Yes.

WvdH: This, he says, is very much the way Tagore reinterpreted the *Mahabharata*, focusing not on the heroic figure of Arjuna, but on the more ambivalent

Figure 9: Savitri (Sushma Seth), Supriya (Rekha) and Subhadra (Supriya Pathak) in
Kalyug (1980)

Karna.[21] It's not surprising you also chose Karna, because you like ambivalent
figures.

SB: Yes.

WvdH: Did you consciously adopt that perspective in the film?

SB: Absolutely. In the *Mahabharata*, Karna is a very interesting figure because
he was born before his mother was married and was then abandoned to be
looked after by someone else. He didn't know that he belonged to the same
family as the Pandavas, that he was actually the eldest brother. When the battle
took place he was the general of the opposing forces, the Kauravas, because he
was a very close friend of Duryodhana. Karna was as great a general, a duellist
and an archer as Arjuna was. And when his mother discovered that he was
going to lead the Kauravas, she told him that she was his mother. He breaks
down, because he can't fight his own brothers – so she really weakens him.
The central issue that fascinated me and continues to fascinate me is that of
a mother who hasn't been a mother at all, who then expects the loyalty of a
son, placing him in a terrible quandary. Karna eventually accepts his loyalty
to his mother without betraying his loyalty to the side he's on and so allows

himself to be killed. That was the central feature of the *Mahabharata* story that is very exciting and very interesting. We often have people who are placed in situations of conflicting loyalties, where the only honourable thing to do is to be sacrificed. So this served as the basis for *Kalyug*.

WvdH: Ashis Nandy also suggested that the two families in the film, unlike in the *Mahabharata*, seemed to be no better than each other.

SB: Yes.

WvdH: In the *Mahabharata* you get a sense that the Pandavas, whatever else they do, are still essentially good.

SB: Actually, even in the *Mahabharata* that is not necessarily so. What ultimately makes the Kauravas fail is essentially a matter of law. You see, there is very little to choose between them. There are, of course, different interpretations. It really is a matter of law. It has a lot to do with the concept of monarchy and what constitutes the rule of law. The fathers of these two clans are brothers. Dritarashtra has one hundred sons, while Pandu has five sons, but Pandu is younger, so Dritarashtra has to be king. However, Dritarashtra is blind and a king has to be whole in every respect. It's like God. You cannot have an idol that is broken or chipped. Pandu also has a problem because he was not the father of his own sons.

WvdH: They were all fathered by the Gods.

SB: Yes. Pandu demands his family's share of the territory they are to rule, which Dritarashtra is willing to give, but his eldest son Duryodhana refuses because these five sons are not the children of their father. So there's a certain legal situation. When they are given their territory, they lose it all by gambling.

WvdH: In the dice game.

SB: Yes. And they're sent into exile. When they return, Duryodhana still refuses them their share. That's what leads to the battle. Neither side is particularly good or absolutely right. The *Mahabharata* is in effect a kind of history of mankind.[22] It's not just a question of good or evil. It's a question of right and wrong. Both are wrong and both are right at different times.

WvdH: But only one side has Krishna.

SB: Yes, only one side has Krishna. Duryodhana asks Krishna what the basis of his choice is. Krishna gives this very long explanation that becomes the *Bhagavad Gita*.

WvdH: But there is no Krishna in your film.[23]

SB: No.

WvdH: This isn't a world in which Krishna could exist?

SB: No.

WvdH: So the film was a critique of materialism.

SB: Absolutely.

WvdH: This critique of materialism wasn't from your point of view a critique of modernity, of the sort of push towards modernization?

SB: No.

WvdH: Some people regard materialism and modernity as the same thing.

SB: I would disagree with that because even the *Mahabharata* is about materialism and certainly not about modernity.

WvdH: I think that people like Ashis Nandy adopt an anti-modernist perspective.

SB: I'm not sure that he is anti-modernist. I think he sees everything in India as a conflict between modernity and tradition.

WvdH: And you don't necessarily?

SB: Not entirely, not if you look at some of the political developments in recent years as far as India is concerned. Some of the new films that have been vastly successful like *Kuch Kuch Hota Hai* [Something is Happening, 1998] have seamlessly combined the two.[24]

WvdH: Was the pre-credit family tree sequence always part of the plan or was it introduced later to avoid the confusion of having so many interrelated characters?[25]

SB: No. It was important to have that at the beginning. You had to know who was who. Then you could relate to the characters. It was also important because we used names that are not the familiar ones in the *Mahabharata* – for example, Bharat is another name for Arjuna.

WvdH: Bharat is also another name for India, isn't it?

SB: Yes. The basic story of the *Mahabharata* was written well before the *Mahabharata* itself was written and that story was called *Vijay*, which means victory. Then there was a further version called *Bharat* and then it became the *Mahabharata*.

WvdH: So the names of the characters in the film are not just common names, they also refer back to the epic story. I wasn't aware of that at all. Why did you decide to use the names from the earlier versions of the *Mahabharata* rather than the more familiar names?

SB: Because otherwise there would have been very strong associations with the original. I didn't want that because everyone would complain that the characters were not like that in the epic.

WvdH: It's like making a film from a very well-known novel and people complaining about how it's not like the book. Furthermore, you mentioned that not all of the characters and their activities in the film are directly linkable to the *Mahabharata*. We talked about Rekha earlier. Why did you choose her for that particular role?

SB: Actually the character of Supriya had to be very attractive. She had to be her own person, as she was in the *Mahabharata*, because she was the wife of all five brothers.

WvdH: She's the Draupadi figure.

SB: Draupadi was what you might call a post-feminist figure. She was very much her own person and she was also a very dominant female, even among the women. All of them, all the brothers, were in awe of her.

WvdH: Supriya's husband was certainly in awe of her and was unable to communicate with her at all. You highlighted her on-going education, in that she was studying for a doctorate and this was indicative of her power, intellectually as well as sexually. In the *Mahabharata*, Draupadi signifies a matriarchal perspective. The *Ramayana* is a more patriarchal story, isn't it?

SB: Of course, it is far more patriarchal. The *Mahabharata* also has a certain historical reference to polyandry. Certain communities in India have been polyandrous and there the women, as in all matriarchal matrilineal systems, have a great deal of power. Supriya is certainly not a victim.

WvdH: No, definitely not. But then very few of your women characters have been. You don't give the film an epic dimension.

SB: No. It's familial in a non-epic way. It's more intimate.

WvdH: Some people have criticized it for not being epic and for not being morally unambiguous.

SB: Yes, but then the moral ambiguity of the *Mahabharata* is very well known. Ultimately, one of the things about morality is the difference between individual morality and social morality. They're two different things. Social morality is often a convention adopted in order to keep society stable. So, when you talk about individual conscience and individual morality it's completely different from talking about social conscience and social morality. The distinction is important because when you talk about honesty you have to ask who is he honest to. He should be honest with himself rather than be simply honest to society. If the two can merge it's perfect. But they don't always merge. A lot of people think that they're honest when they're simply finding ways of doing things that won't affect society too much. The reason why the *Mahabharata* is such a great epic is because it deals with such aspects. For example, what is right action? Is it determined by circumstances or is it an absolute? It is a continually fascinating epic, because it indicates that there are no final answers.

WvdH: Yet there are people, some with particular agendas, who want to claim that the *Mahabharata* defines good and evil as rigid moral polarities.

SB: Yes. Good and evil are very clearly defined in the *Ramayana*, but not in the *Mahabharata*. In the *Mahabharata* you can't say that people are totally evil or totally good, because often many of the decisions they take are because of problems they face at that moment and they need not necessarily be the solutions for all time. Therefore the *Mahabharata* is far more sophisticated and in that sense it will remain modern for ever.

WvdH: The other criticism that I came across is that the film secularizes the *Mahabharata*.

SB: Once again you have to define the secular. In India you can never contrast the secular against the religious as it often is abroad. Secularism in India has been given a completely different meaning. Here it does not have an exclusive meaning; rather it has an inclusive meaning. In India when we say somebody is secular it means that you accept everybody equally. Indian secularism means that all religions are equally respected, irrespective of whether you are Christian, Muslim, Hindu, Parsee or Buddhist. Whatever your own personal preference might be, it does not preclude equal respect for others who may believe differently from you. In India this has been the commonly accepted definition of secularism. And it always confuses people abroad because outside of India when you talk about being secular it means that you separate religion from all temporal activity, particularly those connected with the affairs of the State. We don't believe that at all. You cannot do that with a billion people, because none of them would agree to that sort of secularism. Indians have lived reasonably well together, although certainly not always ideally. Otherwise we would have broken up and destroyed each other over all these many millennia that we have lived here. So here secularism has an all-inclusive meaning as against an exclusive meaning.

WvdH: My question about secularism was triggered by yesterday's interview in *The Times of India* with Ashis Nandy, where he defines secularism as a modern ideology that's been in crisis in India for the last twenty years.[26]

SB: Ashis himself is a secularist of the kind that I have mentioned. He includes rather than excludes. That view always sits uneasily with people from outside

India. We always object when somebody says India is a Hindu country, as against Pakistan, which is a Muslim country. We are not a Hindu country, we are a secular country. There's only one Hindu country in the world and that's Nepal.

WvdH: Bharat and his girlfriend, Subhadra, attend a Kathakali performance, which concludes with a very violent scene. Does that also come from the *Mahabharata*?[27]

SB: Yes. It's a very well-known episode involving Draupadi. As we discussed earlier, the *Mahabharata* is about a battle between two sets of cousins. One set of cousins, the Pandavas, eventually wins, destroying the other set, the Kauravas, and, in the process, they destroy themselves. Yudhistira, the eldest Pandava brother, is a rather reckless gambler and he loses everything. Eventually he stakes their wife, Draupadi, and he also loses her. She refuses to go with the Kauravas. So she is disrobed, and that humiliation is too much for her to bear. She asks Krishna to help and she curses Dushassana, who is the one who humiliated her, and pronounces that when she exacts her revenge she will wash her tresses in his blood. When the battle takes place and when Bhima, one of the Pandava brothers, kills Dushassana, he tears open his stomach and he brings out all this blood. She then washes her tresses in it. That's the episode they are watching.

WvdH: You just mentioned gambling, which in the film is associated with horse racing. Furthermore, the scene where the tax officials rifle through Supriya's underwear seems to refer to the disrobing of Draupadi. These are all little references back to the *Mahabharata*.

SB: Yes.

WvdH: Despite that powerful scene in the theatre, Bharat and Subhadra are basically bored by the Kathakali performance. This is presumably a criticism of their way of life, which has no links back to the cultural tradition.

SB: Yes, of course. It represents one of those ruptures that has taken place between tradition and modernity.

WvdH: After leaving the theatre, they go to a nightclub, which you present in very unflattering terms. The nightclub scene also seems to criticize the relation-ship between the two of them, in that she is a young woman who is interested in dancing and partying, whereas Bharat isn't interested in that at all. It says something about the way in which their marriage has been set up. In terms of age and outlook, she and Bharat's nephew, Sunil, are much more compatible. But that match is not possible.

SB: It's not. As in the *Mahabharata*, Subhadra's marriage to Arjuna [Bharat in the film] is a marriage that will create alliances. Strangely enough, in the

Mahabharata battle, Subhadra's children are eventually killed, while Draupadi protects her child and does not allow him to be killed. He becomes the heir. It is exactly like in *Kalyug*, where Supriya's son, who is at boarding school, is brought back to become the heir.

WvdH: In the film, his uncle and aunt, Bal and Kiran, bring him back and become his 'parents'. The rest of the family has basically disintegrated, including Supriya.

SB: Supriya really loved Bharat and is willing to sacrifice everything for it.

WvdH: This is evident in that very striking scene at the end, where she tells Bharat's wife, Subhadra, to leave her bedroom as she cradles Bharat in her arms. Her character and the way that Rekha plays her suggests a very austere and brusque woman. She's not a very lovable figure, but she is a very powerful woman in terms of her knowledge and her sexuality. She conveys that with a hardness that is really quite interesting. She creates an alienating effect on the viewer.

SB: That's because she wants to be everything. She wants to be wife, lover and mother, excluding everybody else.

WvdH: Yet Bharat sees himself as a person who is in control of his own destiny.

SB: Eventually he has no control over anything.

WvdH: The dominant male relationship in the film is between Bharat and Karan. Their battle with each other is, in some respects, over Supriya, because in the past, Karan had desired her. But their conflict also revolves around Savitri. At the end of the film, when Bharat discovers that Karan is his half-brother, he calls his mother a slut.

SB: As in the *Mahabharata*, Karan was born out of wedlock, and Savitri gave him away. She didn't want her other children who were born in wedlock to know about him. Of course, Karan always missed her – that was his weakness, his Achilles' heel. Bharat and his brothers made their mother use that in order to destroy Karan.

WvdH: Earlier in the film, Savitri tells Karan that he is her son. He is devastated, and after she leaves, he lies on his bed in a foetal position. This is probably the tenderest moment in the whole film, where otherwise tenderness is not really evident. At that moment you associate Karan with Western music, particularly Albinoni's *Adagio*.[28] What link were you making here?

SB: He is a much more sophisticated and broader intellect than the rest of them. He is a far more urbane person than the others. He has a mind that is far more receptive to the world. He's a genuinely tragic human being, like Karna in the *Mahabharata*. Arjuna was considered by far the most intelligent, the bravest and the most accomplished, but he was not as accomplished as Karna. So, the pre-romantic Western classical music was something I thought would be interesting to associate with him, indicating an appreciation of music, painting and culture.

WvdH: A quality not evident in Bharat or the others. But Karan is as ruthless as any of the others, isn't he?

SB: Absolutely. When it comes to power everyone is equal.

WvdH: Talking about paintings, the film really uses décor very strikingly and does so more overtly than do your earlier films.

SB: These are people who would have the money to buy expensive objects. They're also what one might call people of old wealth. New wealth would go in for kitsch, but they don't go in for kitsch.

WvdH: The beauty of this environment tends to overwhelm the behaviour of the people operating in front of it. There's a discord between these sculptures, the paintings and the wall hangings, and the activities the characters engage in. Why did you include industrial relations matters as one of the triggers for the development of the conflict in the film?

SB: It's a question of who holds the real levers of power.

WvdH: The trade unionist, Bhavani Pandey, is no less manipulative than the people who he deals with. It's a very bleak film in that respect.

SB: Yes, it is.

WvdH: I noticed that there was an absence of establishing shots in a number of the major sequences. Bhishamchand's birthday party consists of a series of short scenes of two or three people talking together. One then suddenly becomes aware that a certain person had been in the room all the time. This would have been evident if you had used establishing shots.

SB: It relates to how they themselves perceive the place and the event. How they perceive the party. They're not looking at the others.

WvdH: This technique recurs again when the Puranchands are discussing their appeal and it also occurs in *Junoon*, where we learn in retrospect that a character has been listening to a particular conversation all the time. I don't recall you employing this strategy in any of your earlier films.

SB: Those stories didn't lend themselves to that sort of approach.

WvdH: Finally, just a comment on the song picturization in the film, which occurs during Bharat's honeymoon. It seems to be very similar to mainstream Bombay cinema picturization.

SB: Yes, it was. The song is a pop/rock piece that was popular at the time the film was made.

WvdH: Is it then indicative of the sort of people that they are?

SB: Yes, particularly the girl.

WvdH: She keeps on playing the song from then on. Yet the lyrics of the song are very downbeat for a mainstream Hindi film song.[29]

SB: Yes, absolutely.

WvdH: *Kalyug* is certainly your most pessimistic film.

SB: It would be, yes.

WvdH: Around this time, Aparna Sen made *36 Chowringhee Lane* [1981].[30]

SB: Soon after.

WvdH: What intrigues me about it was that it seems as if your crew was transferred to her film *in toto*.

SB: Yes, it's true. She wanted the same crew. Shashi Kapoor, who was the producer of that film as well, was also keen to keep the same crew, because they had got used to working with each other. I was in Bengal making a film called *Aarohan* [The Ascent, 1982].

WvdH: Was that film commissioned by the Bengal government?

SB: Yes it was. They asked me what subject I would like to make a film on.

WvdH: So it was an open-ended offer.

SB: I was very keen to make a film on land reform, which was something that I have always believed is crucial to any kind of sustained development of this country. Not all the states of the country have had proper land reforms and that has caused many other kinds of problems. And so I was examining the situation of tenant farmers in Bengal, using a story based on real life.[31]

WvdH: It reminds me of an article in the paper some days ago about the burning of a Dalit village, because somebody else wanted the land. This also occurred in *Manthan* and it's obviously still a real issue.

SB: It is. Land ownership has never been fully sorted out. Bengal has finally done it, as have Kerala and Karnataka.

WvdH: Is that why you decided to make the film in Bengal?

SB: Yes, because the land reform programme began there.

WvdH: Did Naseeruddin Shah play the main character in that film?

SB: No, Om Puri.

WvdH: Do you see them as interchangeable actors?

SB: No, they are quite different. I don't think I would ever have cast Naseeruddin for that part. Om was absolutely the person to play that role.

WvdH: The two roles that they play in *Mandi* couldn't be reversed?

SB: No, Naseeruddin Shah couldn't have been the photographer. He would have given it a completely different interpretation.

Notes

1. The autobiography, published in 1970, 'caused a major sensation' (Rajadhyaksha and Willemen, 1999: 239). Hansa Wadkar was a star of both the Marathi and Hindi cinema, working mainly at the Prabhat and Bombay Talkies studios. Her major films were made in the 1930s and 1940s. A sequence from her Marathi musical, *Lokshahir Ramjoshi* (1947), was re-created as the credit sequence song-and-dance number in *Bhumika* (Rajadhyaksha and Willemen, 1999: 307).
2. *Bhumika* is the story of Urvashi, usually called Usha (Smita Patil), a film star, who frequently works with the actor Rajan Kumar (Anant Nag). Her home life is strained, with a husband, Keshav Dalvi (Amol Palekar), who is jealous of Rajan, but dependent on her earnings, and a mother, Shanta (Sulabha Deshpande), who has always been critical of her. Though she loves her teenage daughter, Sushma, this does not save the situation from being intolerable, and Usha leaves in a taxi. As a young girl, Usha was taught to sing *ragas* by her grandmother, but Shanta insisted she find work, because her alcoholic, consumptive father was dying. A family friend, Keshav Dalvi, helped Usha find work as a singer in the Bombay film industry for producer Harilal (Kulbhushan Kharbanda). Usha becomes successful, but constantly wants to stop working; she particularly doesn't want to work with Rajan. She becomes pregnant with Keshav's child and marries him. He eventually insists she resume her film career, since his business is in trouble. Usha accepts a role in a modern mythological film and is forced by Keshav to work with Rajan, who declares to Usha that he loves her. Usha leaves Keshav and moves into a hotel, where she meets Vinayak Kale (Amrish Puri), a rather overbearing fellow hotel guest. She is introduced to Sunil Verma (Naseeruddin Shah), a pretentious film director, who makes a film with her and charms her into a relationship with him. He suggests a suicide pact, but

is unable to go through with it. She meets Vinayak again and he takes her to his mansion in Goa, only telling her when they arrive that he has a son and a bedridden wife. She is upset about this, but nevertheless moves in with him. He confines her to the house until she smuggles out a letter to Keshav, who, together with the police, rescues her. He drops her off at a hotel, where a now adult Sushma comes to see her. She wants her mother to live with her, but Usha decides to remain alone, no longer answering phone calls from Rajan.

3. The genre categories were determined in the 1930s and have not changed substantially since then, although they are so general that internal variation is possible and necessary: socials (films dealing with contemporary life), historicals (dealing with courtly life), mythologicals (primarily adaptations from the *Mahabharata* and the *Ramayana*), stunt films (dealing with *dacoits*, i.e. bandits) and fantasy films (based on Persian stories such as *The Arabian Nights*) (Thomas, 1987: 304–5). The mythologicals constituted the earliest genre (e.g. D. G. Phalke's *Raja Harishchandra*, 1917) and were generally adaptations of Parsee theatre plays of the late nineteenth century. Traditional mythologicals are no longer as popular are they were, although they have continued to be a significant part of the South Indian film industry. Hindi mythologicals moved to television in the 1980s with versions of the *Ramayana* (1986–8, 91 episodes) and the *Mahabharata* (1988–90, 94 episodes), which became phenomenally successful. Modern mythologicals remain popular, with the contemporary life style acting as a 'camouflage' or an allegorical frame for the traditional stories. The films of Manmohan Desai, such as *Amar Akbar Anthony* (1977), *Naseeb* (1982) and *Coolie* (1983), can be labelled as modern mythologicals, as, in a somewhat different context, can films like Benegal's *Kalyug* and Kumar Shahani's *Tarang* (1984). J. B. H. Wadia and Homi Wadia established the Wadia Movietone Studio in 1933 and directed and produced a series of stunt films inspired by the Pearl White serials and Douglas Fairbanks action films of the 1920s and starring Fearless Nadia, India's most famous stunt actress, born Mary Evans in Perth, Australia (Rajadhyaksha and Willemen, 1999: 239).

4. Urvashi was an immortal water nymph who loved King Pururavas and bore him a child. However, she ultimately rejected him: 'Go home; you will never have me, you fool' (O'Flaherty, 1981: 254). Kalidasa, generally considered India's greatest poet and playwright, wrote a play about their relationship, called *Vikramorvasiyam*. Chidananda Das Gupta, discussing the Hindi cinema's obsession with the patriarchal figure of Krishna, contrasts it with Pururavas 'begging Urvashi not only for her continued love, but for his own life' (Das Gupta, 1991: 152).

5. This refers to the Jnanpith Award to Karnad in 1999, which, according to *The Times of India*, was a 'recognition of an artistic sensitivity that has upheld

the virtues of democracy, pluralism and decency in public life' (*Times of India*, 1999: 10).

6. Shabana Azmi was honoured at the 1999 International Film Festival in Hyderabad. In a subsequent interview she nominated *Ankur* as her best film, although her interviewer seems to be unfamiliar with it, assuming that her first films were 'a couple of Manmohan Desai films' (Nair, 1999: 6). The editorial cited in the previous note mentioned *Nishant* and *Manthan*.

7. *Anugraham/Kondura* tells of a young Brahmin, Parasuram, who is given a boon – a root that terminates pregnancy – by a sage, Kondura Swamy, and is told it will retain its power as long as he remains celibate. Parasuram's wife worries about his sanity, but he acquires a following due to his saintly behaviour. However, he secretly desires a village woman, Parvati, who is said to be pregnant. Believing it to be her evil father-in-law's child, Parasuram gives her the root. But she is not pregnant and Parasuram becomes distressed and rapes his wife, who then commits suicide. Parasuram rushes off to find the sage, but he has disappeared.

8. Shashi Kapoor was the youngest son of Prithviraj Kapoor, who starred in India's first sound film, *Alam Ara* (1931), but was more involved in the theatre and set up his own theatre company, while continuing to make films, including a significant role in his son Raj's *Awara* (The Vagabond, 1951). Raj was Shashi's older brother and there was a middle brother, Shammi, who became a major star in the 1960s. As a child, Shashi acted in Raj's *Aag* (Fire, 1948) and *Awara*, but was drawn to the theatre and joined Geoffrey Kendal's Shakespeareana touring theatre troupe, marrying his daughter, Jennifer Kendal. In the 1970s, he played a number of starring roles opposite Amitabh Bachchan, e.g. *Deewar* (1975), *Kabhi Kabhie* (1976) and *Trishul* (1978). He also acted in James Ivory's *The Householder* (1963), *Shakespeare Wallah* (1965), *Bombay Talkie* (1970) and *Heat and Dust* (1983), in Ismail Merchant's *In Custody* (1993) and in Stephen Frears' *Sammy and Rosie Get Laid* (1987). He produced *Junoon, Kalyug, 36 Chowringhee Lane, Vijeta, Utsav* and *Ajooba* (1991, which he also directed), starring in all of them except for *36 Chowringhee Lane* (Rajadhyaksha and Willemen, 1999: 119–21).

9. The Merchant–Ivory team was one of the most successful and long-lasting producer–director partnerships of the last forty years. The American-born James Ivory and the Bombay-born Ismail Merchant first teamed up as director and producer respectively in *The Householder* in 1963; forty years later they were still working together on *Le Divorce* (2003). (Merchant died in 2005.) The third partner of this remarkable production team was the German-born scriptwriter Ruth Prawer Jhabvala, who acquired her Indian name through marriage. Their early films were set in India or were on Indian subjects, e.g. *The Householder* and *Heat and Dust*, but they moved into the 'heritage' film

genre by adapting nineteenth-century American and British novels to the screen, especially those of Henry James, e.g. *The Europeans* (1979) and *The Golden Bowl* (2000), and E. M. Forster, e.g. *A Room With a View* (1986) and *Howard's End* (1992).

10. Geoffrey Kendal acted in *Shakespeare Wallah*, *Junoon* and *36 Chow-ringhee Lane*. Jennifer also performed in these films, as well as in *Bombay Talkie*, *Heat and Dust* and in Satyajit Ray's 1984 film *Ghare Baire*, made just before she died. The 'other sister' was Felicity Kendal, who was also in *Shakespeare Wallah*, but is best known for her television series *The Good Life* (1975).

11. Rekha is one of a number of south Indian actors who have succeeded in the Hindi cinema; others include Vyjayanthimala (*Devdas*, 1955) and Sridevi (*Mr India*). She has starred in a number of high profile courtesan/prostitute genre films, such as *Muqaddar Ka Sikandar* (Blessed by Destiny, 1978), *Utsav* and *Umrao Jaan* (1981), the last considered 'the quintessential courtesan film of the Bombay cinema' (Chakravarty, 1993: 287). Benegal's *Bhumika* and *Mandi* also draw upon the courtesan genre. Rekha's role in *Silsila* (The Affair, 1981), which also starred Shashi Kapoor, was considered controversial, because it was claimed that the film's love triangle mimicked the actual relationship between its stars: Amitabh Bachchan, his wife Jaya Bhaduri and Rekha (Dwyer, 2002: 95).

12. *Junoon* starts with an explanatory title that identifies the historical context. This is followed by a long credit sequence, during which a fakir works him-self into a trance in response to a group of men singing a Qawwali *rang*. He then shouts that the British will perish and subsequently falls to the ground. This is watched by Javed Khan (Shashi Kapoor), who then rides off, stopping outside a large house, where he stares at a young woman, Ruth Labadoor (Nafisa Ali), who becomes alarmed by his behaviour and calls out to her mother. Javed returns home and argues against the aggressive stance taken by his wife's brother-in-law, Sarfraz (Naseeruddin Shah), towards the British. In the middle of a church service, Sarfraz and his men slaughter the congregation, including Ruth's father, but Ruth manages to escape. She, her mother, Mariam (Jennifer Kendal), and her grandmother are given shelter by Ramjimal (Kulbhushan Kharbanda), a Hindu business acquaintance of Mr Labadoor. The sepoys continue to search for them, but it is Javed who breaks into Ramjimal's house and abducts Ruth, her mother and grand-mother. His wife, Firdus (Shabana Azmi), is suspicious of his motives and becomes distressed, as do Ruth and Mariam, when he announces that he's going to marry Ruth. The Labadoors spend some time with Javed's aunt, during which Javed remains insistent. Mariam brokers a deal with him: only if the British are defeated can he have Ruth. After some hesitation he agrees. While Sarfraz and his men repeatedly go off to fight the British,

Javed looks after his pigeons, often watched by Ruth. Sarfraz once again tries to convince Javed to join them, but he refuses and, despite the failure of the sepoys to defeat the British, he insists that he will have Ruth, whose dislike of him continues. Ruth's grandmother dies and Javed arranges for a Christian funeral, where for the first time Ruth seems to respond to him. The sepoys are again defeated, but this time Javed joins them in a fierce battle, in which he is the sole survivor. The townspeople flee the advancing British, but Javed returns to look for Ruth, who, he is told, is in the church with Mariam. Mariam tells him to leave them alone, but Ruth walks out of the church towards him with a smile. He rides off as an end title summarizes their separate fates.

13. Sufism is a form of Islam that embraces 'the mystical, almost pantheistic view of an immanent God'. In the twelfth and thirteenth centuries it gained a mass following, particularly in the 'newly islamicized lands of Asia' (Mansfield, 1992: 70–1). Unlike orthodox Islam, which disapproved of music, Sufism made music an essential component of its doctrine, using singing as a way of approaching God (Jairazbhoy, 1975: 237).

14. 'I firmly believe that the songs seriously hamper the emotional development of the story in a film, however good the literary content [i.e. the lyrics] and however brilliant the musical form of the song.' Amazingly, these words were written by Guru Dutt, one of the greatest exponents of song picturization in the cinema, in an essay called 'Classics and Cash' (quoted in Rajadhyaksha, 1984: 108).

15. Rather confusingly, the film is called *Indian* in Tamil, *Hindustani* in Hindi and *Bharateeyudu* in Telugu.

16. Unlike the film, the book is, apart from the prologue, a first-person account by Ruth (Bond, 2002).

17. Junoon is now Pakistan's most acclaimed rock band, characterized by the Boston Globe as sounding like 'Led Zeppelin with Sufi Muslim poetry' (http://www.junoon.com/articles/art_02.html, accessed 17 October 2005).

18. 'In two high-pitched scenes she pulls out all stops and firmly establishes herself as one of our finest dramatic actresses' (Ray, 1976: 103).

19. *Ulysses' Gaze* could be labelled, like *Kalyug*, as a modern mythological. The film is set in the twentieth century as it follows a film director trying to locate the remnants of the first Balkan film. It becomes a journey back and forth in time that ends up in Sarajevo, a city under siege in the 1990s Balkan conflict. The film alludes to Ulysses' journeys in Homer's *The Odyssey*, but apart from the title there is no literal invocation. Angelopoulos says that 'it is a figurative "match" in the sense that my Odysseus is in a similar situation as that of the Homeric character, but with the difference that my figure's Ithaca happens to be the missing film' (Horton, 1997: 99).

20. Nandy's analysis of *Kalyug* is part of an extensive argument, originally written in 1987, on the relationship between what he calls the Indian art film (exemplified by Satyajit Ray), the middle cinema (Shyam Benegal) and the commercial cinema (a non-auteurist perspective). He precedes the critique of Benegal's film with an outline of Rabindranath Tagore's attitude to the *Mahabharata* as contained in his short play *Karan-Kunti-Sambad* (Nandy, 1995: 216–19). Ashis Nandy is an important and influential Indian public intellectual and a prolific writer on a wide range of subjects, including cricket, science, psychology, nationalism and cinema. In 1998 he edited a book on Indian cinema called *The Secret Politics of Our Desires*.

21. The English title of the play is given as *Karna and Kunti* and it runs to just five pages (Tagore, 1936: 561–5).

22. Similarly, Peter Brook's play and film (1989) of the *Mahabharata* have Vyasa (the 'author' of the epic) identify it as 'the poetical history of mankind' (Bharucha, 1991: 229). Rustom Bharucha's perspective on the play is extremely critical, accusing Brook of invasive Orientalism.

23. Philip Lutgendorf in an online review of the film mentions that there is a character called Kishen (Kishan in the film's credits), which is 'a common variation on Krishna'; he goes on to say that he 'is predictably a partisan of the Pandava-surrogates, but he plays an exceedingly minor role' (Lutgendorf, 2005b: 2).

24. *Kuch Kuch Hota Hai* became one of the biggest hits of the 1990s (both in India and in the Indian diaspora) and won the major prizes at the *Filmfare* Awards (India's version of the Oscars). Its emphasis on urban affluence and youth culture as signs of modernity suggests a modern India, but one 'that never strays far from traditional values' (Kabir, 2001: 47). This can be traced through the change in the relationship between the male protagonist and the female protagonist; as it moves from one of friendship to one of sexual attraction, miniskirts and jeans are replaced by saris.

25. *Kalyug* starts with a visual and verbal description of the family tree (the following second listed names are those used in the *Mahabharata*). Bhishamchand/Bhishma (A. K. Hangal) is the uncle of Khubchand/Dritarashtra (Vinod Doshi) and Puranchand/Pandu, whose father died when they were young. Khubchand is married to Devki/Gandhari (Vijaya Mehta) and they have two sons, Dhan Raj/Duryodhana (Victor Bannerjee) and Sandeep Raj/Dushasan (Akash Khurana). Dhan is married to Vibha (Rajshri Sarabhai) and they have two young daughters. Sandeep is a bachelor. Puranchand/Pandu is dead and is survived by Savitri/Kunti (Sushma Seth), who has three sons, Dharan Raj/Yudhistira (Raj Babbar), Bal Raj/Bhima (Kulbhushan Kharbanda) and Bharat Raj/Arjuna (Anant Nag). Dharan is married to Supriya/Draupadi (Rekha) and they have a young

son. Bal is married to Kiran and they have a teenage son, Sunil. Bharat marries Subhadra/Subhadra (Supriya Pathak), who is Supriya's niece and the daughter of Kishan Chand/Krishna (Amrish Puri), an adviser to the Puranchands. Karan Singh/Karna (Shashi Kapoor) is Savitri's 'abandoned' son and works for the Khubchands. The two families both own engineering companies and they invariably bid for the same government contracts. Recently, the contracts have gone to the Khubchands and this has led to increasing antagonisms between them, especially between Bharat and Dhan. Savitri, Kishan and Bharat decide that Bharat should marry Subhadra, but Supriya objects, saying Subhadra is still a child. On the other hand, Supriya sends her son to boarding school, despite his protestations. Dhan tells Karan that his cousins are all bastards, the sons of a Swami of whom Savitri was very fond. Dhan arranges for the Swami to attend the wedding reception of Bharat and Subhadra, much to the chagrin of the Puranchands. The conflict between the two companies escalates, resulting in the death of Sandeep. Savitri tells Karan that he is her son in an effort to stop the violence, but it only leads to Karan withdrawing into himself. However, Karan does eventually tell her that Bharat is in danger. So Sunil is sent on an assignment instead of Bharat, but is killed by a truck. Bharat rings Karan and says he'll revenge Sunil's death. Karan resigns from his job and visits Bhisham for advice. On his way back his car has a flat tyre and, in fixing it, he is knocked over by a jeep. Savitri tells her sons about Karan, causing Bharat to become extremely abusive towards her. Supriya finds Bharat lying on his bed in a drunken state, tells Subhadra to leave and cradles Bharat in her arms. Bal and Kiran bring Supriya's son back from boarding school and promise to look after him.

26. Nandy goes on to argue that secularism 'doesn't have much of a future', but he then contrasts this definition of secularism, which he identifies with Nehru, with that 'of the likes of Kabir who encouraged and nurtured inter-religious amity and peace' (Jha, 2003: 12). These comparisons suggest that Nandy is talking about two different versions of the concept.

27. Kathakali dance drama comes from Kerala. It literally means 'story play' and has traditionally taken its stories from the *Ramayana* and the *Mahabharata*. It is a spectacular form with striking makeup and costumes, as well as an overt emphasis on eye movements, facial expressions and body gestures (Brandon, 1993: 92). The recent Keralan film *Vanaprastham* (The Last Dance, 1999) portrays the world of Kathakali performers.

28. Tommaso Albinoni's *Adagio for Organ and Strings* (which was also used by Orson Welles in his 1962 film *The Trial*) has become one of the most popular pieces of Baroque orchestral music, along with Vivaldi's *Four Seasons* and Pachelbel's *Canon*; the three are often included together on a single compact disc.

29. What's your problem? What's your grief?
    Did his heart deceive you; he was a traitor.
    What did you get from the deceiver?
    What did you get from the traitor?
    Say, what's on your mind?
    (from the subtitles on the Eros Entertainment DVD)

30. Aparna Sen is the daughter of film critic Chidananda Das Gupta, who started the Calcutta Film Society with Satyajit Ray in 1947. She acted in Bengali commercial films, as well as in films by Satyajit Ray, e.g. *Aranyer Din Ratri* (Days and Nights in the Forest, 1969), Mrinal Sen, e.g. *Ek Din Achanak* (Suddenly One Day, 1988) and James Ivory, e.g. *Bombay Talkie*. *36 Chowringhee Lane* (shot in English) was her first directorial effort and starred Jennifer Kendal as an Anglo-Indian schoolteacher obsessed by Shakespeare. Her second film, *Parama* (1985), attracted the attention of feminist critics for its culturally nuanced representation of women in contrast to Mira Nair's approach in *Salaam Bombay!* (Arora, 1994). Her most recent film, *Mr and Mrs Iyer* (2002, also shot in English) tackles communal issues through the relationship between a Brahmin woman and a Muslim man.

31. *Aarohan* covers a ten-year period (1967–77) of the struggle of a share-cropper, Hari Mondal (Om Puri), to hold on to his land in the face of the machinations of his absentee landlord. He is eventually persuaded by the local schoolteacher to fight the landlord through the bureaucracy and the legal system. He loses everything and is reduced to being a strikebreaking labourer. Only through political action does he manage to register his claim as a sharecropper. Most of his family has had to move to Calcutta to survive, but Hari now sets out to find them and bring them back.

Interview 6
From *Mandi* (1983) to
Antarnaad (1992)

Figure 10: Rukmini (Shabana Azmi) and Zeenat (Smita Patil) in *Mandi* (1983)

WvdH: I found *Mandi* [Market Place] a very interesting, but surprisingly different film.[1] Its range of moods and its bawdiness, particularly in the first half of the film, was handled with a lot of panache. Did you enjoy making that?

SB: I enjoyed it enormously. It was my first ensemble film.

WvdH: Tungrus, the Naseeruddin Shah character, was the servant of this whole group of women and he's interestingly counterpointed with the women, being part of them and yet also in his own world.

SB: Yes, he's in some ways like a eunuch. He's almost sexless.

WvdH: He's the only one who seems not to desire or seek to go to bed with the women. There is a marvellous scene where he is drunk and he walks around in the courtyard singing a song. The scene is quite unlike the rest of the film, being much quieter and more reflective.

SB: The song that he sings is about the same poet I told you about before, that famous king of medieval Hyderabad.

WvdH: The one you used in *Nishant*?

SB: Quli Qutb Shah. But the main thing was that when Tungrus is not drunk, he's the perfect slave. And when he drinks, then his other personality emerges and everything that he knows about everybody comes out, especially about the madam. He also warns her that she's going to come to a bad end.

WvdH: He's a cautious character, quite unlike Rukmini, who throws caution to the wind.

SB: Absolutely.

WvdH: She is an incredibly resourceful woman, willing to try anything, and she seems to always fall on her feet.

SB: Actually, it's very interesting. This story was written by Ghulam Abbas, one of the finest short story writers in Urdu, who moved to Pakistan after Partition. He wrote this story based on an incident that took place in 1929 when Jawaharlal Nehru was the chairman of the municipal board of Allahabad. The board decided that the brothel in the centre of the city of Allahabad should be relocated far away from the town. That brothel was located next to where Nehru was born. The city fathers were offended that this illustrious family lived next to this brothel. The story itself is only about four pages long. So we developed it.

WvdH: *Mandi* seems to be divided in two. The first part is set in the original brothel while the second part deals with its relocation and then its further relocation. It seems that the film changes its mood as well in the second half of the film, expressing a greater sense of anxiety about the characters, even about Rukmini herself as she starts to feel that she's losing Zeenat.

SB: Yes.

WvdH: Were you concerned that the change of mood might break the film in two?

SB: No, once Zeenat goes, then the whole thing's going to collapse. The relationship between these two holds the entire brothel together. Once Zeenat runs away, they all want to leave and start to do their own thing. And so the only person she's left with eventually is the deaf-mute girl.

WvdH: The way this girl comes back, almost as a vision, is very interesting and quite abstract. It's terrible what initially happens to the deaf-mute girl, being sold to the brothel, but she comes back as a replacement for Zeenat.

SB: This is her only home. Her return becomes the beginning for yet another reincarnation of the brothel.

WvdH: There's no hint of lesbianism when Rukmini and Zeenat embrace each other on the bed?

SB: It's not a sexual love.

WvdH: The film also examines the *tawaif* or courtesan role in Indian culture, with the courtesan brothel confounding the traditional stereotypes of women in Indian society.[2] Rukmini runs a brothel but she also performs a particular and significant cultural role.

SB: Traditionally, a brothel was a very important institution within society. Young men were always sent to a bordello to learn social graces. Rukmini sees herself as an influence that helps to refine society.

WvdH: The prostitutes see themselves as more than just prostitutes, particularly Zeenat and Basanti, the Neena Gupta character in the film. The dancing scenes are very beautiful and make one realize that the film is brilliantly photographed. The colours are very bright, but not gaudy at all.

SB: There is a certain richness. It was photographed by Ashok Mehta.

WvdH: Was that your first film with him?

SB: The very first film that he did with me was a documentary in which he was a camera-hand, not a cameraman. This was in 1967 when I was making an anthropological documentary on a tribal community in Madhya Pradesh. The cameraman fell ill with malaria so we had to send him back to Bombay. I operated the camera and Ashok gave me exposures because he knew how to read a light meter. That was the beginning of Mr Ashok Mehta.[3] He went on to become one of the best cameramen in our country.

WvdH: You mentioned the other day that you can't afford him any more.

SB: I can't afford him.

WvdH: The look of the film is quite different to the films photographed by Govind Nihalani.

SB: I didn't want the shooting style to be like the films that I'd done before.

WvdH: By now Govind Nihalani was making his own films, wasn't he?

SB: Yes, he'd already made *Aakrosh* [Cry of the Wounded, 1980].

WvdH: The dance scenes in *Mandi* are choreographed quite unlike those in the popular Hindi film, which would be a lot more hyperactive. You wanted to present it much more traditionally?

SB: Yes. There were no contemporary lyrics – all the songs in the film were poems written by famous poets of the eighteenth and nineteenth century. There was Mir Taqi Mir, a late eighteenth-century poet, who is considered probably the greatest poet after Ghalid, who is a figure like Shakespeare. Then there was a baudy [i.e. bawdy] poet also from the same period, called Insha. This poetry covered the period of the courtesans of India. The style, the renditions and even the musical character of the film came from that period.

WvdH: The music was composed by Vanraj Bhatia, who seems to be particularly good at doing that sort of thing. He doesn't mimic that style, but just composes in that particular tradition.

SB: Vanraj probably knows more about music than anybody else I know in our country. He was trained as an Indian musician when he was a child. Then he started to play the piano, and eventually became a pupil of Nadia Boulanger in Paris, and his contemporaries are all the great composers of the West today. So he's been very much part of the modernist tradition of Western classical music as well. He combines Indian music, Eastern music, Western classical traditions, modern music, and can move from one to the other. Ever since he came back to India, he's been with me. He's worked with me on all my films, except for one or two.

WvdH: I was a little bit puzzled by the long chase of Zeenat and Sushil on the motorbike. Were you attempting to do some sort of a parody?

SB: Yes. It was a kind of a film parody.

WvdH: And what about the Amrish Puri character. Was he an otherworldly figure?

SB: A kind of a Sufi. He's actually an invention of the madam. She is a great believer in Baba Kharag Shah, a Sufi Baba who lived sometime in the past. His spirit keeps emerging and she sees him as the figure who will help her out of her travails and so she builds this little temple for him when they relocate the first time. It is his voice that she hears every time she is in any kind of difficulty and asks for help.

WvdH: Ultimately it's her will that carries her, isn't it? The film focuses on the strength of woman, as do so many of your films. But here it is particularly significant, so that the film becomes a hymn to the power and survival of woman. The two animals in the film, the parrot and the monkey, are used to comment on the characters.

SB: The parrot is a commentator on everybody who comes to that house. In Indian lore the parrot always brings lovers together. The parrot is also a sexual symbol in classical Indian painting. And a parrot also keeps a woman's virtue intact.

WvdH: That's an interesting comment on the film. The parrot belongs to Rukmini, doesn't it?

SB: Yes. In classical Indian literature there is a whole book of parrot's tales.

WvdH: I have heard of that.

SB: The book was originally in Sanskrit, but there is a Persian version, an Arabic version and a Central Asian version. The book starts with a merchant buying a parrot for his wife to keep her virtue intact. Every time she wants to go and meet her lover the parrot engages her by telling her stories. He invariably tells a love story, actually an erotic story, which prevents her from meeting her lover.[4]

WvdH: It's an early version of the *The Arabian Nights* story collection, which uses a similar strategy. Is the monkey, which frightens everybody except Zeenat, representative of something or is it purely a technique to narrate that little scene?

SB: Just a technique.

WvdH: After *Mandi* you made the two documentaries on Nehru and Satyajit Ray that we talked about earlier. Then came *Trikal*. What does the title actually mean? It's translated in English as 'Past, Present, Future'.

SB: That's what it means in Hindi also. Three epochs, meaning past, present and future.

WvdH: Was it the last film that you made with Blaze?

SB: Yes, the last one.

WvdH: In some ways it is a more typical film, but in other ways it's very unusual. The protagonist is an outsider, although he is an insider returning to a community and reflecting upon it. So he's both an outsider and an insider, but even when he was an insider, he was an outsider because he was not of a suitable caste to be able to marry the young woman. Was it important for you to have that outsider perspective?

SB: Yes, because it was a question of discovery. The main character looks at this house and he compares it to a Ming vase. It's just a vase but it tells the history of an era. Similarly, this house represents not only what he experienced as a youth but much of what he has become and what he is. So he goes back to this village to locate this house. The story is set in the last few years before the Indian army

Figure 11: Poster for *Trikal* (1985)

took over Goa in 1960–1.[5] It also deals to some extent with Goan history and with the attitudes of the Hindu and Christian communities. There were a lot of forcible conversions at that time – an issue very much in the news today[6] – and the inquisition in Goa was terrible, particularly in the mid-eighteenth century. There was also the Rane revolt. The film is a blending of fiction with reality because that house where I shot the film was built in 1680. It belongs to Mario Miranda the cartoonist, who is a friend of mine. I wrote the original story and I became fascinated by that house and by the family, which lived there for hundreds of years. All this is also connected with the history of Goa itself, because Mario's great great grandfather was one of the people who captured the rebel Rane and handed him over to the Portuguese governor.

WvdH: Like Maria's grandfather in the film.

SB: Like the grandfather, yes. It turned out he was the wrong Rane. He was kept in the basement, where the nephew, who was actually fighting to make Goa independent from the Portuguese, is hiding in the film.

WvdH: The figure of the nephew, Leon, is linked to the Ranes. He appears in the house just after the Rane disappears. This provides the link between the present of the film, 1961, and the events of 150 years earlier. It's really the story of a minority community.

SB: But a very substantial minority. Goa is 45 per cent Christian and 55 per cent Hindu, whereas there are only 2.3 per cent Christians all over the country. Goa has probably some of the best laws in this country – it's the only part of India that has Napoleonic laws.

WvdH: Because of this cultural mix there is an emphasis on Catholicism and Catholic ritual, which might have seemed strange to some of your audiences.

SB: The intention was to show that India is a very extraordinary country because everything is represented, including cultural baggage such as these rituals which have been given up by the Catholic church elsewhere some time ago, but continue in Goa.

WvdH: That's always an interesting phenomenon. The same occurs in Australia. For example Italian migrants have brought traditions from Italy and have held on to them, while back in Italy, they have changed.

SB: It's like Indian communities living in Surinam and the West Indies. In Surinam they speak a kind of Hindi that is very archaic – that kind of speech was used in one part of India in the nineteenth century. Languages have evolved tremendously here, but there it has remained in a time warp.

WvdH: My Fijian-Indian friend in Australia told me that the Indians in Fiji didn't look up from their reading of the *Mahabharata* to notice what was happening in the country in which they were living. The film has a wonderful opening that integrates the past and the present. It's much more complex than it appears on the surface as you have the man bringing the coffin across the green field intercut with Ruiz coming in the car to the village. They seem to be co-temporal, but it becomes clear after a while that they're not.

SB: That's when the flashback actually begins.

WvdH: Yes. He walks into the past. When he walks into the room I was reminded of a Visconti film, *The Leopard* [1963], as Ruiz and we see this extended family sitting around the dead body on the bed.[7] It's a very rich opening to the film and complicated in its temporal relationship.

SB: Recently, I've been reading Jorge Amado, the Brazilian writer, who says in one of his novels that there was always literature, even before the ability to write.[8] So that coffin and this chap meeting, while I wasn't conscious of it at that time, is very similar in terms of imagination. Ruiz recovers that memory.

WvdH: He then tells the story of himself as a young man, but he is not always a very attractive figure. This is typical of your way of dealing with characters, where the person with whom we enter a story is not necessarily to be totally identified with.

SB: No.

WvdH: You always have this sort of slight separation between identification and criticism. Ruiz is often unconcerned about the feelings of other people. Even at the end, when he comes back to his adulthood, his interest in his son is negligible. He leaves there, not having learnt very much about himself or about the past in which he was involved. He's an educated urbanized man, who is ultimately disregardful of the world in which he was brought up. Is this lack of interest in the past characteristic of Indian culture today?

SB: Yes, it is. People are certainly not interested in history.

WvdH: They're interested in Goa but only as a tourist destination. You don't show it in a touristy way in the film.

SB: Not at all.

WvdH: It must have been difficult because it's so visually attractive.

SB: Yes, but the other Goa is even more attractive. It also has a cultural character that has developed over a period of time, which, if we are not mindful, can so easily be destroyed. And it has taken a long time for that cultural character to evolve. In the film the priest is concerned about this Catholic family being kept away from sin and about the matriarch's séances. She's very Catholic, but at the same time she sends her annual tribute of coconuts and rice to the temple.

WvdH: That cultural syncretism, of being able to encompass multiple traditions, is a significant characteristic of Indian society.

SB: It is particularly important in the Indian situation.

WvdH: The matriarchal figure, Maria, is stuck in the past. If Ruiz is not interested in the past, she is stuck there with her dead husband.

SB: She doesn't mind the fact that her husband was a womanizer of the worst possible kind and that he really didn't care for her.

WvdH: The film also shows that in calling up the past, one doesn't necessarily get the past that one seeks. There is another past that rises to the surface – it is not welcome, but it has to be faced. And do you think that Donna Maria faces it in the film?

SB: She does eventually because she finally says that she's not willing any more to call up the past. Then the figure from the Chinese opera comes and tells her that there are only four elements and that she'll return to them.

WvdH*:* Similarly, the ghosts that are haunting the house, the Ranes, keep bubbling up to the surface because they cannot be denied either. The political situation of 1961 also raises the whole question about cultural identity, as the men talk about whether they are Indian or Portuguese.

SB*:* Which is why the various things that Maria does make her very typically part of this culture – she couldn't be Portuguese in that sense. While there's confusion in other people's minds, there's none in her mind. There's confusion in Leon's mind because ultimately he goes back to Portugal, although he was fighting for the independence of Goa. All these various positions are part of the process of evolution of a national consensus, about who we are, what kind of people we are. It's a debate that continues. It doesn't end.

WvdH*:* The visualization of the Ranes gives the film a touch of Latin American magic realism, doesn't it?

SB*:* Years before that I'd been reading a lot of Latin American work, by writers like Amado, Márquez and that Peruvian writer Llosa.[9] The Goan imagination itself has been shaped by this kind of Latin or Portuguese influence – the way Goans see their own history has some reverberations of Latin America.

WvdH*:* How was the film received in India?

SB*:* I'm afraid it wasn't successful at all in the cinemas. Somebody from the press asked me why I had made a foreign film.

WvdH*:* The irony is that you were making a film about India and Indian identity.

SB*:* The odd part is that on television it's been very successful and it keeps being repeated. In recent years, people have liked this film very much, but when we released it in the cinema, it just collapsed. It did receive commercial distribution in Japan, where it did well for some strange reason.

WvdH*:* The version I saw was in Hindi. Was it also made in Portuguese?

SB*:* No it wasn't. We did subtitle it in Portuguese and it was shown in Portugal. Naseer [Naseeruddin Shah] came with me and we presented the film in Lisbon.

WvdH*:* The characters talk in Hindi, but is that the local language?

SB*:* The film actually should have been made in Konkani. It's my home language as well.

WvdH*:* I'm surprised to hear that because your original language is Telugu, isn't it?

SB*:* Actually it was Urdu because I was born and brought up in Hyderabad. The languages there were Telugu, Urdu and several of the other South Indian languages, but my parents came from the southwest coast, south of Goa –

the Malabar Coast. So my home language was one of the several dialects of Konkani.[10] In fact my family's temple is in Goa.

WvdH: So you already had a strong affiliation with Goa. That was why the subject was of great interest to you.

SB: Yes it was.

WvdH: That brings us to *Susman* [The Essence], which once again was funded by a group of co-operatives.

SB: Yes. It was funded by all the handloom co-operatives of the country. The idea was to tell their story and I chose to tell a story about a particular economic matter. The second largest trained human resource of the country, after the farmers, are weavers. Ever since mill cloth became the common cloth for people to wear, particularly since the second half of the nineteenth century, the problems of the handloom weavers started to grow. And handloom weaving was the most important industry that India had from the pre-industrial economy onwards. After that came handicrafts and various other things. It was therefore the first to be hit by industrialization. In India the handloom weaving skills were passed on from parents to children and it's been the family profession over many centuries for a very large number of rural families. It developed into a great art. Indian textiles were exceedingly well known all over the ancient and medieval world and also a large portion of the modern world. It's only when mill cloth became common and cheaper and quicker to make that their livelihood started to be hit. When India became independent, one of the most important problems to deal with was how to keep the art and craft of handloom alive and yet fit it into the industrial economy. And that problem has really not been solved. We still have a very large number of people engaged in handloom, but we have not been able to provide them opportunities for a better livelihood. That was the reason for making that film. There are certain qualities of cloth that you will never get from anything other than handloom. The move from general cloth making to the special kinds of fabrics which handloom can make has been and continues to be a very painful one.

WvdH: Did the co-operatives approach you with this project?

SB: Yes, they did. Because I had made *Manthan* they felt that I would probably be able to make a film that would project their situation. I have always had an interest in issues that concern the social condition of our people and I have always liked making films on subjects of this kind.

WvdH: Did the relationship between you and the co-operatives work as well as it did in *Manthan*?

SB: Yes it did, except that they were not capable of distributing the film, or getting it to people. So the film could not be released as widely as *Manthan* was.

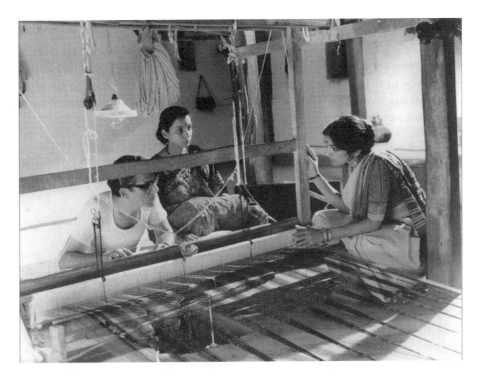

Figure 12: Publicity photo of Ramulu (Om Puri), Gauramma (Shabana Azmi) and Mandira Rai (Neena Gupta) in *Susman* (1986)

It remained, unfortunately, on the festival circuit but did get some distribution. Eventually it was shown on television, but even then it didn't get the kind of exposure it needed.

WvdH*: Susman* starts with documentary shots of the wonderful patterns of the weavings. It continues in the documentary vein except that the voice-over starts to criticize certain things in the weavings. What made you start the film in that way?

SB*:* The handloom is constantly identified as one of the great traditions of India, through Festivals of India and various other exhibitions. So the film starts as a kind of fashion show where this lady buys material from various handloom weavers through middlemen. Then we move into the story of a particular weaver who is given an order for a Festival of India show and then into the life of that weaver.

WvdH*:* So the film starts with the promotional aspect, turns to the difficulties and realities of production and finishes with the exhibition stage. It's almost like a film in that respect – looking at the various stages of its existence. But the majority of the film is devoted to the production process.[11]

SB: There is also the issue that whenever something is produced traditionally, it is defined as a craft and not necessarily an art.

WvdH: Ramulu, the weaver in the film, seems to accept a certain level of dispensability, in that, having completed the weavings, he no longer has a role to play, whereas Mandira, the exhibition designer, asks for him, implying that he is more than a craftsman.

SB: That she does. But the fact remains that one is more readily given credit for being an artist if one is urban. This is reinforced at the official level, because handloom comes under the Ministry of Industry, whereas painting comes under the Ministry of Culture. So handloom is separated from culture.

WvdH: Typical of the way in which you approach film, you set up the handloom versus the powerloom, just as you contrast the middleman versus the co-operative relationship and consider how the craftsman/artist fits into that particular economic structure. But these relationships are not polarized into good versus evil.

SB: When the government of India felt that handloom weavers had to earn more, they didn't suggest that the value of handloom be greater than the value of mill cloth. While handloom should be considered a specialized kind of artistic creation, the solution suggested, particularly in the late 1950s, was that power-looms be provided so that a handloom weaver could produce more yardage to augment his income. Now this is no real solution to the problem of handloom weavers. It is a solution only in so far as it helps the handloom weaver to create more yardage. But then creating more yardage can actually be much more efficiently done by the mills. So this peculiar solution was actually ridiculous. What it did do was to move a lot of handloom weavers into the powerloom sector, where they were open to much greater exploitation. It still operated on the level of a cottage industry where they couldn't organize themselves as a trade union, while mills had very strong trade unions to look after the rights of the workers. In the powerloom sector there is no such security, no such support to see that they're not exploited. So the handloom weaver, whose earnings were slowly drying up because he wasn't producing enough and his product did not have the kind of markets that were necessary to keep him above a survival level, moves into a situation where he is now open to another kind of exploitation without a support system like a trade union. Ramulu's son-in-law goes to work in a powerloom, but soon discovers that it's worse, not better, than the situation he had left. So it's a question really for the policy makers to find a solution to this perennial problem, because the problem is fairly serious. If handloom is raised to the status of an art, lesser number of people can concentrate on the type of weavings that the mills cannot produce.

WvdH: So this is a quality/quantity relationship?

SB: Yes.

WvdH: I now understand why there were those stop-work scenes in the power-loom areas, which dealt with worker organization and strikes.

SB: They were getting organized so that they would have some strength to function against the owners of the powerloom, who today are very exploitative, while a mill owner cannot exploit his workers in the same way.

WvdH: The chaos that surrounded the powerloom activities was contrasted to the handloom world, although that was not all peace and harmony either. The problems here were mainly the personal relationships within the family itself.

SB: It was also a question of simple survival, because this work isn't bringing them enough to make a livelihood. And even if it is, there is another kind of exploitation. The only way they can reach a market is through traditional middlemen who would like to keep them totally dependent on them.

WvdH: So the other structural problem of the industry is the one between the co-operatives, which presumably represent the weavers, and the middlemen, like Ramulu's uncle in the film, who are basically trying to retain them as servants. And yet the co-operative seems to have difficulty in getting its own house in order, doesn't it?

SB: Yes.

WvdH: It seems to be tied to the middlemen as well.

SB: Yes. It's a very complex problem. The handloom co-operatives haven't been as successful as, let's say, the milk co-operatives, because they are not their own masters. They do not employ marketing executives. The milk co-operatives work well because all the officials are employees of the farmers. While here it's the opposite. It's they who control these people. So that is why the handloom co-operatives haven't worked as well.

WvdH: And into this situation comes another of your outsider figures, the exhibition designer, who is sympathetic to the handloom industry, and her boyfriend, Seth, the middle-class technocrat who sees handloom as a craft that can easily be replaced by technological development. He comes off fairly poorly in the film, doesn't he?

SB: Yes. It's my personal view that whatever concepts of modernity and development you have, you must have the human being at the centre of it. For progress to have validity, it must have the human being at the centre of it. Otherwise, what's the point of this progress?

WvdH: Mandira is a middle-class character who sticks by Ramulu despite all her middle-class reservations about his family stealing the cloth, because she can't understand that their survival instinct is so powerful. She remains a very positive figure. Although in that final scene in France, where the French journalist interviews her and Ramulu, she becomes his mouthpiece and insists on presenting the official line. She moves from a personal relationship to an institutional discourse.

SB: By interpreting, her concern moves away and is no longer central, whereas his concerns remain very simple and straightforward.

WvdH: The scene is very nicely constructed with him behind her, slightly out of focus and he remains there as a mute presence. Much as Bindu is the mute presence in *Manthan*. She co-opts him on behalf of the ideology of the Festival of India programme.[12]

SB: This was one of several ideas that the government of India considered, about which I'm very ambivalent.

WvdH: I also remember the debate about Satyajit Ray's films. The government wanted to acknowledge him as a great film director when his work was being shown overseas because it was to the credit of India, but yet what he showed of India was not necessarily to the credit of India.

SB: Yes, exactly.

WvdH: There was Nargis' outburst against *Pather Panchali*, accusing Ray of peddling poverty.[13] Have you similarly been attacked?

SB: Oh yes. Constantly, from the beginning up to now. It's always been like that. That will change when we eventually become confident of ourselves. The urban middle-class mind does not have the sense of confidence that it requires not to feel ashamed of what we are.

WvdH: Not having to apologize to anyone about it.

SB: Reality shows itself in so many different ways. So this has always been a problem, particularly for filmmakers who are concerned with the nature of reality in this country.

WvdH: I thought about your type of filmmaking when I watched this film, because while they are very different situations, the battles of the handloom industry and independent filmmaking are similar. In that respect the mill cloth production system is like the commercial cinema, where quantity is more important than quality.

SB: Well yes, that's an interesting way of looking at it.

WvdH: But I'd like to now come back to the family situation because that is the most interesting part of the film – the relationship between Ramulu and Gauramma, his wife, and their different desires. She is solely concerned with getting her daughter married off, whereas his craft is powerfully important and yet it is also that which destroys him, or boxes him in, as he says.

SB: He is what one might call the quintessential artist. His art is his life. She is different. She has to look after her family. To her, that is a very important factor, while for him that is a factor but the predominant thing is his art.

WvdH: Yet he obsessively insists that his son shouldn't follow in his footsteps.

SB: Yes, because he's afraid of that kind of relationship. His art has taken over his life, but he doesn't want someone else of his own family to be in his predicament.

WvdH: This is the idea of the artist driven almost unwillingly to do what he has to do.

SB: Yes – he's compelled to do it. He can't do anything else.

WvdH: The music in the film, with the weaving rhythms, seems to accentuate that even more.

SB: Yes. One of our most famous Sufi Bhakti figures in India was Kabir, who was a fifteenth-century weaver and considered a saint. And his couplets were very well known and have a strong mystic significance. They're always about being one with your creator, without any intervention in between. It's a very Sufi Bhakti concept.[14]

WvdH: Like the mystical tradition in the West where there is a direct relationship with God.

SB: This is a tradition in India too. So Kabir was a weaver himself and all the songs in the film are his poems.

WvdH: They talk about weaving and life, and the relationship between the two.

SB: Weaving is such a wonderful metaphor for life.

WvdH: The patterns that are created. The threads that come together.

SB: And the rhythms of the loom.

WvdH: The musical rhythms were almost syncopated – slightly out of phase. They weren't exactly mimicking the weaving movements. Were there two composers for that film?

SB: There were. One was one of our most well-known classical singers called Pandit Jasraj. He sang a couple of them and the rest were done by Vanraj Bhatia.

So you had Jasraj and Vanraj! Jasraj's son was the nominal composer for Jasraj's singing, but actually it was Jasraj himself.[15]

WvdH: I did some reading on Kabir and noted that he was a Sufi who saw no distinction between Islam and Hinduism.

SB: He was one of the great bridges between Islam and Hinduism. There were many, but he was among the most important because he could move without any kind of problem from one to the other, because of his belief that the essence of all religions is the same – a very Sufi and Bhakti concept. And Kabir lived at a time when the Muslim invasion was in full force in India, when the social and political problems were tremendous, when the country was going through a major upheaval.

WvdH: Did you use his poetry in another film as well?

SB: Yes, I've also used Kabir in *Mandi*.

WvdH: I noticed that Anand Patwardhan in *Ram Ke Naam* [In the Name of God, 1992] quotes him as well.

SB: Yes, he's used a lot of Kabir.

WvdH: In many respects, Ramulu is your most developed male character, perhaps apart from Gandhi. He's the still centre in the film. He hardly speaks in the middle section of the film and his resistance is palpable. But he is all forgiving and is so pleased that his daughter comes back, even though he's not allowed to show it, since he believes that she should be with her husband. I think he is one of your most complex male figures and a very admirable one at that. Would you see him in that way as well?

SB: Yes, he's the kind of character that I'm most fond of because he is, in some ways, at peace with his maker, if one has to use a religious kind of example. His experience is very deeply felt and he doesn't have to state his commitment.

WvdH: Was it therefore crucial that the film not end with the interview with the Frenchman, but with him at the loom?

SB: It had to end with him at the loom, because it's the loom that makes him whole.

WvdH: So denying himself the opportunity to weave was also a terrible ordeal for him.

SB: Absolutely, he denied that to himself.

WvdH: The relationship between him and his wife, and his brother and his wife, was quite acrimonious at times, but I was very impressed by the way you constructed the *mise-en-scène* of their conflicts. Did you build that particular house as a set or was it an actual house?

SB: It was an actual house but we re-organized things there. It was a house in a village of weavers. In fact, Om Puri asked me whether he could live in the village and not in the hotel with the rest of us in Hyderabad. It was about forty kilometres from the city to this particular village called Muktapur where we shot the film. And it's the centre of some wonderful forms of weaving. Not only did he stay with a family for the entire time we shot the film but he learnt to weave and he created enough yardage for me to have a shirt, for him to have his own shirt and for my wife to get a whole dress made, as well as items for a couple of other people. He became a very good weaver by the end of the film. He really got into that whole rhythm and into the character of these people – that's one of the reasons I think why he gave such an incredibly convincing performance.

WvdH: Returning to the house again, the way in which you stage the action in depth, as in *Bhumika*, is most impressive. You cut from one side of the action to the other as figures move into different positions in relation to each other, which comments on their relationships. Do you actually sketch shots and scenes the way Satyajit Ray did?

SB: I don't feel the need to do that. Once I've got the geography of the place in mind, I know how I want to use the spaces there. So I don't normally need to make drawings. Sometimes I do but that's only to explain a particular aspect to the production designer, the art director or sometimes to the cameraman before we start shooting – the character of shots and movements of people. But these are mostly diagrams rather than drawings.

WvdH: Yes. Have you always had that ability to visualize?

SB: Yes. I've never had any kind of problem there. And it's developed over the years. I normally break down my shots on the set and give it to the assistant. Once I've set up the *mise-en-scène* I know where the camera's going to be placed for each shot and what bits of speech and other things accompany it.

WvdH: What is the meaning of the film's title?

SB: 'Susman' is the life force. It's a word that Kabir used.

WvdH: Like the thread in the weaving.

SB: Yes.

WvdH: Could we have a brief discussion about *Bharat Ek Khoj* [The Discovery of India]? What triggered your interest in such a major enterprise?

SB: I wanted to do one of three things – the *Ramayana*, the *Mahabharata* or the story of India. At that time, Indian television was expanding and others had taken the *Ramayana* and the *Mahabharata*,[16] so I decided that I was going to do a history of India.[17] I settled on Nehru's work simply because his book *The Discovery of India* had a particular reason to be written. He was trying to define India as a nation. We have defined our country in many ways, starting with Ashoka 2300 years ago.[18] Of course we also had mythological definitions. Akbar later tried to give it a political definition but Nehru wrote this book when he was in jail before India became independent.[19] And it became very important to him to define what the Indian nation was, independent of Western history. The concept of a nation is essentially a European one – after the Hundred Years War nations got defined in very specific ways, by ethnicity, by religion, by language, and so on. Now India can't be defined in those ways. It is almost continental in size, it has many different kinds of people, many different ethnic strains and as many languages as you have in whole continents. You also have all the religions of the world represented in India. Nehru was trying to work out a definition of India as a nation and therefore he needed to go back in history to the origins and the evolution of the country, because the diversities of India are mind-boggling. He was trying to locate what were the factors that kept this country together and stopped it from splitting into little units. Our society is not homogeneous, yet in all this heterogeneity there's always been something that kept it together. Nehru's book was an exploration of those factors and I felt that this was a wonderful book to base my series on, to tell the story of India. *Bharat Ek Kho*j really literally translates as 'India – The Search'. A search for India.

WvdH: Right. Not the discovery of India.

SB: Not the discovery of India but a search for India. His book had no references because he was in jail. He did have a historical adviser, E. P. Thompson, whose view was very interesting, but Nehru was attempting to write a history for the first time in India from an Indocentric point of view.[20] During the colonial period when history became a very important subject of study for the colonial masters as well as for the colonial subjects, the history of India was written from a Eurocentric perspective. It was seen from a European point of view, which was condescending, patronizing and often downright arrogant, culturally speaking. So Nehru was attempting to remove that Eurocentric colouring in his telling of history and it was therefore a seminal work.[21] There was much that he did not really know about, particularly relating to South India. I employed twenty-two historians, authorities in their own periods, as my consultants and advisers and we proceeded to fill in those blanks and also to correct Nehru where he was factually wrong. In *Bharat Ek Khoj,* Nehru is the commentator, quoting from the book as he takes us through Indian history in person. Where his book is unclear or where he might be wrong or where he does not know, I have another voice in contradiction to him – this voice is spoken by Om Puri. The series was in fifty-three parts totalling fifty-three hours. We started from the beginning and went on till India became independent, just before which Nehru published his book. I stopped there since he was going to be the person who took us through Indian history. Like Nehru, the series was interested in studying the evolution of Indian culture and the rise and fall of several civilizational processes in the country. This brought in literature, music, architecture, fabrics, styles of clothes. The whole thing was very exciting for me to do because you can do this sort of thing only once in a lifetime.

WvdH: You would only want to do it once in a lifetime!

SB: It also gave one an opportunity to look at literatures of the past – ancient, medieval and modern. We also looked at how Indian culture was such an absorbing, accumulating culture and not one that rejects. There are rejections today but these are marginal movements. The essential mainstream of Indian culture has been one of absorption and accumulation.

WvdH: And that includes the colonial period, the European period?

SB: Absolutely.

WvdH: As well as Islamic and other influences. The episode of the series that I've seen was constructed in the form of tableaux, which incorporate a number of cultural issues.[22] Does that remain your strategy throughout?

SB: Not necessarily. In that episode I was making comparisons between history and how myths are created – the need to make mythic history. This was important because people have different definitions of history and then history itself is written and re-written, revised constantly in terms of contemporary need. So those were aspects that I also wanted to bring in. There are other episodes that present the stories of kings and queens, of dynasties falling and growing.

WvdH: Shama Zaidi mentioned to me that you decided not to dwell on the great figures after the 1857 Mutiny and concentrate instead on what you might call a people's history. Was that to avoid having contemporary figures in the film?

SB: No. One could have had contemporary figures, but here we had the op-portunity and the material available to tell the people's history, which is far more significant than the story of dynasties and kings and queens. But not enough material had been available for earlier periods. Whenever it was available, we did use it. For instance, with the consolidation of Moghul power in India during the reign of Jahangir and Shah Jahan, India became the leading trading power in the world. Indian value-added commodities were traded in the West, which is what brought the West to our shores. Here we did have some material where we could tell the story in terms of the people, rather than kings and queens.

WvdH: You mentioned earlier that every generation has to re-tell its past, its coming into being. I suppose you did that as well in the late 1980s. You took this book, which was finished in the late 1940s before Partition, but your perspective could not remain innocent of that.

SB: No, it couldn't remain innocent of that. It therefore became particularly important to locate the processes that actually led to Partition, without going beyond 1947.

WvdH: Do you think that it was fortuitous that you took on the project in the late 1980s?

SB: It was. We had a national consensus about our nation, our people, our country, our democracy and our constitution. But this consensus is now being questioned in different ways. This concept of national consensus has come back into public discourse in a way it hasn't for many years. Perhaps the time has come to again examine our definitions.

WvdH: Yes. What it is to be an Indian.

SB: Yes. The Hindutva is one way of defining it.[23] Whether it has major support can only be proved when elections come along. It might just be a minority that is pushing its views forcibly because those people happen to be in government now[January 1999].

WvdH: I haven't seen *Antarnaad* [Inner Voice, 1992].

SB: *Antarnaad* is actually a very interesting story of a non-governmental agency, which has very strong religious beliefs and takes a Gandhian route to change the lives of people. These people go into the countryside and try to develop people's self-esteem as the basis for changing themselves. This programme of self-esteem was worked out by a man called Pandurang Shastri Athavale. It is again that whole catalyst thing. It's the story of two villages in the Punjab – a fishing village and a farming village – and their conversion. Both these stories are true. Athavale's work has been quite extraordinary – about 15,000 villages in Gujarat have now become Swadhyay, which is this process of developing self-esteem.[24]

WvdH: And as you said, it's a very Gandhian movement, because Gandhi always saw the village as the centre of Indian societal development.

SB: Yes, because 75 per cent of India continues to live in villages and unfortunately our public discourse marginalizes that 75 per cent. Gandhi was very aware of that, so he always brought the village into focus. Athavale does the same thing. But then all so-called 'progress' and 'development' has always been a process of polarizing the rural from the urban. So in India, being largely a rural country, such polarization can only be seriously damaging.

WvdH: Did you initiate this project yourself or were you contacted?

SB: The Swadhyayees asked me whether I thought it was a subject that I would like to make a film on. So this too was made in a similar way to *Manthan* and *Susman*. Pandurang Shastri said that whoever put money into the film would be given shares for that amount. Once the film started to make money they would get their money back – which is what happened. The Swadhyayees also distributed the film themselves.

WvdH: That's more like *Manthan* than *Susman*.

SB: It earned them over £100,000 in Britain and about $300,000 in the US. It was shown in Kenya, Uganda and South Africa apart from India. So it was quite profitable for the people who put money into the picture.

Notes

1. *Mandi* is the story of Rukmini (Shabana Azmi), who is the madam of a brothel, which she tries to characterize as a centre of courtesan culture, particularly through Zeenat (Smita Patil), who sings for the clients, and Basanti (Neena Gupta), who specializes in Kathak dancing. Tungrus (Naseeruddin Shah) is the establishment's servant and guardian, although when drunk he curses his and Rukmini's predicament, prophesying the destruction of their world. There are two other men who spend a lot of time in the brothel: the local policeman, who lives with one of the prostitutes, Kamli, although he actually desires Zeenat; and the photographer, Ramgopal (Om Puri), who sets out to photograph the women in provocative poses, particularly Zeenat. A new girl, Phulmani, is sold to Rukmini, who is unaware that she is a deaf-mute. Phulmani herself is confused and frightened and tries to run away. The house is bought by a local businessman, Gupta (Kulbhushan Kharbanda), who wants to re-develop the site. He colludes with a moral campaigner, Shantidevi, to move the brothel out of town and to place the underage deaf-mute in a home. Zeenat and Basanti perform at Gupta's house; Gupta's daughter is betrothed to Sushil, the son of the town's mayor, Agarwal (Saeed Jaffrey), but Sushil is mesmerized by Zeenat, whom he keeps visiting at the

brothel, despite Rukmini's objections. As a result of Phulmani attempting suicide, Rukmini and her prostitutes are jailed. Agarwal provides bail, as he is grateful that Rukmini has brought up Zeenat, who is actually his daughter from a liaison with a prostitute who has since died. The brothel is re-located on land owned by Gupta, but business is poor, until Rukmini prays at a nearby grave of a Hindu saint. Suddenly, everything improves and major building activity is undertaken by Gupta in this once desolate place. This leads to Rukmini being forced out again. Rukmini tells Zeenat that Sushil is her half brother, but Zeenat nevertheless runs away with him, although she disappears as he is trying to fix up his broken-down motor bicycle. Rukmini is distressed by her loss of Zeenat and leaves the brothel together with Tungrus. On the way to a pilgrimage site, she prays at a small shrine and looks up to see Phulmani running towards her.

2. Chidananda Das Gupta traces the figure of the *tawaif* through Indian culture and Indian popular cinema, suggesting that its cinematic representation is based on North Indian ('Hindi belt') conceptions of women (Das Gupta, 1991: 126–64). Sumita Chakravarty employs feminist film theory to argue the contradiction in the courtesan film genre in terms of female subjectivity; she goes on to propose that *Mandi* (and *Bhumika*) 'problematize the conventions of the courtesan film' (Chakravarty, 1993: 296).

3. Ashok Mehta went on to photograph *Trikal*, *Susman* and *The Making of the Mahatma*, as well as *Mandi*. His first feature credit was on *36 Chowringhee Lane* and his best-known film is probably *Bandit Queen*. He was also the cinematographer of *Gaja Gamini* (2000), the painter M. F. Husain's obsessive tribute to the film star Madhuri Dixit, and of *Aanken* (2002), the very successful Indian version of Quentin Tarantino's *Reservoir Dogs* (1991). He directed his first film, *Moksha*, in 2001.

4. The book is called *Sukasaptati*, or 'The Seventy Tales of the Parrot' and was compiled in India no later than the twelfth century (Irwin, 1995: 67).

5. *Trikal* starts in the present, with the return of Ruiz Pereira (Naseeruddin Shah) to the house of the prominent Brahmin Catholic Souza-Soares family, with whom he had stayed twenty-four years earlier, just before the Indian army liberated Portuguese Goa in 1961. The house is now deserted, but he recalls the gathered family mourning the death of the patriarch, Ernesto Souza-Soares, all those years ago. There was his wife, Maria (Leela Naidu), her daughter, Sylvia, and her husband, Lucio, their grown-up daughters, Anna and Aurora, and their two young sons, Ernesto's illegitimate daughter, Milagrenia (Neena Gupta), who is now Maria's maid, and Ruiz Pereira as a young man. Also present are Renato and his wife Amalia, who have come from Portugal to negotiate a match between their son Erasmo and Anna. Finally, there is Dr Pereira, Ruiz's uncle. Ernesto's death delays the likely engagement and Maria will only decide after consulting her dead husband. She conducts a

number of séances, with Milagrenia as her medium. Instead of contacting her husband, a figure called Vijay Sing Rane appears in front of her. He complains that her grandfather beheaded him, mistaking him for Kustoba Rane. As Maria awakes, she sees her nephew, Leon, in front of her. He has escaped from a Lisbon jail and seeks sanctuary for a few days. A later séance results in the appearance of Kustoba Rane, who accuses Maria's family of treachery and collusion with the missionaries in massacring his family, as well as moving into his house. Leon and Anna fall in love, and Erasmo and his parents, realizing that the match is no longer possible and that Goa is about to be taken over by the Indian army, return to Portugal. Ruiz was also in love with Anna, but this was not reciprocated and found unacceptable by Maria, because of the lower status of Ruiz's family. Ruiz's sexual desires are directed towards Milagrenia, whom he makes pregnant. Leon and Anna elope and Sylvia, Lucio and the rest of their children also depart. Ruiz is sent to Bombay by his uncle, leaving only Maria and Milagrenia behind. In a final apparition, a Chinese opera figure chants about Ernesto having now mingled with the elements of earth, water, fire and air. Back in the present, Ruiz discovers that Leon and Anna have now bought the house and that Milagrenia had a son. He drives away, contemplating the power of memory.

6. The issue of conversions to Christianity became headline news in January 1999, when the Australian missionary Graham Staines and his two sons were burned to death in their jeep as they slept. This act was ostensibly in response to Hindus being given money to become Christians and is linked to the rise of Hindu nationalism in the 1990s. It is a complex and highly emotive issue (see e.g. Sathe, 1999).

7. Luchino Visconti's 1963 film is an ode to the end of an era and of a social class. It contains numerous darkly lit tableaux of the extended Salina family.

8. Jorge Amado's novels are mostly set in the Brazilian northeastern state of Bahia, most famously in *The Violent Land* (1945). His 1969 novel, *Tent of Miracles*, combines social criticism with an exuberant evocation of the heterogenous elements of Brazilian culture. Many of his novels have been made into films, most notably *Tent of Miracles* (Nelson Pereira Dos Santos, 1977).

9. The Colombian novelist Gabriel García Márquez is perhaps the best known of the Latin American 'magic realist' writers. He won the Nobel Prize for Literature in 1982. His best-known novel is *One Hundred Years of Solitude* (1967). A number of his books have been made into films, including *No One Writes to the Colonel* (Arturo Ripstein, 1999), *Erendira* (Ruy Guerra, 1982) and *Chronicle of a Death Foretold* (Francesco Rosi, 1987; and, most remarkably, as *Bloody Morning* by the Chinese woman director Li Shaohong in 1990). Mario Vargas Llosa is a Peruvian novelist of complexly structured narratives, such as *The War at the End of the World* (1981).

10. The Konkanis are the inhabitants of the Konkan coastal region in Maharashtra, just north of Goa. In 1622, a Christian book, *The Doctrine of Christ*, was published in Konkani, 'widely believed to be the first printed book ever published in an Asian language' (Rao, 1996). Well-known Konkanis include Guru Dutt, Lata Mangeshkar, Girish Karnad, Shyam Benegal and Narsing Rao Benegal, who helped draft the Indian Constitution.

11. *Susman* is set in the village of Pochampalli in Andhra Pradesh, which is considered a leading centre of *ikat* weaving. Mandira Rai (Neena Gupta), the designer of an exhibition of Indian textiles in Paris, is convinced by the village middleman or 'master weaver' Narasimha (Kulbhushan Kharbanda) to offer an order for two saris to the skilled handloom weaver Ramulu (Om Puri), who is bonded to Narasimha. Ramulu's wife, Gauramma (Shabana Azmi), insists, against Ramulu's will, on keeping some of the silk for a wedding sari for her daughter, Chinna (Pallavi Joshi). Mandira discovers this third sari and accuses Narasimha of trying to sell her exclusive designs. Narasimha in turn berates Ramulu, who feels humiliated and refuses to continue with the order. Seth, Mandira's boyfriend, who works as a textile mill official, tries to convince her of the irrelevance of the handloom in an industrialized society, but she argues for the cultural importance of handloom weaving. The local village weaving co-operative, set up to support the actual weavers, is itself involved in corrupt practices with middlemen like Narasimha. Ramulu's brother, Laxmayya, and his wife, Janaki (Ila Arun), live with him, but they are always fighting and Janaki is suspicious of her husband's interest in one of Ramulu's workers. Chinna accompanies her new husband, Nageshwar, to his powerloom set-up in Bhiwandi (in Bombay), but tensions develop between the powerloom owners and the textile workers, culminating in violent rioting, in which Nageshwar is injured. In the meantime, Chinna returns home and seems to re-activate Ramulu, who now finishes the two saris for the exhibition. At the same time, the corrupt co-operative secretary is finally charged, leading to the possibility of a more weaver-friendly organization. Mandira invites Ramulu to the Paris exhibition, where he tells a journalist about the joy of working with one's hands. Mandira gives the journalist a more formal statement about the aesthetic importance of supporting the handloom craftsmen.

12. The Indian government launched a number of state-sponsored cultural festivals abroad in the 1980s. They were begun by Indira Gandhi and became great commercial successes. It has been suggested that they were part of a project to present 'India abroad as a craft nation – a global cultural reserve where vital traditions of folk arts and crafts, music, and dance are maintained' (Greenough, 1995: 241).

13. Nargis was a major star of Indian cinema of the 1940s and 1950s, especially remembered for her roles in Raj Kapoor's films and most famously in

Mother India, after which she retired and entered parliament for the Congress (I) Party when Indira Gandhi returned to power in 1980. In her first speech, she attacked Satyajit Ray for emphasizing India's poverty in his early films in order to win acclaim in the West (Robinson, 1989: 326–8). Salman Rushdie, in *The Moor's Last Sigh* (1995), provides a rather more satirical perspective on this celebrated event (Rushdie, 1995: 173).

14. Bhakti, which refers to devotion to a personal god, was at the centre of a transformation of Hinduism from the thirteenth to the seventeenth century, away from ritual and liturgies to meditation and mysticism. Kabir (1440–1518) was probably born a Muslim and conceived of God in personal and experiential terms. As a result Muslims considered him a Sufi, whereas Hindus saw him as an exponent of Bhakti. He remained a weaver all his life and his poetry is 'a poetry of the people: it is unpolished and has a rustic, colloquial quality, yet it is pervaded with a profound symbolism and often reaches great lyrical power' (Jordens, 1975: 274–5).

15. Pandit Jasraj is considered the 'foremost exponent of the Mewati *gharana* (style or school of music)' and his singing is marked 'by the presence of bhakti (devotion)'; he has also composed the music for operas, ballets and films (Jasraj, 1993).

16. The ninety-one episode *Ramayana* was made by Ramanand Sagar for Doordarshan (the state-owned television channel) in 1986–8 and the ninety-four episode *Mahabharata* was directed by B. R. Chopra in 1988–90 for the same channel.

17. *Bharat Ek Khoj* is a fifty-three episode series produced by Doordarshan that 'traces the crucial and significant landmarks in the evolution of the great Indian Civilization; a unique combination of multicultural, multireligious and multi-ethnic communities constituting a pluralistic society unparalleled in the entire world. The episodes sometimes use the technique of a documentary, at other times drama, in their narratives. The episodes are anchored by the actor Roshan Seth who plays the role of Jawaharlal Nehru' (Benegal, 2002). Episodes 5 and 6 are devoted to the *Mahabharata* and episodes 7 and 8 to the *Ramayana*.

18. 'This astonishing ruler, beloved still in India and in many other parts of Asia, devoted himself to the spread of Buddha's teaching, of righteousness and good will, and to public works for the good of the people' (Nehru, 1960: 86). Santosh Sivan's recent film *Asoka* (2001) trades historical accuracy for spectacle and romance in an account of the emperor's more violent life before his conversion to Buddhism.

19. 'Akbar was the third of the Moghul dynasty in India, yet it was in effect by him that the empire was consolidated ... It was in his reign that the cultural amalgamation of Hindu and Moslem in north India took a long step forward ... The Moghul dynasty became established as India's own' (Nehru,

1960: 163, 164). The best-known and best-loved rendition of Akbar in the cinema is that portrayed by Prithviraj Kapoor in *Mughal-E-Azam* (1960), although the film is also a spectacle and a romance, focussing on Akbar's son's devotion to the palace maiden, Anarkali.

20. Partha Chatterjee characterizes Edward Thompson (and his co-author of their 1934 book, *Rise and Fulfilment of British Rule in India*, G.T. Garrett) as 'two liberal British historians sympathetic towards the aspirations of Indian nationalism' (Chatterjee, 1993: 14). In *The Discovery of India*, Nehru quotes from this book and from Thompson's solo work, *The Making of the Indian Princes* (1943), on several occasions.

21. When *Bharat Ek Khoj* was re-screened on Doordarshan in 2001, a reviewer not only criticized Shyam Benegal's series as 'entirely anachronistic', but also accused Nehru's book of providing 'a faithful narration of the Euro-centric view of Indian history'. Furthermore, Nehru is labelled an 'autocratic ruler', whose ideologies of 'agnosticism ... secularism ... and socialism ... have caused such a great havoc' (*Times of India*, 2001). The website at which this document was accessed belongs to the Bharatvani Institute, 'an organization providing an ideological defence of Hindu religion and culture' (http://www.bharatvani.org).

22. This was episode 24: The Delhi Sultanate and Prithviraj Raso, Part I. Shyam Benegal had suggested that I view this episode.

23. Hindutva refers to the political ideology of Hindu nationalism, a phenom-enon that arose in the nineteenth century as a reaction to colonialism, secularism and modernism. It sought to devalue the other cultures of India, particularly Islam, and to reinterpret Hinduism in masculinist and martial terms (Nandy et al., 1995: 56–61). Anand Patwardhan's film *Pitru Putra Aur Dharamyudh* (Father, Son and Holy War, 1994) sets out to examine the links between communal violence and masculinity. One political manifestation of Hindutva was the destruction of the Babri Masjid at Ayodhya in December 1992; another was the rise of the BJP (Bharatiya Janata Party), which constituted the central government of India from 1998 to 2004.

24. *Antarnaad* is structured as a series of trips over a few years by three Swadhyayees, Arvind (Kulbhushan Kharbanda) and two companions, to a farming village and a fishing village. The trips are separated by a series of short scenes situated in Arvind's home, where his wife, Ragini (Shabana Azmi), and his widowed mother have a rather tense relationship. Arvind also realizes that he has been neglecting Ragini and eventually takes her on the third and fourth trips that he and his companions make to the two villages. It turns out that she is to play an important part in turning the villagers towards individual and social transformation.

Figure 13: Poster for *Suraj Ka Satvan Ghoda* (1992)

WvdH: *Suraj Ka Satvan Ghoda* [The Seventh Horse of the Sun] is the first NFDC feature that you made and is a co-production with Doordarshan. What was attractive to you about the novel it was based on?

SB: It's what one might call a modernist novel, written in the 1950s by Dharmvir Bharati, who was one of our more remarkable literary figures in the Hindi language. This novel tells the story of a 'wanabee' writer, Manek, who has never written anything, but is very free with his opinions about everybody else's writing. He belittles what was the most remarkably successful love story ever told in contemporary Indian literature – a novel called *Devdas*, which is the story of Devdas' self-destructive love for Parvati. It's almost like a Sufi love story. Devdas became the archetypical hero figure, later stereotypical hero figure, of practically every commercial Indian film until Amitabh Bachchan started the angry young man phase.[1] The central character in the novel scoffs at the Devdas character and he decides to tell a series of stories, which, strangely enough, reaffirm rather than reject this Devdas myth. The novel also interested me greatly in terms of its form. Cinema has found it very difficult to do what literature has found ways of doing. For example, you can go backwards and forwards seamlessly and you can indicate people's perceptions of each other. For instance, a parent and a child relationship freezes at a particular moment in time and remains that way through to the end of their lives. In my relationship with my father, there was a defining moment that took place perhaps when I was twelve years of age. So whenever I met my father, I continued to be twelve years old for him, even when I was thirty-five. Similarly, he continued to be what he was at that defining moment rather than what he was when I met him again. Relationships get frozen in time, but this is very difficult to characterize in the cinema, whereas it can be done in literature. There is also the issue of simultaneity. In one of the stories Manek tells, he sees himself as a pre-pubescent boy, in another as a late teenager, while in a third as an adult. When you put them all together, you suddenly realize that these events were actually simultaneous happenings. He was more or less the same age when all these stories actually took place. So it's a question of how you perceive your own self in different relationships – you choose to be an adolescent in some relationships, an adult in other relationships and a pre-pubescent in yet other relationships. All this exists in the novel. I wanted to find a form where I could do this in film. It was a complete break from anything else that I had done before and therefore very exciting too.

WvdH: The other day you said that *Bhumika* was very complex in its structure, but this film is even more complex.[2]

SB: Much more so.

WvdH: There is clearly the need for Manek to remain the same age and be played by the same actor because you want the different ages to be seen as perceptions rather than as age states.

SB: It's happening more or less in the same time frame.

WvdH: Did that require a very detailed scripting process?

SB: Yes, but most scripts of mine are quite detailed. It was a very exciting process of both scripting and filming.

WvdH: Early on in the film, the novel *Devdas* is mentioned by a character, but the storyteller Manek disregards him. Behind Manek's head is a picture of Tagore and this seems to propose an alternative view. Tagore represents a very different sense of the romantic to that of the melodramatic figure of Devdas. Tagore remains a presence in the film even though he is not referred to at all.

SB: No, he's never referred to. Tagore represents a particular literary tradition, as does *Devdas*' author, Saratchandra Chatterjee. Both were contemporaries.

WvdH: And both were Bengalis. I think that I enjoyed this film more than any other of your films, because I'm interested in the process of storytelling and the involvement of storytellers in their own stories. Can the stories be separated from the storyteller? In a sense, the film says, it can't.

SB: You'll always weave yourself into your stories.

WvdH: There is the weave metaphor again. As the film goes on, Manek becomes more and more trapped inside his own stories.

SB: Until he almost dissolves in his own story at the end of the film.

WvdH: That's right. The distinction between the storytelling and the story totally collapses in that traumatic scene at the end when Satti confronts him with what he's done to her both as a character and as a storyteller. In the first part of the film there does seem to be a distinction between what he's talking about and his presence in the story. One of his three friends to whom he is telling the story is called Shyam. Is that significant?

SB: No, that is the character's name in the novel.

WvdH: It's just that Shyam becomes the writer at the end of the film.

SB: Yes. One of the interesting things about the novel is that we are not told who is the narrator of the stories that Manek Mulla is telling. So I had to create a character.

WvdH: He was also the person who was in the art gallery, looking at the paintings by Gulam Mohammed Sheikh, who was also an academic.[3]

SB: He used to teach art at the Baroda School of Fine Arts.

WvdH: What was the relevance of those paintings in relation to the film?

SB: He has a similar multi-faceted view of things. When you look at his paintings there are always stories within stories. He also paints himself in his pictures. I found that an increasing parallel with the story of *Suraj Ka Satvan Ghoda*.

WvdH: From the few paintings that I've seen and the ones that you show in the film, he seems to combine elements of the Indian miniature tradition with the European paintings of someone like Chagall.

SB: Yes. He combines them, but it's strongly rooted in the miniature tradition.

WvdH: Perhaps in the same way that your work is Indian, but also very conscious of the narrative and filmic traditions of the West. In the first story, the woman's name is Jamuna, which, as I understand it, is the name of the actress who plays the Parvati role in the first Devdas film.[4] Is that the name of the character in the novel as well?

SB: Yes.

WvdH: And Tanna is the Devdas figure. They are the archetypal couple in the Devdas tradition, although it seems to me that Manek quickly assumes the Devdas role himself.

SB: But he's the betrayer rather than the betrayed.

WvdH: This reverses the original situation. Are the caste differences between the characters also reversed in relation to the Devdas story?

SB: Yes.

WvdH: So Manek is already the betrayer in the first part of the film?

SB: Yes.

WvdH: In the second story, which is about the horseshoe, there's a scene that is initially confusing. We hear a wedding procession passing the storyteller's house. He calls his three friends to the balcony, and as they look down, you cut to the story. The point-of-view shot thus joins together those two stories. For a moment we've lost our bearings.

SB: Yes. This process of moving from the telling of the story to the story itself is something we do so easily when we speak. The mind has this way of travelling, and I was using film to travel in that same fashion.

WvdH: That way of joining together the story and storytelling process is most adventurous.

SB: You'll find I did that earlier in *Trikal*.

WvdH: Yes, that's right. You joined the past and the present through the coffin. But here it is developed much more elaborately.

SB: Much more elaborately.

WvdH: This leads to a real surprise in a later story when the now married Lily talks to someone we can't see. A cut reveals that it's Manek. In a sense you've led us up the garden path, as, I suppose, storytellers are wont to do.

SB: Yes. It's the manner in which storytellers use the different means at their disposal.

WvdH: As well as Manek, the storyteller, there are the three listeners who are also interpreters of the stories in the film. This creates a multi-layered effect, because the viewer of the film is also an interpreter. Was this a parody of different interpretative strategies?

SB: It was a parody, but it also represents the process of analysis, in which you are both a listener and a participant. So these three are also critics and they are dealing with current ideological beliefs.

WvdH: One of them takes the Marxist view, while Shyam undertakes these elaborate dream interpretations, almost Jungian dream interpretations, which are quite horrific. You don't undercut these interpretations – they're as valid as any of the other interpretations.

SB: They have a validity.

WvdH: Shyam's descriptions keep referring to severed limbs, which suggest to me the severed stories of the film. The story between Lily and Manek includes songs that are given the Hindi film picturization treatment.

SB: Yes, because the imagination is affected by the Hindi film – even his storytelling is affected by the Hindi film.

WvdH: As well as the *Devdas* reference in this story, you also refer to a character called Devsena, who comes from a novel called *Skandgupta*.

SB: It's a very famous novel written in the early part of the twentieth century.

WvdH: The final story of Satti is a familiar one in your films – the middle-class man and the servant girl. It doesn't surprise me that you end the film with that particular relationship because it is the one that's most preoccupied with failure and disappointment.

SB: Yes. And betrayal – the urban middle-class betrayal of the rural community.

WvdH: It is embodied in the poems that Manek and Satti recite to each other. His is a rather mannered personal poem. Her poem is about the archetypal experience of daughters leaving home.

SB: That's right.

WvdH: She devalues her poem but it's the more important one. Your sympathy, I presume, lies with her.

SB: Yes.

WvdH: Neena Gupta gives a marvellously broad performance that ultimately becomes quite tragic. The three children in the film are all fathered in somewhat strange ways. Are they all Manek's children?

SB: They're not, but he does take on the guilt of their existence.

WvdH: In that respect Satti's boy is representative of all those little boys. Are you happy with the film?

SB: I'm quite happy with the way the film turned out.

WvdH: I imagine that it would have been quite a difficult film for audiences to come to terms with.

SB: To some extent, but on repeated viewings, people seem to have liked the film. It had a much greater exposure through television, and it's been repeated frequently on television. When it was first shown, it didn't have the kind of response that I thought it would have.

WvdH: Because of the frequent references to Indian literature and popular culture, audiences outside of India would have found the film difficult.

SB: Definitely. *Suraj Ka Satvan Ghoda* has never been commercially released outside of India. But it has been seen by festival audiences and it's had a pretty good response on the festival circuit.

WvdH: How did *The Making of the Mahatma* come about? From Shama Zaidi, I got the impression that it was started well before the Mandela government came to power in South Africa.

SB: Well before the general elections took place. It happened soon after Mandela was released. Fatima Meer, a political activist and a member of the ANC, came to India and wanted to meet me. She had written biographies of the young Gandhi in South Africa and of Nelson Mandela. She and her husband were very close to Nelson Mandela – her husband had his power of attorney during all those years he was in jail. She wanted to know from me if I would like to make a film on either Mandela or the young Gandhi. I felt that I would be more competent to make a film on the young Gandhi rather than on Mandela because I didn't know enough about Mandela at the time. South Africa was a very crucial period in Gandhi's life because those twenty-one years made Gandhi what he became. If it wasn't for his South African experience, neither his philosophy nor his

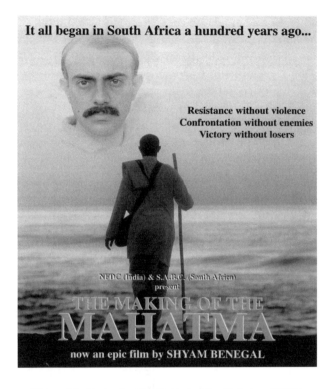

Figure 14: Poster for *The Making of the Mahatma* (1996)

political strategy nor his tactics nor his methods nor his own principles of living would have seriously found any kind of crystallization. Funnily enough, that experience of Gandhi's is the least known anywhere in the world and least of all in India. The exception is South Africa, where he was a great inspirational figure. The Congress Party that he formed in South Africa eventually served as the inspiration for the African National Congress. For the first fifty years of its existence, the African National Congress followed Gandhian principles of civil disobedience and non-violence – what they call passive resistance. It's been acknowledged by everybody, including Nelson Mandela, that Gandhi played a seminally important role for the South African Liberation Movement. Fatima Meer's book was called *The Apprenticeship of a Mahatma*. The funding was partially to come from South Africa and partially from India. At that time the South African part actually was meant to be privately funded. The script took a long time to do and there were lots of fights between Fatima and I. I then got Shama Zaidi involved in the scripting. So there was this three-way scripting process. After Shama had finished with her part of the drafts, Fatima did her own draft. Finally I did my final draft of the script. By that time the elections took place and Nelson Mandela became President. The funding then changed slightly and the South African Broadcasting Corporation decided to put money into the picture. So on our side there was the government of India through the National Film Development Corporation and on the other side the South African Broadcasting Corporation. A fair amount of research was done in both India and South Africa, but research wasn't too difficult largely because the Gandhi archives are amongst the most exhaustive for any single Asian leader. The film was shot in South Africa and, except for my cameraman, some of the actors and the costumes that were done by my daughter Pia, the rest of the cast and crew was South African.[5]

WvdH: Was the fact that it was a co-production the reason why you shot the film in English?

SB: No. The Indian diaspora to South Africa really started in 1862. Indians had been taken there as indentured labourers even earlier, but from 1862 it became organized and whole communities of Indians were sent there to work in the plantations. This developed into a substantial South African Indian population, which came from different regions and so spoke different languages. In South Africa they all started to speak in English. This is why the film was shot in English.

WvdH: They would have used English themselves. This issue of the different backgrounds of the Indians was taken up in the film.

SB: There were three kinds of Indians. There were the indentured labourers, virtually slaves, who were taken there to work on the farms. Then there were people who were seeking work under the colonial administration. They were known as passenger Indians. They weren't there under any kind of disabling contract, but they usually did very ordinary jobs, maybe waiters and clerks. And then there were the people who were called the free traders. The trading community came from the west coast of India, while the indentured community were from very poverty-stricken areas of South India as well as from Central and Eastern India, from Bihar and places like that. The passenger Indians were mostly South Indians but they had a certain amount of education. So the Indian community was stratified there as well. The Indians were segregated by the colonial and the Boer administrations, but they also had their own stratification, all of which caused many complications. The blacks were down at the bottom, the Indians were above them, the coloureds were above them and then the white man was on top of everybody else.

WvdH: There was also a tension between the Boers and the English. Gandhi in the film, as no doubt in life, continually tried to find ways of making all of these groups meet each other, from Smuts down to the African jailer.

SB: Although he found it very difficult to get the Africans to join his own movement and he eventually suggested that the Africans should form their own movement, which they did with the African National Congress, the ANC.

WvdH: There were a couple of places in the film where you had him discuss issues with some of the Africans, like the pastor in the fields.

SB: The Reverend John Dube, who was a very interesting figure because he was one of the founders of the African National Congress.

WvdH: As is your wont, Gandhi was not presented as a simple saint. He was not an unblemished figure.

SB: No, he was not.

WvdH: You felt it was also necessary to tell the story of Gandhi's personal life.

SB: Absolutely. He may have had many virtues, but he was a normal human being with flaws and problems. He was also a man with an incredible will and with a searing honesty.

WvdH: Searing is right!

SB: Particularly towards himself. This made him different from everybody else because he was self-critical, apart from being critical about everybody else. Whatever he wanted to propagate, he'd tried it out on himself. He would never ask anybody to do what he wouldn't do himself. That's what got him the kind of following he did get.

WvdH: But it was also by an unbending logic. Not even his wife or his children got in the way of that logic.

SB: He couldn't allow that to happen. His wife was a person of great strength herself. She eventually became his most devoted disciple, but she did create space for herself. She didn't allow him to walk all over her.

WvdH: Is this why you create some space for her on the soundtrack in the film?

SB: Yes.

WvdH: Even though she ends up primarily talking about him, she is given a voice in the film. But she doesn't talk about herself.

SB: One of the interesting things was that she was totally unlettered and she resisted learning from him. That was her kind of defiance. She did learn how to read and write very much later in life. In fact, a little before she died, when they were both in jail in the Aga Khan palace in Pune, he used to do daily lessons with her. But in the early years she did resist him because she didn't want to fully come under his influence.

WvdH: She was much more traditional than him and she had her own sense of hierarchies which he resisted strongly, including the hierarchy of caste.

SB: In everyday life, she was also much more pragmatic than he was. He was very pragmatic in his politics but in his home life he wasn't terribly sensible.

WvdH: There are some scenes that illustrate how they worked out their relationship. There's also Gandhi's unwillingness to bend to the authorities, who refuse to allow him to see his very sick wife. From a personal point of view, Gandhi doesn't come off very well in those situations.

SB: But he is not being selfish. It depends on which way you look at him. His wife is dying and they are using that to blackmail him and he is unwilling to be blackmailed. If he bent in front of them there, then he would have to do so for ever. He then wrote her a letter which was very loving in many ways but which also showed him as the kind of person he was.

WvdH: This whole matter comes up again later when he comforts the woman whose husband was killed on the march and he makes a statement to the effect that it will only be when women like his wife are widows that the suffering will end. He wants to bring it back to himself all the time.

SB: Yes.

WvdH: Gandhi's detachment from sexual desire, as I understand it, goes back to his guilt for being so sexually demanding of his wife when they first married.

SB: That's casually mentioned in his autobiography. Every interpretation takes that as a very key moment. But I don't necessarily think that is so. For somebody in his mid-teens making love to his wife, hearing that his father has died in the next room, a terrible sense of guilt connected with sex is not surprising. But it is not that simple. It had much more to do with a sense of sublimation of sex, a concept that exists in one of the philosophical schools of India.[6] This is the idea of the sublimation of sex by depriving oneself of it, of celibacy as a transcending of sexual desire. So this was something that came to him partially through his own religious training and partially through a person I've not dealt with in the film. He was a man called Raychand and Gandhi had met him when he returned from England. Gandhi acknowledged his influence on him. Raychand wasn't very much older than Gandhi, but he died at the age of thirty-two. He was a Jain and self-denial is a very important aspect of one school of Jain belief.[7] This also partially explains some of the concepts of self-denial that Gandhi adopted as part of his principle of living. Gandhi also talked about there being enough in the world to meet everybody's needs but not enough for everybody's greed. He would often use this expression. Some of these ideas come from Raychand as well. So I wouldn't give that much credibility to a simplistic Freudian interpretation.

WvdH: The film includes the 'Vande Mataram' song and, at the end, the African song, which makes it very contemporary.

SB: Of course, the 'Nkosi Sikeleli Africa' is the South African national anthem. There's also another song, a black workers' song, a miners' song, which became the rugby anthem during the World Cup.

WvdH: Vanraj Bhatia told me that he re-scored 'Vande Mataram'.

SB: He re-scored it. It was written in the early 1890s by Bankim Chandra Chatterjee.[8] It was used as a song to rouse people against the British partition of Bengal in 1905. Later the South African Indian Congress took over this song for Gandhi's long march. It was called the Big March and was the first political long march in history.

WvdH: Why did Vanraj Bhatia re-score it?

SB: He re-scored it because the original tune is very quiet. It's not rousing enough.

WvdH: India is ever-present in the film but it's invisible. The ending of the film suggests the move across the sea to India.

SB: Gandhi himself said that his battle was to be fought there, and not in South Africa.

WvdH: The rising sun and the beach thus represent India but also the future.

SB: He left South Africa and came to India, became the most important leader of the Nationalist movement, turned it into a mass movement and took India to freedom.

WvdH: Would you ever want to tell the rest of his story?

SB: That part of the story has been told by Richard Attenborough.[9]

WvdH: Was his film in your mind when you were making your film?

SB: Not at all. My image of Gandhi was very different from his.

WvdH: The film that I was reminded of was a John Ford film, *Young Mr Lincoln* [1939].[10] I don't know whether you've seen it.

SB: I saw it many years ago as a child.

WvdH: It is the making of a President, as yours is the making of a Mahatma. The end of the Ford film, where Lincoln walks up the hill under a thundering sky, is a bit more melodramatic than your ending, but your film is more like it than like Richard Attenborough's film.

SB: I was more interested in the evolution of Gandhi, which for Attenborough was a prelude that is dispensed with in the first fifteen minutes and then he concentrates on Gandhi the leader. Gandhi was already the Mahatma when he came back to India. He didn't change from 1914 to 1948, when he was assassinated. His evolution had already taken place.

WvdH: He is, of course, another outsider – an educated middle-class man who comes into a community and attempts to cause change in it.

SB: Yes. He's a catalyst figure.

WvdH: It seemed to me that the *mise-en-scène* is much simpler than many of your other films. It's much more pared down.

SB: I didn't feel that it needed to be elaborate. I didn't want to lose the focus on how he was evolving.

WvdH: So the film style itself needed to be simple and more transparent?

SB: Yes.

WvdH: Quite unlike *Suraj Ka Satvan Ghoda*, which is rather baroque. Rajit Kapur [who plays Gandhi] seems to have become your favourite male actor at the present time. What does he mean to you at the moment?

SB: He is a very important new actor because he has quite extraordinary talent and has great capabilities. He's also extremely versatile. It is a very important thing for me to find an actor like that, with that kind of commitment.

WvdH: He's the film director in *Samar* [Conflict]. Is he at all like Shyam Benegal, film director?

SB: He's much more nervous and wants to decide everything very quickly as a director. I've created that kind of a figure because his concerns are very much more specific to the film he's making rather than to the life around.

WvdH: So the film examines the issue of how one relates to one's subject.

SB: That's it.

WvdH: Is that your first film shot in widescreen?

SB: No. *Sardari Begum* [1996] was. *The Making of the Mahatma* was a widescreen film too, but it wasn't anamorphic widescreen. *Sardari Begum* was the first anamorphic film. It is now very difficult to get distribution in India if you don't use cinemascope widescreen. Indian audiences, and also distribution interests and exhibitors, prefer to show a film that covers the entire screen.

WvdH: So it is just accepting the inevitable.

SB: And therefore constructing your visual conceptualization to suit this kind of film. You fit your visual concepts to meet the requirements of that format.

WvdH: Watching the beginning of *Samar*, I noticed that your compositions encompass two or three main figures in the frame and there is much less cutting than before.

SB: You don't have to cut so much.

WvdH: *Samar* was, like *Hari-Bhari* [Fertility, 2000], financed by the Ministry of Welfare, wasn't it?

SB: *Hari-Bhari* was financed by the Ministry of Health and *Samar* by the Ministry of Social Welfare.

WvdH: In both cases the money came from the NFDC.

SB: This is because government departments can't deal with private individuals.

WvdH: So, once again you're working with an organization, whether it's the handloom industry or the dairy farmers, about a particular social issue. But again you want to take a fictional approach with a complicated story that underlines a social problem.

SB: Yes. *Samar* deals with a subject that is very important for me – the situation regarding untouchability in India today. It's been over fifty years since we passed affirmative action legislation to bring this whole community of people, who number between 15 and 18 per cent of the population, into the mainstream. They had no rights whatsoever. They were consciously denied any kind of normal human rights because they were supposed to do menial work and

Figure 15: Ramesh Singh (Yashpal Sharma), Murali (Ravi Jhankal) and Uma (Rajeshwari Sachdev) in *Samar* (1999)

remain invisible. So we passed some quite revolutionary legislation in the early years of India's independence. It was now time to evaluate how far we had come. We still frequently hear of atrocities against Untouchables. In some ways these atrocities have become worse because they are now challenging the system, because now they do have some rights and they're trying to make use of those rights. That brings them into direct confrontation. There was an incident of an atrocity that took place against an Untouchable in a little village in Madhya Pradesh, a state where a lot of these developments haven't actually percolated. The *Thakur*, the chief of the village, together with the *Panchayat*, the village council, decided to punish an Untouchable who had gone into a temple. In earlier times, they were not allowed to go into temples, but now they have a constitutional right to do so. This young man went into the temple to thank God for having cured his wife of an illness. He was seen by the village priest, who complained to the *Thakur*, who then decided to punish him publicly by urinating on his head in front of the whole village. It was a most humiliating kind of punishment. This caused a tremendous amount of furore and led to the entire Untouchable community there objecting loudly and, in turn, to the caste Hindus of the village boycotting them. The government then had to step in, but the problem is still going on. This happened in 1991 and I decided to make a film about this in 1998. So seven years after this incident took place I went to that village and met all the people who were affected by this. The *Thakur* had died, but the man against whom this atrocity was committed was still there. I wanted to get some insight into changing attitudes towards Untouchables. So I decided to take that story and shoot it in that village, with the actual people there plus actors who played the roles of the actual people – a film within a film. Urban actors played the roles of those people in the village, who also appear in the film. You see the actor and you see the actual person. Now, this led to many things. One was that the urban actor was himself an Untouchable, but he's lived in urban India and had never experienced this. So there is his perception as against the perception of the Untouchable living in the village, their attitude to each other and to the village, and the village's attitude to this group of people who had come a long way to make a film. Finally, there was the attitude of the director who's making the film. It becomes clear that the urban middle-class attitude towards these atrocities is completely different from the attitude of the people in the village.

WvdH: So this was the way you complicated the social issue in this film?

SB: Yes. The idea was to look at the situation today – seven years later and also fifty years later. I enjoyed making it as a film within a film, because it allows many more points of view than if you were just to tell a story.[11] After all, this story has been told many times in Indian cinema. I myself have made several such films thirty years ago.

WvdH*: Ankur* and *Nishant.*

SB*:* I didn't want to make another film like that, because it doesn't say anything new. Hopefully this approach was much more insightful.

WvdH*:* Were the rural Untouchables in the film the actual people from the village or were they actors themselves?

SB*:* There were actual people and some actors.

WvdH*:* So, in some cases you had three different levels of people – the actual social human beings in the village, actors playing some of them and then actors playing them in the film within the film. I noted that the film was very well regarded at the national film awards.

SB*:* It won the best film award.

WvdH*:* What did the Ministry of Welfare want to convey about this issue?

SB*:* They wanted to highlight the fact that there's a long way to go. For these things to disappear, certain mindsets have to change. Mindsets usually change only when there's so much pressure that they can't resist the pressure. People on their own don't change their mindsets, unless they're forced to. In this case, the mindset will only change slowly, because things that have gone on for over three or four thousand years are not going to come to an end in fifty years.

WvdH*: Hari-Bhari* [Fertility] is also about mindsets.

SB*:* Yes, *Hari-Bhari* deals not just with women's rights and the empowerment of women, but also with women's reproductive rights. By and large, this right is exercised by the men, not just in India, but the whole world over. A country like India has a large base population and our population is growing more than

Figure 16: Hasina (Surekha Sikri Rege), Ghazala (Shabana Azmi) and
Salma (Rajeshwari Sachdev) in *Hari-Bhari* (2000)

it should. Instead of having zero population growth, we are growing at the rate of 2.2 per cent annually. This is a huge amount when you have over a billion people. In a place like the United States it doesn't matter. The United States has a growth rate of about 2.8 per cent, but nobody talks about population control in a place like the United States. Everybody talks about it here. It's also not right to automatically assume that all families should be small. You know it's a matter of individual choice, of a family's choice. How can anybody say they shouldn't have more children?

WvdH: Mao Zedong tried.

SB: So now the Chinese have one-child families, which are not very natural for them, because their family system is as strong as ours. Anyway there are real problems to be faced with a large population that cannot be supported by the land in which they live. So one of the important components of trying to keep the population under control is for women to become conscious of the fact that they have a right. It is not the man's right. It is the woman's prerogative, because she is the one who is going to bear the child and nurse the child, and she has the greatest influence on the child as it is growing up. So she must have the right to decide whether she wants to have a child or not. *Hari-Bhari* was meant to be a film that would create a debate and so persuade people to see it. I set it within a Muslim family. Although we have the largest Muslim population outside of Indonesia, no country that calls itself a Muslim country has such a large population of Muslims as India does. Pakistan doesn't and Bangladesh doesn't. In places like Pakistan and Bangladesh, the mullahs can talk from the pulpits about reducing the population growth. But in India, minority rights groups would object if the mullahs were told to do that. Minorities always feel threatened in a country where the majority belongs to a different religion. In India, the minorities cannot be pushed around. The population problem is slightly greater among the Muslims than it is among the Hindus. When Pakistan was formed, the cream of the Muslim population went to Pakistan. The wealthy people also went, but the poor were left behind and they had very little education. The mullahs have a certain amount of power over the community, because the Muslim political leaders also left after Partition, leaving those left behind leaderless. So the person who gives the sermons in the mosque becomes the leader. The film was set in a Muslim family, because the problems in a Muslim family are slightly different from problems in a Hindu family.

WvdH: Unlike *Samar*, this film was not based on an actual event.

SB: It was based on a series of case histories. The Population Council in this country is a non-government organization. They produce a lot of case histories from different parts of India annually to find out what the situation is and what people think about these issues. So I put a number of case histories together in a story of five women of different ages in a single family. It's a story about a house, where these five women live together. The film is the story of each one of them. It concentrates on women's experience. In some ways, it's an examination of the rights of women in comparison with men's rights – economic rights, social rights, individual rights, physical rights and rights over their own bodies. The film did very well in the marketplace and it's often shown at conferences. Non-government organizations use it in poorer neighbourhoods in different parts of India.[12]

WvdH: This sort of use is reminiscent of *Manthan*.

SB: Yes.

WvdH: Was there any criticism in India that the film concentrated on a Muslim family?

SB: Certainly not. On the contrary, it was much appreciated. The majority of people who came to see the film were Muslims, particularly Muslim women, who came to the cinemas in large numbers in their *burqas*.

WvdH: I'm very taken by your last two films, *Hari-Bhari* and *Zubeidaa*. They're very different to your earlier films. Did you ask Shama Zaidi to script *Hari-Bhari*?

SB: Yes, she scripted it.

WvdH: Was this because the film was concerned with women's issues?

SB: No, it was because she's been a long-time collaborator of mine. But she could also bring more insight into a Muslim family, being a Muslim herself.

WvdH: The end credits indicate that the film was shot and processed at Ramoji Film City. Is that outside of Bombay?

SB: It's about forty kilometres outside Hyderabad. It's a huge studio complex, bigger than most Hollywood studio complexes. It's on a lot of almost 2,000 acres. It has many studios and open lots. It has production equipment, editing rooms, recording studios and laboratories. So I completed the whole production there. I built that whole small town, shot the film, edited it, recorded the soundtrack and brought the finished film back here.

WvdH: Did you enjoy working in such a controlled environment as opposed to working on location?

SB: Definitely. There's much less strain and stress, because it's all in one place.

WvdH: It is also an ensemble film, being about the five women in that family. As in your other ensemble films, you have assembled a number of skilled actors, who can spark off each other. The best known is Shabana Azmi.

SB: There is also Nandita Das, who starred in *Fire* [1996] with Shabana Azmi. She was very good. The others are also very good.

WvdH: The young actor who plays Salma, Rajeshwari Sachdev, was in one of your earlier films too.

SB: Yes, *Suraj Ka Satvan Ghoda*.

WvdH: As you were saying before, the film explores ingrained traditional values about sexuality and choice, without making moral judgements about the characters.

SB: I wasn't making any moral judgements about them. I was relating them to their environment and also the compulsions within the environment, including the weight of their backgrounds.

WvdH: These characters move through various moral states. Afsana, for example, is steeped in selfishness, but at other times she becomes a much more positive figure. Was it important to you to have such character ambiguity?

SB: Yes.

WvdH: Other characters, like Afsana's husband Khurshid, seem to be set on destroying the family by attempting to break it up.

SB: But even if he tries to break it up, it isn't that he wants to break it up. It's because he wants to do something different.

WvdH: Khurshid's desire to move to the city also alludes to the issue of urbanization.

SB: Yes. He represents the urbanization process, as does his wife, and it is embodied in the idea of them living as a nuclear family.

WvdH: In tension with the extended family that the film concentrates on?

SB: Exactly.

WvdH: Do the women in the film really develop awareness of family health matters and of their rights? Or do they hear what's being said but don't necessarily absorb it?

SB: They do absorb it in different ways. But in a patriarchal system, the decision-making is often left to the man. Most people do not pay too much attention to things about which they do not have a right to make a decision. There are characters in the film who are like that.

WvdH: Such as the Shabana Azmi character, Ghazala. Her doctor tells her about fertility and family planning, but she is much more interested in what a woman in the doctor's waiting room tells her about the miraculous child-bearing properties of the ashes from a local shrine.

SB: Yes. Exactly.

WvdH: The film has an optimistic ending, which is encapsulated in Salma's freedom song about kite flying. But in some ways, it's an illusory optimism because Salma's freedom was brought about by chance – the illness of her grand-mother, Hasina. Salma was about to be married off in line with the traditional arrangements.

SB: To some extent yes, but there is already a process of learning adopted by some of the women. Najma loses her baby and then decides to have an operation to stop having further children, but she can't move out of her traditional mindset when it starts to affect other people. When she hears about their maidservant's unmarried niece being pregnant, she says that the girl should be thrown out of the house.

WvdH: Yes, that's right. She also tells Salma that there is no point to her having an education, because it is unnecessary for women.

SB: Yes. Najma is learning, but she's not applying it to other people. This is a common problem, not only in traditional society, but everywhere.

WvdH: But she does learn. She takes action on her own behalf.

SB: The grandmother's illness does enable the learning to be applied to others.

WvdH: Yes, even though Salma is almost about to be recycled in the traditional way, exactly like her grandmother was, when she was forced into marrying a much older man. Yet, the grandmother, Hasina, can't see this, even though she said she was going to help Salma.

SB: Hasina was very bitter about her own marriage, because her husband did not leave her the *mehr*. When Muslim men get married they have to pledge a certain amount of money, which is called *mehr*, for the wife, to provide for her in case of divorce or death. In spite of this bitterness, she will follow the same pattern.

WvdH: The same thing happens in *Zubeidaa*. In that respect, women become the enforcers of tradition, which they force upon their own daughters. It's patriarchy by default.

SB: Absolutely. This is one of the biggest problems. Real empowerment is achieved when women are no longer the enforcers of the patriarchal system. That is the critical change that is required.

WvdH: There is an inkling of that in Khaleel, Najma's husband, when he de-clares, after her operation, that he accepts whatever his wife decides to do. He is quite a positive male character in that respect, isn't he?

SB: Yes. He is.

WvdH: He doesn't seem to want to be the spokesman for patriarchy.

SB: Although he is the patriarch of the family. But he has a certain flexibility. After all, not all patriarchs are monsters.

WvdH: He's therefore a more significant contributor to this process of empowerment than his brother, Khurshid.

SB: Khurshid's solution is to opt out of taking any responsibility for changing things. Khaleel sees his responsibility not just to his own wife and children, but also to the whole family.

WvdH: As does his wife, Najma. She's the cement that holds that whole family together. None of the other women do. Why is there no separate story about Rampyari, the maidservant? You probably wanted to focus on the family itself, but she is a significant female character.

SB: I did not want to address her situation in this film, but she would have similar problems within her family.

WvdH: But she would bring the perspective of a maidservant, presumably even more desperately poor than the family she works for. So her role is purely to underline certain points in relation to that particular Muslim family, such as her niece becoming pregnant and Ghazala being thrown out of her own home by her husband.

SB: Yes.

WvdH: The buffalo sub-plot is there both as a parallel fertility narrative and as an illustration of the significance of the buffalo to the survival of such a community. Its milk is desperately needed for their overall health and especially for the pregnant women. Hasina, the grandmother, is not the cement that holds the family together, but she is a sentinel figure who constantly sits outside the house and watches what is going on.

SB: She's a kind of traditional guardian spirit.

WvdH: But she rarely interferes in the lives of the family members.

SB: Eventually she does speak up to insist that her granddaughter is much too young to be married off. So despite her traditional attitude, she does exercise good sense, when it comes to it. It's not traditionalism or modernity; it's just simple good sense.

WvdH: Hasina also wants to keep insisting that all the decisions that are made in this family have to be made as family decisions rather than as individual decisions. But don't you want people to make more individual decisions?

SB: Yes, of course. Otherwise how are they going to face the future? Traditional family systems are breaking up. One of the casualties of modernity and progress is that they destroy what is actually a very stable system. This fragmentation has to be faced. The alternative is one of remaining steeped in nostalgia.

WvdH: This new situation requires the family to learn how to deal with their social problems and health. This also leads to health workers and doctors intruding upon family secrets or circumstances that are often held at bay. This is highlighted when the health worker arrives and asks about Najma's baby. It becomes obvious that there is real aggression towards the health workers from the family. Did such a response arise out of the way that Mrs Ghandi and her son dealt with birth control?[13]

SB: Yes, that took place in 1973. It became an absolutely traumatic experience for people. Suddenly, out of nowhere, it recalled Stalin's collectivization plan.

WvdH: It must have set back the whole population control programme years and years.

SB: It set it back by about thirty years.

WvdH: Undoubtedly, conservative groups would have made the most of this situation.

SB: They did – political use was made of it.

WvdH: The health worker in the film, while presented as a positive figure, is ultimately sent away without benefiting the family at all. The film is divided into a series of chapters named after the women of this family. Some of them are flashback stories, the first one of which reminded me of the way flashbacks were used in *Suraj Ka Satvan Ghoda*. This episode is called 'Ghazala's Story' and it ends at the exact point where the film itself starts, thus creating a lovely circular structure. Hasina's story is a more traditional flashback, while the other stories are woven into the narrative's present tense. Hasina's story also brings to light the rather brutal discussions about money that precede a matrimonial agreement, one from which the women themselves are basically excluded. This is graphically demonstrated as the camera tracks from the women surrounding the bride-to-be, Hasina, to the men as they decide the financial arrangements.

SB: It is another instance of patriarchy in action.

WvdH: As is the financial bargaining that takes place between Ghazala's husband and her brother about the husband's recompense for taking her back. Once again the woman is being sold from one man to another man for certain gains.

SB: Absolutely.

WvdH: There is a scene at the end of Hasina's story, where Salma arrives at the house to move in with her mother's family, which is particularly interesting in the context of the film having been made in a studio, where you could use tracking shots more than you could on location. It starts with a semi-circular tracking shot across the women, who are 'trapped' in a family portrait. This is followed by a closer version of the same thing, this time only of Hasina, Ghazala and Salma – three generations in tears, comforting each other. It's a very melodramatic moment, almost like a soap opera.

SB: Yes, it is. But there is a certain truth to it, because they come together and there's a bonding. There's a great deal to be said in a patriarchal situation for female bonding. Because of the pressures of patriarchy, there's always greater female bonding.

WvdH: There is also the bonding between Khurshid and his wife Afsana. The one thing that they have going for them is a joy in each other's sensuality, which is not evident in any of the other couples.

SB: With the others, the pressures of life have squeezed it out of them.

WvdH: Afsana keeps talking about having more children and insisting on her role as a mother, but she also has this desire for sex and sensuality. Such ambiguities are part of your character construction. The same applies to Khurshid, who is very selfish, but also generous.

SB: He's impulsive and generous in a very funny sort of way. He wants money from his family for himself, but he ends up spending it on the family, buying a replacement buffalo for the family and a colour TV set for his wife.

WvdH: He's going to have to start saving money all over again.

SB: He's willing to break up the family to get this money and then he spends it on something that he's not going to get anything out of.

WvdH: Afsana seems to disappear from the film once she's been persuaded to return to her husband.

SB: She's now accepted her role and her situation of being part of the family. Earlier she resisted dealing with them at all, living above and removed from the rest of the family.

WvdH: Finally, I want to talk about the songs in the film because it seems to me that there's a real change occurring in your use of songs. They're much more distinct sequences, although not separate from the narrative.

SB: No, but they are also traditional songs, sung in families. Because they're sung constantly, a lot of them tend to lose their meanings. When you pay attention to the meaning you realize that these are songs that actually help them to deal with their life situations. Many of the work songs are like that too. In Chhatisgarh, which was part of Madhya Pradesh, but is now a state in its own right, there are countless such songs. When the farmers transplant rice plants, they have a song, which they sing as a group. The words of the song say that if the water is above your ankle, then what you plant is going to rot and if it is below your ankle, it will burn. They don't pay any attention to the words they're singing while they're transplanting, but it's a lesson in farming technique, saying that the water should be exactly at ankle depth – not more and not less. There are also some beautiful children's songs, which are lessons in science. There is one about water tanks, in which rainwater is collected. The water then fell in love with the sky. The heat of this love caused the water to evaporate. It became a cloud in the sky and went looking for the sky but found nothing, because it was just a void. So not having found a lover, the cloud started to weep and came down as rain. It's a little science lesson. There are also songs that relate to relationships, to tragedies and to the status of women.

WvdH: Like the songs here about the tragedy of being a female or about women's powerlessness. The song under the credits seems to be a nursery rhyme about black and white colours.

SB: It's not a nursery rhyme, but a song that mothers sing to their daughters as they are growing up. It tells them not to wear black and not to wear white. Instead, they should wear coloured clothes. Black is the colour worn when married and white is a sign of mourning and the colour widows wear. This song is from the Deccan, from Hyderabad.

WvdH: You treated the songs much more filmically than in the past, much more as significant components of the film, while still part of the narrative.

SB: They function as commentaries. They're almost like a chorus in a play.

WvdH: I thought of them as crystallizations of their emotions, somewhat like Guru Dutt's approach, suspending the narrative, but not rupturing it, which is what often happens in the commercial cinema. These are 'voice-over' songs that lament the situation that they're in. To that extent the songs, except for the last one, are not really about empowerment. They're more about the traditional world in which the women were brought up.

SB: But sometimes the action is the opposite of what the song says.

WvdH: Yes, that's right. I think that's most interestingly done in the second last song. It starts in the bedroom of Salma and her mother, Ghazala, who are in conflict about Salma's proposed betrothal. It's a dialogue song between a mother and her daughter, which extends to a lament about all the women in the house, each of whom is visualized in her own bedroom.

SB: The song is about the river Ganges, which is a light-coloured river, and the Yamuna, which is dark, but eventually they meet and become one.

WvdH: That's like the black and white imagery of the opening song, where neither colour is desirable, but their combination might be.

SB: Yes.

WvdH: I'd like to move on to the Khalid Mohamed trilogy. How did your relationship with Khalid Mohamed develop and how did you decide to make a trilogy of films together?

SB: Khalid Mohamed is a well-known film critic and the editor of the magazine *Filmfare*. He wasn't particularly fond of my films. In fact, he was always very critical of my work. He never wrote a single good review of any of my films. *The Times of India* newspaper used to have a small column, in which people were asked to write about something that affected them deeply. Khalid wrote a little piece about this great aunt of his, Mammo. I was very moved by that story and I telephoned him and told him that I would like to make a film about Mammo. He offered to write the script and eventually the film was made. When he wrote that story for the newspaper, Mammo had not returned after she'd been deported to Pakistan. She'd been deported more than twenty years earlier, and he didn't even know whether she was still living or not. When he wrote the script, she had still not returned. But when I was ready to shoot the film, she came back. That became the film's epilogue. After I completed that film, he told me that he had another story of a distant aunt of his. This story became *Sardari Begum*. Sardari Begum's story was also an unfortunate one in the sense that she was an unwitting victim of a Hindu/Muslim riot. She came out on the balcony to look at what was happening downstairs and was hit by a stone on her temple, as a result of which she died. This turned into a very interesting film because she was a Thumri singer – Thumri is a north Indian light classical form of singing.[14] It gave me the opportunity to use some very good Thumris in the film. Of course, the subject closest to Khalid's heart was the story of his mother. He hadn't told this story to anybody at all. In *Mammo* we touched upon it. Khalid's father had abandoned him and later his mother had also left him to become the second wife of the Maharajah of Jodpur – the present Maharajah's father – and then she and the Maharajah had died in a plane crash. This film, called *Zubeidaa*, was mounted on a bigger scale, because there were many popular elements in the story. I had some problems making the film because the first wife was still living.

WvdH: Is this the Mandiri Devi character in the film?

SB: Yes. She was very worried that I might show the family in a bad light. I sent her the script and then everything was fine.

WvdH: Even though you showed her brother-in-law, Uday, as a lecherous, nasty man?

SB: Yes, but he was an invention. There was no such person. That didn't worry her.

WvdH: So these films weren't really conceived of as a trilogy from the beginning.

SB: No, it just happened, and since the characters are related to one another, it became a trilogy by default. *Zubeidaa* also introduced some other changes. I engaged a new music director, A. R. Rahman, who is now an exceedingly popular composer and who also has a new huge following outside of India.[15] He's written the music for Lloyd-Weber's *Bombay Dreams*, which is the most successful musical in the London West End for the last ten years. *Zubeidaa*'s music became very popular, because he wrote some very beautiful songs for the film and produced a pretty good background score. As well, I used a main-line star in Karisma Kapoor, who played the main part, and a fairly popular star, Manoj Bajpai, who played the prince. As a result, the film went into what one might call the popular cinema circuit.

WvdH: I'm sure that many people would have said that you'd sold out.

SB: No. Nobody did. In fact, the film was held up as an example of the direction in which popular cinema should move.

Figure 17: Publicity photo of young Riyaz (Amit Phalke), Mammo (Farida Jalal) and Fayyazi (Surekha Sikri Rege) in *Mammo* (1994)

WvdH: *Mammo*, I think, would also have been a popular film.

SB: Yes, because of its subject matter.[16]

WvdH: And also the performance of the actor playing Mammo, who is reminiscent of the Shabana Azmi figure in *Mandi* – a very strong woman character. The subject matter is treated in complex ways and has many ramifications.

SB: It has, because its main feature is borders. It's about India and Pakistan. It's about a country being split, relationships being split, families being split. That is what Indian audiences recognize and also Pakistani audiences. Although it's on the illicit circuit in Pakistan, the response there has been quite tremendous.

WvdH: The film shows that one can make a difference if one really wants to. There's that resourcefulness again.

SB: It's also very ironical and it's very sad that Mammo can only live in India when, on the basis of a death certificate that is drawn up for her, she becomes invisible.

WvdH: Mammo's strength is her ability to confront the history of Partition and the word Partition. Her identity was determined for her rather than one that she chose to have. She was told she is Pakistani and not Indian. Whereas for you the borders are more fluid than that, aren't they?

SB: Yes, they should be.

WvdH: Yes. The little boy who becomes the writer is based upon the life of Khalid Mohamed. The little boy is sometimes quite aggravating in his intolerance and I felt that his grandmother shared that intolerance as well. What was the dynamic operating between the three of them?

SB: The grandmother was unwilling to talk about her daughter, whose marriage had failed, who was abandoned by her husband and had died. Furthermore, her husband had abandoned the boy to the care of the grandmother. So she was deeply resentful about that whole thing and kept the boy completely out of it, isolating him from his own immediate family. The grandmother has withdrawn on account of that bitterness and this has affected the boy. Mammo lightens the whole thing up, since she has no such inhibitions.

WvdH: She has no inhibitions whatsoever. She can talk to anybody about anything. When the young boy thinks of his mother, he can only think of her in Hindi film terms. This is also linked to the fact that she was an actress for a while.

SB: Yes, she was a sometime actress.

WvdH: The move between the past and the present is done very simply by means of the doorbell. And again you confront, as in earlier films, the past and the present. The framing device of an adult looking back on his past and learning from it, or maybe not learning that much from it, was previously used in *Trikal*. It's a way of re-experiencing what one has become. However, we don't really learn much about the adult writer in *Mammo*.

SB: No, because you don't know too much about him as an adult. It's Mammo who he wishes to recover.

WvdH: She almost appears as a wish fulfilment. He asks his grandmother for the letters and, as he reads them, Mammo enters into their lives. Once again you employ the song commentary technique, this time using the poems of Faiz Ahmad Faiz.[17]

SB: He's one of the great Urdu poets, who mourned the demise of a united India. He was a Pakistani and he suffered greatly under various Pakistani regimes. The first song, which is about borders, was written by Gulzar.[18]

WvdH: The search for Mammo is like a Hindi film picturization, but done in a totally unconventional way. They look for her in the mosques of Bombay and the music provides a powerful sense of loss. The writer is a typical Benegal figure who provides a perspective on the events, like many of your other protagonists. You mentioned that *Sardari Begum* is about Khalid Mohamed's great aunt and that the three films are linked to each other, but there is no reference to her in *Mammo*.

SB: No, but there's a reference to her in *Zubeidaa*. She's the one who entertains the Rajput princes in the tent.

WvdH: The structure of *Sardari Begum* appears to be similar to the other two films, in the sense in which it's a reporter or a writer investigating or reminiscing about some event in the past.[19]

SB: *Mammo* is different, but *Sardari Begum* and *Zubeidaa* have a similar form. In *Sardari Begum*, there's a reporter who investigates Sardari Begum's life and turns out eventually to be Sardari Begum's niece, although she doesn't know this. In *Zubeidaa* it is the son who's trying to find out about his mother, because his grandmother refuses to tell him about her. This was already mentioned in *Mammo*.

WvdH: In *Sardari Begum*, the focus is on the Thumri singer and her conflict with other members of her family. In that sense, she's rather like Zubeidaa as well.

SB: Yes. She does rebel and run away from home. She does things that are not normally done in a traditional Muslim family.

WvdH: She also works in the film industry as a playback singer.

Figure 18: Zubeidaa (Karisma Kapoor), Victor (Manoj Bajpai) and Mandira Devi (Rekha) in *Zubeidaa* (2000)

SB: Yes, she does.

WvdH: One of the reviews of the film I read said that Vanraj Bhatia's music was too classical.

SB: The music was very good actually and also very successful with audiences.

WvdH: You mentioned that one of the reasons you enjoyed making the film was to concentrate on the musical performances.

SB: Yes.

WvdH: I imagine that *Zubeidaa* would have been your most expensive film to date.

SB: No. My most expensive film was *The Making of the Mahatma*, but the film I'm making now, *Netaji* [the film's release title is *Bose: The Forgotten Hero*, 2005], will be more expensive.

WvdH: The difference between *Zubeidaa* and *The Making of the Mahatma*, of course, is that *The Making of the Mahatma* is about a man who is poor, whereas *Zubeidaa* has a sense of wealth about it, in terms of the costumes and the palaces, and so gives the impression of being an expensive film. I understand that you approached a number of other actors for Zubeidaa's role.

SB: Yes. Although in my own mind, Karisma Kapoor was the person who I wanted. We just wanted to be absolutely sure. She is a very popular star.

WvdH: She's from the Kapoor family, isn't she?

SB: Yes. She is Raj Kapoor's granddaughter. Most people tried to dissuade me from using her because she was doing all these very light parts and nobody thought that she was a capable actress. She gave a very good performance indeed.[20]

WvdH: What could you see in her that made her your choice for the role?

SB: I saw a certain kind of impulsiveness in her. I wanted a person who had great depth of feeling but also tended to be impulsive in her actions. When she's determined to do something, she'll do it, come what may.

WvdH: Like running away with the prince and leaving her son behind, whatever the cost to herself. What about the person who plays the prince, Manoj Bajpai?

SB: He looked like a Rajput prince. A lot of people don't know what Rajput princes look like – they think they look like tall, fair Punjabis. I knew him to be a good actor, although all his popular roles were of him playing hoodlums.[21]

WvdH: I remember him from *Satya* [The Other Side of Truth, 2000].

SB: But I was getting him to play something that was exactly the opposite – a cultivated aristocrat.

WvdH: You also used Rekha again in the film. Why did you feel that she would be good for the role of the first wife?

SB: Because she's a very accomplished actress. She had worked with me twenty years earlier in *Kalyug*. She has a wonderfully ability and she was the right age to play the part.

WvdH: She comes across as a woman who's very much part of that world, and totally comfortable in it. And yet she recognizes that Zubeidaa has something that she can never attain. Is this the first film for which Vanraj Bhatia hasn't written the music?

SB: No, the second film. He didn't write the music for *Aarohan*.

WvdH: I understand that the music for *Netaji* is also by A. R. Rahman.

SB: Yes.

WvdH: Does this mean that you will not be working with Vanraj Bhatia anymore?

SB: Not at all. Vanraj Bhatia will be doing the music for the next film.

WvdH: Why is A. R. Rahman more appropriate for these two films?

SB: Because there is a certain popular quality that I want for the films.

WvdH: I can understand that. I've liked some of the Mani Ratnam films that he scored.[22]

SB: Yes. He's very, very good. He puts a lot of very interesting colour in the music here.

WvdH: In some other films he's scored, I felt that there was at times too much repetitiveness in his music.

SB: That is not the case in *Zubeidaa*.

WvdH: One of the consequences of using him, it seems to me, is that you are now also using famous playback singers, like Lata Mangeshkar.

SB: Of all the playback singers for the film, only Lata hadn't sung for me before. In fact she told me that I'd been making films for thirty years and hadn't called on her until now, when, as she said, she had grown old.

WvdH: But her voice doesn't sound old.

SB: No. She has a very young voice. She's now seventy-three [in 2003].

WvdH: It's remarkable how she's able to maintain what could be described as a virginal sound.

SB: Which she has. I've used her sister Asha Bhonsle in *Junoon* and in *Mandi*.

WvdH: Another of *Zubeidaa*'s playback singers, Kavita Krishnamurthy, is one of the up-coming stars, isn't she?

SB: Oh no. She's been around for a long time. She's very good. She sang two songs for me in *Bhumika* in 1976. She was an up and coming playback singer then.

WvdH: Maybe she's up and coming in comparison to Lata Mangeshkar!

SB: Yes, but she's been a popular singer for a long time, although she never received the same level of attention as Lata. But then, there's only one Lata, as there's only one Amitabh Bachchan.

WvdH: Given Khalid Mohamed's filmic interest, is it significant that Zubeidaa is also the name of the actor who starred in the first Indian sound film?

SB: No, it's not significant. It was his mother's name. There were two Zubeidaas in Indian films. There was the one who sang in the very first sound film, *Alam Ara*.[23] There was another Zubeidaa who was in films in the forties. Then, of course, the Zubeidaa in my film also acted in a couple of films before she gave up everything.

WvdH: *Zubeidaa* also reminds me of *Bhumika*. Both films have a strong woman, who is being constrained by social norms, fights against them, but does not overcome them.

SB: That's more the case in *Bhumika* than in *Zubeidaa*. Zubeidaa becomes a victim. In *Bhumika*, even if she's victimized, Usha chooses her life of independence.

WvdH: Interestingly, she also passes her convictions on to her daughter, even if, finally, Usha can't make the jump herself. Like in *Hari-Bhari*.

SB: Yes.

WvdH: The beginning of *Zubeidaa* immediately presents a totally different world to any of your other films. There is Lata Mangeshkar's voice, A. R. Rahman's beautiful melody and the bright red scarf floating through the air. It's like no other opening sequence of yours. It is, of course, a magical world, a fairy world. The film starts as a fairy story and ends as one, but the bulk of the film is not a fairy story at all.[24]

SB: The grandmother objects to her daughter's behaviour for most of the film, but at the end she says that she doesn't want to think about all that, because for her Zubeidaa will always remain a fairy princess.

WvdH: There is a strong 'once upon a time' quality to the beginning of the film, with Zubeidaa's son, Riyaz, watching the scarf falling on Zubeidaa's grave.

SB: Yes, because, as a child, he had imagined her as a fairy princess and that's the memory he wants to keep for himself despite the real story of her life, which he discovers as an adult.

WvdH: The first quarter of an hour of the film is steeped in this nostalgia, including Riyaz's maid singing to him about the fairy princess, Zubeidaa. This is then rather brutally shattered when the film cuts to the adult Riyaz, when a different narrative, an investigative story, takes over. But the opening of the film is about nostalgia, dreams and memory – the awakening of his memory of her. You were fairly bold in giving away the whole plot at the beginning.

SB: I didn't see that as a problem. If a producer had insisted that I couldn't do that, I wouldn't have made the film for him.

WvdH: It's not as if the film is plot-driven. When Riyaz, identifying himself as a film reporter, sets out to find the missing reel of the film in which Zubeidaa performed, I was reminded of *Citizen Kane* [1941] and continued to be on and off during the film. Did you set out to make such a connection?

SB: Not consciously, but it's one of the films that I admire greatly. It's one of the great films of the world. But I don't think I consciously thought in those terms, because it's a common enough pattern – such a structure doesn't only occur in *Citizen Kane*.

WvdH: I agree, but there were times when I thought of that film, such as when Riyaz visits Rose. It reminded me of the reporter talking to the drunk Susan Alexander in the bar at the beginning of *Citizen Kane*. Riyaz's grandmother, Fayyazi, is very reluctant to tell him about his mother, as she was in *Mammo*. She resents him finding anything out about her.

SB: She resents all the people she thinks took her daughter away from her, made her into somebody else and destroyed her. She blames Rose. But then she has another reason for blaming Rose because Rose was her husband's mistress.

WvdH: Rose later makes the point that Zubeidaa is strong because of her father, whereas her mother was weak. Fayyazi wants to cocoon her grandson and she literally wants to mother him, to be his mother – as she tells Zubeidaa she is going to be. She wants a child who she can call her own, as she could never call Zubeidaa her own. Zubeidaa's rebelliousness and impulsiveness are qualities that Fayyazi doesn't have at all. She comes across as quite a sad figure, doesn't she?

SB: She was a sad figure, but she was also a sympathetic figure. Life has treated her badly and her husband really didn't care for her too much either. She suffered her husband's neglect and later she was almost a doormat as far as her daughter was concerned. She doesn't want that situation to occur with her grandchild.

WvdH: Unfortunately, in both *Mammo* and this film, she is eclipsed by domineering and extrovert characters, like Mammo, Zubeidaa and Rose. In that sense she is almost a tragic figure.

SB: Her personality is also one that withdraws into herself rather than reacts.

WvdH: Unlike the character she plays, the actor, Surekha Sikri Rege, who was also in *Mammo* and *Hari-Bhari*, has great screen presence.

SB: She's a tremendous actress.

WvdH: Has she been in many films other than yours?

SB: Not too many, but she's an extremely well-known theatre actress from Delhi, although she now lives in Bombay. She does a lot of television work.

WvdH: In many of her scenes in *Zubeidaa* she comes across as a very beautiful woman.

SB: Yes.

WvdH: Very different to Karisma Kapoor's beauty or even Rekha for that matter. The other woman, Rose, is very much a liberated woman.

SB: Yes, she is in many ways. She's Anglo-Indian and, without having the strong traditions of either side, that allows her to do what she wants. Even when she's an old woman, she's living entirely by herself in a small, poor tenement with her cats.

WvdH: This also introduces a double standard, in which Suleiman is obsessively overprotective of his Zubeidaa but has no problem with Rose's behaviour.

SB: None at all. These are two different things. They're in two different compartments.

WvdH: It is not an issue about women for him, it's about daughters. The liberated Rose is also the instigator of Zubeidaa's liberation and freedom. Rose leads her towards this fairy prince, but Zubeidaa is unable to articulate her feelings about him or about herself. There's an interesting scene which occurs after Rose, Zubeidaa and Victor go to the Taj Hotel for dinner. He expresses his feeling for Zubeidaa and she is totally unable to respond. She runs outside and neither Victor nor Rose is able to 'revive' her.

SB: She's unable to function in such a situation, because she's been forced to live a life in which she's not allowed to make any choices of her own. It is his falling in love with her that changes things for her. If that hadn't happened, she would have continued to live at her parents' home with her little son and do what her parents wanted her to do. So this new situation is difficult for her. Rose is her road to freedom.

WvdH: Is Victor also her road to freedom?

SB: Yes.

WvdH: But he also becomes her controller; he becomes like her father.

SB: Absolutely. He is bound to tradition in the same fashion.

WvdH: So first she's cocooned in her parents' house with her son and later she's cocooned in Victor's house by herself. She's trapped in both worlds.

SB: Yes. This is what she fights against.

WvdH: She comes into contact with Mandiri Devi, who has sympathy for Zubeidaa, but who is also an enforcer of tradition.

SB: Absolutely.

WvdH: She wants to constrain Zubeidaa within a role that she's unwilling to occupy. What role does the invented character of Uday play in relation to these conflicts?

SB: He has ambitions of his own. Being the second son, he'll never have the throne, but he also feels that whatever little share of this world he may have will disappear once Zubeidaa arrives at the palace. Victor gives her the forest house, but Uday insists that it belongs to the family and that Victor can't just take a unilateral decision.

WvdH: While not a major theme in the film, there were interesting references to the issue of Muslims returning from Pakistan to India after Partition. The way it's dealt with in *Zubeidaa* is almost the opposite of its treatment in *Mammo*. Here Suleiman has encouraged and helped his friend to come back, but his friend is dissatisfied and unwilling to accommodate himself to the new environment.

SB: During Partition there were huge population movements. Muslims went to Pakistan and Hindus came here. Many of the Muslims who left here were under no pressure to leave – people who had been living in Bombay were not displaced in any way. But some of them did decide to go, feeling that Pakistan was their country, because they were Muslims. Many of them felt lost in Pakistan, because where they came from was their home and where their friends were. So, a number of them returned to India. This continued until the mid-1950s. Some of those who returned discovered that they had lost what they had before and returned to Pakistan again. Suleiman's friend came back, because Suleiman did help him, but he wasn't satisfied with things here, although his son had found work in a hospital. He wanted to return to Pakistan and expected his son to accompany him, which he was willing to do. But the son, Mehboob, was by now married to Zubeidaa. Suleiman was upset that his friend wanted to go back, but he definitely wouldn't allow his daughter to go.

WvdH: Meḥboob was a rather weak character, very much willing to do whatever his father wanted. Mehboob's father assumed that, having decided to return to Pakistan, Zubeidaa would accompany her husband. Suleiman's refusal does make him a slightly more positive character, given his otherwise unpleasant personality.

SB: Except that it was not a particularly good thing to do. She didn't want to go to Pakistan, but the fact was, she would eventually have gone with her husband and their child. But her father was insistent.

WvdH: There was also the related question about how the child was to be raised if Zubeidaa took him with her to Jodpur. Fayyazi tells Victor, who is a Hindu, that the child must be brought up as a Muslim.

SB: This is an important issue for Muslims, as it is for Catholics, that the child's religion should not be tampered with.

WvdH: The only other reference to religion that I can recall occurs during the 1952 election campaign, when Victor tells Zubeidaa that she cannot come with him while he is electioneering.

SB: Because he might lose votes. She would have been a liability, particularly that soon after Partition. Muslims in India at that time were under great suspicion, but that suspicion vanished after 1971, after the third war that we had with Pakistan. Pakistan split into Bangladesh and West Pakistan. For the majority of Indians, the formation of Bangladesh was a vindication of what they had always believed – that a country couldn't be created on the basis of a religion. It seemed to confirm the view of India as a nation that is not based on any religion. A nation has to be inclusive; it has to bring together all ethnic groups and religions. So, religion as the basis for a nation seemed ridiculous. That is what happened to Pakistan. It split in spite of the fact that both West Pakistan and Bangladesh were populated by Muslims.

WvdH: You also raise the issue of the politics of the mid-1950s, in terms of the relationship between the Rajputs and the Congress Party.[25]

SB: There were about 530 princely states in India under the British and all those states were nominally autonomous in the sense that they had some power, although essentially all the power rested with the British. But when the British left India, one of the things they told the princes was that they could remain free if they wanted to or they could join India or Pakistan. The choice did not in fact exist, because the Nationalist movement saw them as feudal entities that had no place in a modern state. Soon after Independence, the Indian Home Minister, Sardar Patel, persuaded all of these states to join the Indian Union.[26] There were only three states that initially did not: Junagadh – which is in Gujarat – Kashmir and Hyderabad. These three said that they wanted to be independent. When Kashmir said it wanted to be independent, Pakistan sent their forces into Kashmir, which made the Maharajah of Kashmir, who was a Hindu, sign an accession treaty with India. Pakistan has still not accepted this. Hyderabad tried to hold out for about a year with a lot of machinations on the part of the British, but then India simply sent in its army and took it over. The French gave up their territories quite easily but the Portuguese didn't and Goa did not become part of India until 1961.

WvdH: You deal with this in *Trikal*.

SB: Yes. So that's the background to the politics in the film. The first elections took place in 1952 and in 1950 the princes called a Conclave of the Princes of Rajasthan, because most of the princely kingdoms were in Rajasthan. They wanted to opt out of the Union and regain their freedom, since they had been rulers for thousands of years. But the Maharajah of Jodpur, Raja Vijandra Singh, who also called himself Victor, disagreed and proposed they stand for election. If they won the elections, then they would still be the head of state.

WvdH: He was very confident, wasn't he? He said that if he nominated a stone to stand for the election, it would win.

SB: It was a statement that he actually made and he did win with the highest margin in that election. He recognized that he had to deal with India. This was in late 1952, and he was on his way to Delhi to present his credentials to Nehru when he and Zubeidaa died in that plane crash. The present Maharajah, Raj Singh, took over as a minor from his father and, just a month ago [January 2003], celebrated the fiftieth anniversary of having ascended the throne.

WvdH: The end of the film seems to leave the cause of the plane crash ambiguous.

SB: He was a very fine pilot and the weather was fine. So why did the plane crash? His first wife blamed his enemies, saying they sabotaged the plane. In her diary, Zubeidaa writes that she didn't want Victor to change and that only in death would she be with him for ever. This suggests that she caused the plane to crash.

WvdH: There was an intimation of this when, during their honeymoon, she grabs hold of the plane's controls.

SB: To this day nobody knows how the plane crashed.

WvdH: Apart from Mandiri Devi, there seemed to have been a concerted attempt by the rest of the Maharaja's family and staff to erase Zubeidaa's existence.

SB: The first reason was that she didn't come from a princely family and was thus a commoner. Secondly, they didn't want to admit to the fact that she was married to him, because then her son would be among the heirs.

WvdH: So Khalid Mohamed was never accepted as an heir?

SB: No. They wanted to keep it in the family and erase her memory altogether.

WvdH: In looking at the films as a trilogy, it is immediately apparent that there are plot inconsistencies. This is most obvious in terms of Riyaz's age at certain key events. Similarly, in *Zubeidaa* Riyaz's father never contacted him whereas in *Mammo* there was some contact.

SB: The connections between the two films are not that important and are not crucial to what I was saying. The films look at events from different directions.

WvdH: The film has quite a number of songs.

SB: There is the wedding song, which is an actual wedding song ['Mehndi Hai Rachnewali'/The henna has coloured your palms red], the song that is sung at that Gangaur festival among princely families ['Hai Na'/The path is strewn with fragrant air], the Thumri which is sung at the princes' Conclave ['Chhodo Mori Baiyaan'/Listen to me my love], the fairy tale song that the maid sings to Riyaz ['Pyaara Sa Gaon'/Far away in a mango orchard] and her own song, which she wrote in her diary and which her son imagines her singing when she and Victor were courting ['Dheeme Dheeme'/I hum softly].

WvdH: There is also the song from the film in which Zubeidaa starred ['Main Albeli'/You are romantic]. Was that done in the style of the time?

SB: Yes, that of the early 1950s.

WvdH: It is quite different to the Guru Dutt type of song picturizations.

SB: This is a more popular type. Guru Dutt in his time was not considered terribly popular, only becoming so after he died.

WvdH: The wedding or henna song sets up a counter-point between the words, which glorify marriage, and Zubeidaa's unhappiness and frustration. Her rebelliousness is evident in her taking her father's gun and putting it to her head. But it disappears as soon as her father arrives. His look crushes her dissent and not a word is spoken. The film then cuts to the wedding itself. Much of the impact of this scene is derived from the power of Amrish Puri as an actor. His stare is quite forbidding. His persona does not just derive from the many films he's made with you, but also his villain roles in the popular Hindi cinema.[27]

SB: Yes.

WvdH: The song that Zubeidaa sings to Victor as a declaration of her love and adoration is the most typical Hindi film song in the film.

SB: It is a very typical Hindi film song and the lyrics are very much of that period.

WvdH: You acknowledge the genre to the extent of having the required costume changes.[28]

SB: This comes from Riyaz reading Zubeidaa's diary and imagining their courtship.

WvdH: In *Mammo* you also have him imagining his mother singing a film song. So he's imagining it as a popular Hindi song?

SB: Yes. That is what he has grown up on.

WvdH: But at the same time the way you shot the number is quite unlike the typical Hindi film song. It doesn't have any fast cutting.

SB: No, but then there was no fast cutting in the films of that time, unlike the frenetic pace of song editing in current films.

WvdH: The song under the credits recurs throughout the film and functions as Zubeidaa's voice-over ['So Gaye Hain'/The memories of my heart].

SB: Yes. It asks for someone to awake the memories of her heart, and this is what her son, Riyaz, does in the film.

WvdH: Correct me if I'm wrong, but isn't it unusual to have more than one playback singer singing Zubeidaa's songs? I thought that typically one singer, say Lata Mangeshkar, would sing all the songs for a particular character in a film.

SB: Not necessarily, and here there was no reason for it to happen.

WvdH: Earlier you noted that the film has been regarded as a model for future Hindi films. What did you mean by that? In what sense is *Zubeidaa* a possible prototype for a different sort of Hindi film?

SB: In the way that the songs relate to the narrative. Songs are so much part of the form of Indian cinema itself. Not having songs would weaken the classical structure of an Indian film. Furthermore, the chances of a film doing well or being popular with audiences are reduced enormously if you don't have songs. Very few American films are made in ways that deviate from the traditional characteristics of the American cinema. In the same fashion you can't do without songs in the Indian cinema. Otherwise you remain on the margins and never move into the popular mainstream. So if you've got to use songs, it's best to use them as films did in earlier times. At present, songs function simply as interludes. They're not part of the main narrative of the story. Often songs, even the lyrics, have no connection whatsoever to the narrative. In that sense they're more like the 1930s Hollywood musical. This approach has run its course in Indian cinema. It is possible, once again, to have songs as part of the narrative, so that the film remains an integrated entity.

WvdH: You've always had songs in your films, but they often function as a commentary on a particular moment in the movie, as in *Nishant*. But over time, the songs in your films have come more to the fore.

SB: Yes.

WvdH: Will there be songs in *Netaji*?

SB: To some extent, because there are some very famous marching songs. Subhash Chandra Bose was very musical himself. He had a very good singing voice and was very fond of both Indian music and Western classical music. He had a huge music collection.

WvdH: How does Khalid Mohamed feel about your films now?

SB: He seems to have liked these three films.

WvdH: Has it made him re-think his views of your other films?

SB: I don't know. I haven't really asked him.

WvdH: Khalid Mohamed's own first film, *Fiza* [2001], seems to be a more typical Hindi film than *Zubeidaa* was.

SB: Yes. It was. He planned to do it that way. He was, quite understandably, deeply affected by the riots that took place in the wake of the Babri Mosque demolition in December 1992. So he wanted to deal with a story of a community that is pushed against the wall. It tends to create undesirables. It creates terrorists. He didn't want the terrorist in the film to be an absolutely black figure, like the way President Bush has characterized them. There's a reason why they have come about. It wouldn't have happened if there was more social justice in the world. He wanted to make it in a very popular genre to get broad exposure for the film.

WvdH: Consequently, the songs often have nothing to do with the plot. The film also has comedy items, with the very popular Johnny Lever.[29] However, it has a strong female Muslim protagonist, who controls the narrative. She is going to find her brother and she will do it on her own terms. It is unusual for a Hindi film to have such a strong female figure.

SB: Of course. It's very unusual.

WvdH: Karisma Kapoor also plays this woman, but does so quite differently to the way she plays Zubeidaa. She doesn't have quite that edginess we discussed earlier. There is one song in *Fiza* that is interesting to compare to *Mammo* – the song at the Haji Ali Mosque.[30]

SB: They sing Qawwalis there. Haji Ali was a Sufi master, who lived in the four-teenth century, although the mosque was only built in the nineteenth century.

WvdH: The song in *Mammo* is a narrative song, with Riyaz and his grand-mother searching for Mammo. Khalid Mohamed's song is very much a song performance.

SB: Yes. It's also an affirmation of what might be called the essential Islamic value of tolerance.

Notes

1. Amitabh Bachchan was and remains India's most loved and most popular film star. He started his career in the late 1960s, but it was his role in *Zanjeer* (1973) that led to the 'angry young man' label, further elaborated in films like *Deewar* (1975), *Sholay* (1975), *Trishul* (1978) and *Agneepath* (1990). No longer a young man, his recent films have him adopting more patriarchal roles, e.g. *Kabhi Khushi Kabhie Gham* (2001) and *Aanken* (2002). Much

has been written about his persona and his presence in Indian cinema as a 'parallel text' (Mishra, 2002: 125–56). Sudhir Kakar set out the prevailing male archetypes in Indian cinema in the following terms: the Majnun-lover (duplicated in the Devdas-lover) in the 1950s, e.g. Dilip Kumar in *Devdas* (1955); the Krishna-lover in the 1960s, e.g. Shammi Kapoor in *Junglee* (1961); the good–bad hero based on Karna in the *Mahabharata* in the 1970s, e.g. Amitabh Bachchan (Kakar, 1989: 35–8).

2. *Suraj Ka Satvan Ghoda* is framed by Shyam (Raghuvir Yadav) walking through an art gallery recalling the times he and his friends met at Manek Mulla's house to listen to his stories. In the first story Manek (Rajit Kapur) tells, he lives next door to a young woman, Jamuna (Rajeshwari Sachdev), who loves Tanna (Riju Bajaj). Jamuna's family disapprove of Tanna, because he is of a lower caste, and Tanna himself is unwilling to stand up to his father, Mahesar Dalal (Amrish Puri). Jamuna transfers her affection to Manek. Manek then tells the next story. Jamuna marries a rich but old landlord. Tanna marries a girl from a rich family, but is unable to forget Jamuna. Jamuna remains childless, until her carriage driver, Ramdhan (Ravi Jhankal), gives her a ring made from a horseshoe. She has a son and within a few years her husband dies. Ramdhan promises to look after her and her son. Manek meets Ramdhan at a railway station and tells him he now has the job at the Mail Service that Tanna had before he died. Manek's friends interpret the story in various ways. Manek says that the next story is about Tanna. Jamuna wants to marry Tanna, but her parents refuse and Tanna is unwilling to leave his father. He fails his school examination and finds a job in the Mail Service. His father arranges his marriage to Lily (Pallavi Joshi), who befriends Jamuna. Lily leaves Tanna and goes to her mother's house to give birth to a son. Jamuna, her son and Ramdhan meet Tanna at the railway station, where Tanna is struck by a train. He dies in hospital in the presence of Jamuna and Lily. Manek's friends argue about the meaning of this story too. Manek says that the next story is about a girl called Lily. Lily is sobbing and Manek comforts her, saying he loves her but that she will leave him. Lily prepares for her marriage to Tanna. Manek's final story is about Satti (Neena Gupta), the adopted daughter of a disabled soap maker, Chaman Thakur (Lalit Tiwari). Satti is strongly attracted to Manek and tells him Chaman has sold her to Mahesar, Tanna's father. She asks for his help, but he refuses. Manek's friends accuse him of treating the women in his stories badly. They go to a teashop, where Manek turns around to see Satti holding a little boy. As she returns to Chaman sitting on a cart, Manek follows her. In the art gallery, Shyam recalls that Manek disappeared.

3. Gulam Mohammed Sheikh is one of the foremost contemporary Indian painters. He is also a poet and an essayist, frequently writing about the relationship between European painting and Indian art (Sheikh, 1983: 43–52; 1993: 143–54; 1997: 7–32).

4. I am referring here to the 1935 film version. In fact, the first film adaptation of *Devdas* was made in 1928 by the Bengali director Naresh Chandra Mitra (see Interview 2, note 8). Apparently, there are seventeen versions of *Devdas* in various regional languages, including a 1982 Bangladeshi version by Chashi Nazrul Islam (Etem, 2002: 93-4). The recent Hindi version by Sanjay Leela Bhansali was one of the big hits of 2002. The 1935 version was made in both Bengali and Hindi, with different actors performing the title role (P. C. Barua and K. L. Saigal, respectively), although Jamuna played Parvati in both films. Ashis Nandy in an essay on this version's director, P. C. Barua, mentions that 'For playing the role of the heroine, he chose Jamuna, a woman who had lived at the margins of respectability and with whom he had fallen in love. They got married in 1934 itself, when *Devdas* was being made' (Nandy, 2001: 146).

5. *The Making of the Mahatma* starts in 1892, when Gandhi (Rajit Kapur) tells his wife Kasturba (Pallavi Joshi) that he's taking a job as a barrister in South Africa for a few months. On arrival, he discovers that Indians are regarded as 'coolies', positioned well below Europeans. He helps set up the Natal Indian Congress to fight a bill that would deny local Indians the right to vote. Gandhi leaves for India, only to return with Kasturba and their children in 1896. Once again, he is accosted on arrival in Durban. In 1899, the British are fighting the Boers and Gandhi argues that the Indians must support the British, as they claim to be British citizens. Gandhi and family go home to India, but he returns to South Africa upon hearing that the British are restricting Indians from owning property. He becomes involved in running a newspaper and decides to live on a farm. In 1904, Kasturba and some of their children join him. Now the British are fighting the Zulus, but, once again, Gandhi insists they support the British, despite the worthiness of the Zulus' cause. He is strongly affected by the sufferings on the battlefield and tells Kasturba that he wants her to help him wean himself from desire. In 1906, a meeting of Indians decide to oppose a bill requiring them to carry identity passes. Gandhi proposes *satyagraha*, passive resistance. He is jailed and taken to General Smuts (Paul Slabolepszy), who says that if they undergo voluntary registration, the act will be repealed. Gandhi is set free, but many Indians refuse to register, whereas Gandhi does, because his objection was against compulsion. However, a new bill demands compulsory registration and Gandhi is jailed again. Told that Kasturba is very ill, he is offered freedom if he pays the fine. He refuses, but is let out and attends Kasturba, who accuses him of selfishness and of sacrificing his family. He meets Smuts, but rejects legislation to bar Asians from entering the country. Gandhi proposes a *satyagraha* march and is repeatedly arrested, but international attention keeps him out of jail. He shaves his head and now wears a *kurta*. He again meets Smuts, who now agrees to many of his demands. Gandhi says

he's returning to India and embraces Smuts. As he walks towards the sea, Kasturba, in voice-over, says that he regrets leaving South Africa after twenty-one years and considers himself a South African-Indian.

6. Gandhi himself refers to *brahmacharya*, or celibacy, as a vow that covered fasting in the broadest sense of the word, and he quotes from the *Bhagavad Gita* about the disappearance of yearning (Gandhi, 1982: 302–4). Sudhir Kakar has written in detail about Gandhi and women (Kakar, 1989: 85–128). *Brahmacharya* is an aspect of traditional Hindu ideas about acquiring inordinate strength and purpose (Lannoy, 1971: 386).

7. Gandhi devotes a chapter to Raychand in his autobiography (Gandhi, 1982: 91–3). Jainism is an Indian religion, having a strong ethical system, based on five vows: '(1) abstention from injury to living beings (*ahimsa*); (2) speaking the truth (*satya*); (3) not stealing (*asteya*); (4) chastity (*brahmacharya*); and (5) limiting one's possessions (*aparigraha*)' (Upadhye, 1975: 106). It is remarkable how close these principles are to those of Gandhi.

8. Bakim Chandra Chatterjee was a Bengali novelist and polemicist. He was a Hindu and Bengali nationalist, focused on devotion to the Motherland. In his most famous novel, *Anandamath*, he wrote a hymn called 'Bande Mataram' or 'Vande Mataram' (Hail Mother/land) (Masselos, 1993: 107–8). The title became the national cry during the *swadeshi* (buy Indian-made goods) movement and is constantly used by the nationalist Sandip in Rabindranath Tagore's 1916 novel *Ghare Baire* and in Satyajit Ray's 1984 film adaptation. It was proposed as India's national anthem, but eventually Rabindranath Tagore's 'Janaganamana' was chosen (Nandy, 1994: 89).

9. Richard Attenborough's film, *Gandhi* (1983), is an expensive spectacular epic of the life and death of a 'great man' in the mould of *Lawrence of Arabia*. It was controversial in India not just because of the film's interpretation of Gandhi and its 'rejigging' of history (e.g. the Amritsar massacre), but also because it was partially funded by the National Film Development Corporation and employed many technical people from the Bombay film industry (Chakravarty, 1993: 191).

10. There are other similarities between *Young Mr Lincoln* (1939) and *The Making of the Mahatma*. Both protagonists were lawyers (court cases are major dramatic moments in both films) and both were assassinated. At the end of both films, the final music is strongly linked to nationalist goals: 'The Battle Hymn of the Republic' and 'Vande Mataram', respectively.

11. *Samar* focuses on Nathu (Kishore Kadam) and his wife Dulari (Rajeshwari Sachdev), who are Dalits. The upper castes, led by the village headman, Chamak Singh (Ravi Jhankal), treat the Dalits like animals and restrict their access to the village well. Nathu complains and the government installs a separate hand pump for them. Chamak is furious and beats Nathu. Here it becomes clear that a film crew is shooting this scene. The director, Kartik

(Rajit Kapur), constantly talks to Murali Singh, the actor playing Chamak, and to Kishore, the actor playing Nathu, about their performances. The 'real' Nathu (Raghuvir Yadav) is also on the set, persistently giving his comments on what is being portrayed. Kishore is himself a Dalit and is very self-conscious about it, a fact that Uma, the actor playing Dulari, constantly discusses with him. Murali gradually becomes as intolerant as his character, Chamak. In the film being shot, Chamak stops the Dalits from working. Dulari has a sore hand and is told it is leprosy. Nathu goes to the temple asking for her to be cured. Unbeknownst to Chamak, Nathu finds work in a nearby town. A doctor tells Dulari that she only has a skin rash, which can be easily cured. On his return, Nathu returns to the temple because Dulari is cured, but Chamak sees him there and beats him severely. On the film set, Kishore complains about Murali's aggressive beating and the two engage in a fight. Uma tries to calm Kishore down. Kishore then refuses to do the scene where Chamak urinates on Nathu, because, he believes, Murali will only try to humiliate him. The 'real' Nathu tells Kishore it is only make-believe and that it was he who had to actually endure it. Murali becomes more intolerant and Uma accuses Kishore of a similar prejudice towards the upper castes. In the film, Nathu makes a formal complaint against Chamak. This leads to a public hearing in the village and the police are ordered to arrest Chamak. The film crew leaves, but the relationship between Kishore and Murali has not improved. The film ends with the Dalits returning to work.

12. *Hari-Bhari* starts with Ghazala (Shabana Azmi) returning to the family home after her husband has ejected her. Because the family is poor and the house is already overcrowded, she is welcomed reluctantly by her mother, Hasina (Surekha Sikri Rege), her brother, Khaleel (Lalit Tiwari), and his wife, Najma (Alka Tridevi), and her sister-in-law, Afsana (Nandita Das). The first episode is called 'Ghazala's Story'. Ghazala's husband, Munir (Srivallabh Vyas) is a womanizer and demands that Ghazala bear him a son. She has not been well and her daughter Salma (Rajeshwari Sachdev) accompanies her to the doctor, who discusses her illness in the context of her supposed infertility, suggesting that her husband may be infertile. Munir responds aggressively and throws Ghazala out of the house. The second episode, 'Hasina's Story', starts with Hasina as a young woman. Her sister dies in childbirth and she is forced to marry her sister's husband, who is a much older man, and bring up their baby. In the present, Munir takes Ghazala back for a price. On her return, Munir again insists on his virility and fertility, resulting in both Ghazala and Salma leaving and moving into the family home. In the third episode, 'Najma's Story', Najma is pregnant again and Hasina's younger son, Khurshid (Rajit Kapur), returns home. His wife, Afsana, wants to join him in the city, but he doesn't have enough money

to buy a house. He asks Khaleel for his share of the family property. Najma gives birth to a girl, but both are unhealthy and undernourished. A health worker talks to her about sterilization, but Afsana insists it is against their religion and tells the health worker to leave. Munir arrives and forcibly takes Salma home. Khaleel eventually gives Khurshid a large amount of money. Najma's baby dies and she decides to have a sterilization operation. The family objects, but Khaleel accepts her decision. In the fourth episode, 'Afsana's Story', Khurshid tells Afsana that he has had a vasectomy. She is very upset and leaves him, but is eventually enticed back. In the final episode, 'Salma's Story', Munir returns Salma to Ghazala, because he intends to marry again. Ghazala suspects that Salma is pregnant, but the doctor determines that her missed periods are due to Salma being anaemic. Najma now suggests they have Salma married, but Salma wants to finish her education first. The women hear of an available middle-aged widower and arrange a meeting. However, Hasina becomes ill, possibly with cervical cancer and Salma's engagement is postponed. Salma is relieved and returns to school.

13. Initially, the family planning programme was based on persuading people to reduce the number of children and to encourage voluntary sterilization, but Indira Gandhi's son, Sanjay, initiated a more ruthless campaign. 'In many areas sterilization became *de facto* compulsory and authoritarian: health workers would descend on villages and sterilize all males, willing or not; country buses would be stopped for the same end' (Masselos, 1993: 262). Salman Rushdie in *Midnight's Children* refers to the slum clearing and sterilization programmes of the 'Sanjay Youth volunteers' (Rushdie, 1981: 414).

14. Thumri is derived from Bhakti 'romantic-religious literature', in which the text is paramount and the singer engages in melodic improvisations (Jairazbhoy, 1975: 232–3).

15. A. R. Rahman (or A. R. Rehman) has been the most influential and prolific Indian film composer since the 1990s. He started in the Tamil film industry and it was his second film, *Roja* (1992), that drew him to the attention of the Hindi film industry. His first Hindi film was *Rangeela* (1995), while the best known is probably *Lagaan* (2001). He has composed the music for Deepa Mehta's Indian-based films, *Fire* (1996), *Earth* (1998) and *Water* (premiered in 2005), although for *Water* his involvement was confined to the songs. For *Fiza* (2001), he only composed the Qawwali song. All the Mani Ratnam films from *Roja* onwards have been composed by him.

16. *Mammo* starts with a dream that Riyaz (Rajit Kapur), a writer, has about his great aunt, Mammo. He asks his grandmother, Fayyazi (Surekha Sikri Rege), about her. She says that Mammo wrote to her many times, but she never replied, despite them being sisters. Riyaz asks to see the letters, which

plead with Fayyazi to allow her to live with them. The doorbell rings, and as Riyaz answers it, he is a boy opening the door to Mammo (Farida Jalal), who's come to stay with them. Mammo tells them that she was happy in Pakistan after her husband took her there, but things changed once he died, when his family treated her as a servant. She managed to arrange a temporary visa for herself, but hopes to make it permanent. Mammo also talks about Zubeidaa, Fayyazi's daughter and Riyaz's mother, who wanted to be a film star, but was married off at an early age. Fayyazi doesn't want Mammo to mention any of this, but Mammo continues, whispering so that Riyaz doesn't hear it, that Riyaz's father is still alive. The third sister, Anwari, and her husband arrive in Bombay, and Fayyazi, Mammo and Riyaz go to their hotel. There is tension between Anwari and her sisters, and the subject of Riyaz's father being alive is now raised in front of the boy. Riyaz is angry with Fayyazi and runs away. Fayyazi tells Mammo that his father remarried shortly after Zubeidaa's funeral and that she made Riyaz believe his father was dead too. Riyaz eventually returns home and he and Fayyazi make up. He writes to his father, who replies that he wants no contact with him. Mammo manages to extend her visa and organizes a surprise birthday party for Riyaz, who is most upset by it, because he did not want his school friends to know how poor they were. This offends Mammo, who now leaves. Fayyazi and Riyaz look for her throughout Bombay and finally find her in a mosque. Mammo and Riyaz attempt to bribe immigration officials to enable her to stay in India permanently, but it fails and the police deport her to Pakistan. In the present, Riyaz mentions that this occurred twenty years earlier and they have heard nothing from Mammo since. Once again, the doorbell rings. It is Mammo, who again intends to stay. Fayyazi is concerned that she might still be deported, but Mammo shows them her death certificate and says that she is now invisible.

17. Faiz Ahmad Faiz (1911–84) was a major influence on Salman Rushdie, particularly in terms of 'the double-sided conception of the writer's role, part private and part public'. Rushdie also describes how his aunt saved Faiz's life in the days following Partition (Rushdie, 2002: 431–4).

18. Sampooran Singh Gulzar is a prolific Urdu poet, lyricist, scriptwriter and director. His early work includes the lyrics for *Bandini* (1963) and *Guddi* (1971), while recent examples are *Dil Se* (1998), *Satya* (2000), *Fiza* (2001) and *Saathiya* (2002). Two recent films he directed, *Maachis* (1996) and *Hu Tu Tu* (1999), have tackled the subject of political violence.

19. *Sardari Begum* begins with Sardari Begum (Kiron Kher; Smriti Mishra as the young Sardari) singing in her room. She is disturbed by shouting in the street and goes to her balcony to investigate. She witnesses a violent confrontation between Hindus and Muslims and is accidentally killed when a rock hits her on the head. A journalist, Tehzeeb Abbasi (Rajina Rai Bisaria),

is sent to investigate the riot by her editor and lover, Mark d'Cruz (Ashok Lath). Tehzeeb becomes interested in Sardari Begum, particularly when her father, Jabbar Abbasi (Shrivallabh Vyas; Syed Khurshi as the young Jabbar), attends Sardari's funeral service. Later he tells her that Sardari was his sister and relates to her how Sardari left home to become a Thumri singer. Sardari auditioned for a rich landlord, Hemraj (Amrish Puri), whose mistress she became. Now intrigued, Tehzeeb, despite Mark's disinterest in the story, attempts to talk to those who knew Sardari. She finds Sardari's daughter, Sakina (Rajeshwari Sachdev), but she won't talk. However, Sakina's companions tell Tehzeeb that Sardari trained Sakina in Thumri and that Sardari fell in love with Sadiq Moosvi (Rajit Kapur). Tehzeeb finds Sadiq, who eventually married Sardari and encouraged her into becoming a recording artist and playback singer. In time, their relationship soured. Eventually, Tehzeeb manages to talk with Sakina, who tells her that Sardari was very demanding and domineering, but also independent. Returning to the moment prior to her death, Sardari makes Sakina promise to become a Thumri singer. Tehzeeb leaves Mark and strikes out on her own, just as Sardari did years earlier. Sakina, now alone in the house, sings in her mother's room.

20. Karisma Kapoor (or Karishma Kapoor) began her career in the early 1990s. She worked with the popular comedian Govinda in the mid-1990s, e.g. *Coolie No. 1* (1995), and with Aamir Khan in *Raja Hindustani* (1996). After *Zubeidaa*, she made *Fiza* (2001), which is discussed later in this interview. Karisma is a member of the fourth generation of Kapoors in the Indian film industry. She and her sister Kareena are the first women of that illustrious show business family to work in movies. Kareena starred in *Asoka* (2001).

21. Manoj Bajpai began his career as a *dacoit* (bandit) in *Bandit Queen* (1994). In *Satya* (2000), he won a *Filmfare* award for his role as a Bombay crime boss. He teamed up with Karisma Kapoor again in *Fiza*, although not in a major role.

22. Mani Ratnam (or Mani Rathnam) is the most lauded commercial film director of the last ten years. His early films were made in a number of South Indian languages, but it was his Tamil film (also dubbed into Hindi) *Nayakan* (1987), starring Kamal Haasan as a Tamil gangster in the Bombay underworld, that established him as a major director. His political trilogy *Roja* (1992), *Bombay* (1995) and *Dil Se* (1998) (the last film was actually made in Hindi) was very successful, as well as controversial. His recent film *Kannathil Muthamittal* (2002) tackles the contentious issue of the Tamil conflict in Sri Lanka and its impact on Tamil Nadu. Ratnam's films are often said to be influenced by the MTV aesthetic, and he introduced a technical competence into the film industry that has had a major impact throughout the Indian cinema.

23. *Alam Ara* (1931) introduced the centrality of song and dance to Indian cinema, a phenomenon that the popular Indian cinema has retained to this day. Its star, Zubeida, was a Muslim princess, whose mother, Fatma Begum, became India's first woman director. Zubeida became identified with courtesan roles, as later did Meena Kumari (*Sahib Bibi Aur Ghulam* and *Pakeezah*) and Smita Patil in Benegal's *Bhumika* and *Mandi* (Rajadhyaksha and Willemen, 1999: 241, 253).

24. *Zubeidaa* starts in 1952, with a boy, Riyaz, watching a red scarf falling on a grave and then running to his grandmother, Fayyazi (Surekha Sikri Rege), standing nearby with his maid. Returning home, Fayyazi tells her husband, Suleiman Seth (Amrish Puri), that he should have attended his daughter's funeral, but he says he could not. In 1980, the adult Riyaz (Rajit Kapur) is searching for a reel of film in which his mother, Zubeidaa (Karisma Kapoor), starred in a song-and-dance number. In flashback, Suleiman finds out Zubeidaa is working in a film studio, one that he used to own. He rejects her pleas to continue as an actor and marries her against her will to the son of his friend, whom he has helped to return to Bombay from Pakistan. Zubeidaa has a child, but when her father-in-law insists she return to Pakistan with him and his son, Suleiman refuses to let his daughter leave India. The couple divorce and Zubeidaa languishes in her parent's house with her son, Riyaz. A few years later, Rose Davenport (Lillete Dubey), Suleiman's mistress, takes Zubeidaa to a polo match, where she meets the Maharaja of Jodpur, Raja Vijandra Singh, who calls himself Victor (Manoj Bajpai). They fall in love and marry, intending to live in Victor's palace, but Fayyazi won't let her take Riyaz, whom she insists on bringing up. In 1980, Fayyazi refuses to tell Riyaz about his mother, but Riyaz finds Zubeidaa's diaries and learns of her life in Jodpur. After their wedding, Victor and Zubeidaa fly to his palace in his two-seater. There, Zubeidaa meets Victor's first wife, Mandira Devi (Rekha), and his brother, Uday Singh (Raahul Maharya). Mandira teaches her court decorum, but Zubeidaa finds it very constraining. She becomes wary of Uday, who tries to impose himself on her whenever Victor is away. Victor decides to contest the 1952 elections and travels throughout his electorate with Mandira. Zubeidaa remains behind and feels left out, accusing Victor of hiding her because she is a Muslim. Victor wins his seat and sets out to fly to Delhi with Mandira to talk to the newly elected Congress government. Zubeidaa insists on going with him and runs to the plane, forcing Mandira to remain behind. After Victor and Zubeidaa take off, the plane crashes and a red scarf falls from the sky. In 1980, Riyaz receives a parcel from Mandira Devi, which contains the missing film reel. Riyaz and Fayyazi watch Zubeidaa's song-and-dance performance.

25. The 'north-western Indian kingdoms [were] ruled by Rajputs, feudal dynasties of Kshatrya [the warrior caste] clans...They were a haughty and aristocratic class, brought up from boyhood to enjoy the art of war, hunting and hawking' (Lannoy, 1971: 69). The Congress Party, led by Jawaharlal Nehru, won India's first general elections in 1952. While they won 74 per cent of the seats in the Lok Sabha (House of the People), however, they gained only 49 per cent of the votes (Masselos, 1993: 239).

26. Ketan Mehta made a film about the last five years of Sardar Patel's life, called *Sardar*, in 1993. It was produced by Shyam Benegal, scripted by Vijay Tendulkar and the music was written by Vanraj Bhatia (Rajadhyaksha and Willemen, 1999: 515).

27. Amrish Puri made over 140 films, starting from his early films with Girish Karnad and Shyam Benegal. He already played a threatening figure in Benegal films like *Nishant* and *Bhumika*, but this became more stereotypical in mainstream films like *Hum Paanch* (1980). This reached an apotheosis in *Mr India*, in which he played a maniacal blond dictator called Mogambo. In later years he took on softer, more patriarchal roles, e.g. *Dilwale Dulhania Le Jayenge* (1995) and *Pardes* (1997). He continued to make films with Benegal on a regular basis until his death in 2004.

28. Arbitrary costume changes (typically only of the lead female performer) and locale changes within song picturizations have increased dramatically since the early 1990s. Benegal adopts the former strategy, but not the latter, and then only in this particular number. One of the most remarkable manipulations of both costumes and places occurs in Mani Ratnam's *Dil Se*. Rachel Dwyer discusses settings and costumes in Hindi film in some detail, ascribing consumerism as a possible explanation for the phenomenon (Dwyer and Patel, 2002: 60, 93).

29. Johnny Lever is one of the most popular comedians in contemporary Hindi cinema and has performed in films such as *Karan Arjun* (1995), *Raja Hindustani* and *Asoka*, as well as *Fiza*. None of these films are comedies (as the films of Govinda are) and Johnny Lever's comedy spots function as 'autonomous segments', much the way that songs and dances do. His roles in these films and his name are in a film tradition going back at least as far as Johnny Walker (who had significant parts in many of Guru Dutt's films) and later comedians such as Tony Brandy and Johnny Whisky (Rajadhyaksha and Willemen, 1999: 239).

30. Haji Ali Mosque is a spectacular edifice located at the end of a long causeway on the west coast of Bombay. During high tide, access from the mainland is cut off. This song, a Qawwali, called 'O Beloved Haji Ali', with lyrics by Shaukat Ali, was composed by A. R. Rahman, whereas the rest of the songs were written by Anu Malik. The song in *Mammo* has lyrics by Gulzar and music by Vanraj Bhatia.

Interview 8
On Present and Future

WvdH: The film that you're working on now is called *Netaji* [the film's release title is *Bose: The Forgotten Hero*]. Netaji means leader, doesn't it?

SB: Yes, and Subhash Chandra Bose was called Netaji.

WvdH: Is this going to be a biographical film like the Gandhi film?

SB: To some extent, yes. It deals with the last five years of his life, from 1940 until 1945, when he disappeared, in the sense that his plane took off and there was a crash. There is doubt as to whether he actually died in that crash. In fact, even now there's a commission set up by the government of India. This is the third commission.[1]

WvdH: He'd be a bit old now, wouldn't he?

SB: If he were actually alive, he would be 105. But I'm not really concerned with that. What interests me is what happened before the plane crash. He had been in jail in Calcutta after he had been thrown out of the Congress Party.[2] Because he was ill, he was put under house arrest, from where he escaped across India into Afghanistan, without credentials of any kind. There he was helped by the Italian Embassy, given a passport and an Italian name – Count Orlando Massotta. He made his way through Central Asia to the Soviet Union, where he sought help from what he regarded as a true anti-imperialist power. This was before Operation Barbarossa, before Germany attacked Russia. The Russians did not want to deal with him and so he made his way to Berlin, where the German Foreign Office gave him diplomatic status. There he raised a small force with German prisoners of war from the British Indian Army in North Africa, captured there by Rommel. He created a small Free India legion in Germany. He was protected by the German Foreign Office from having too much to do with the Nazis, because they knew that he would rub the Nazis up the wrong way. But he did meet Hitler and was rather disappointed with the meeting. He decided to leave Germany, because two things disturbed him immensely. One was the fact that he didn't expect that Germany would attack Russia. Secondly, he felt that by doing so there was no hope that Germany would ever be able to help him fight the British in India. Eventually he managed to get a U-boat from Kiel in the North Sea and was taken through the Allied blockade, through the North and South Atlantic and around the Cape of Good Hope. Near Madagascar, he transferred to a Japanese submarine. This is the only time in maritime history that anybody has transferred from one submarine to another in the high seas. Then he went to Southeast Asia and met Tojo, who offered him much more help than the Germans had done. He raised an army again consisting largely of the prisoners of war from the British Indian Army. The Indian prisoners of war became members of the Free India Army, because they were extremely disappointed with the British. When the British left Malaysia and Singapore, they literally abandoned their Indian troops. There was a British colonel called Colonel Hunt, who surrendered his army and himself to the Japanese. He told the Indian troops that they had been loyal to the Empire, but that now they should transfer that loyalty to the Japanese. The troops felt they were being treated like cattle. So they unhesitatingly joined the Free India Army, the Indian National Army. Bose arrived and took over that army and expanded it. He arrived in Nagaland in Northeast India from Burma, where he met Aung San, Aung San Suu Kyi's father, who had started the Burma Independent Army. Bose then captured part of Nagaland. He was trying to move into the plains of Assam when the battle of Midway took place in the Pacific. Now the Japanese were directly threatened by the Americans. So, much of the Japanese Army, from which he was hoping to get logistical support, were sent back to Japan. But he fought on without air cover, without heavy artillery and without armoured trucks. He was fighting with 303 rifles against Field Marshall William Slim, who had under him the British Army, the British Indian Army, the Australians and the Americans. Eventually when he was captured, Slim congratulated him on fighting so valiantly with so few resources. When Japan surrendered on 15 August 1945, Bose was in Singapore. He drove from there to Bangkok and then to Saigon, aiming to return to Russia. On his way there, his plane crashed in Taipei. I think he died, but it has not been proved that he did. He was supposed to go to Darhan in Mongolia, where the Japanese general accompanying him was being sent by the Japanese government to surrender Bose's Japanese forces in Mongolia to the Russians. The Russians came into the war against Japan five days earlier. They were very opportunistic. They were neutral to Japan until five days before the Japanese surrender, in order to get the Kuril Islands, which are still in contention. My story ends with his taking off from Saigon.

WvdH: It's clearly a great adventure story.

SB: Yes, it's a great adventure story. But he's also a remarkable figure in the Indian Nationalist movement because he found a way that would have prevented Partition, if he had lived that long. So he's a fascinating figure of Indian history.

WvdH: He stands in contrast to Nehru, doesn't he?

SB: He and Nehru were rivals, yet Bose was a Congressman till the very end, even after he was expelled. But he considered Gandhi to be his leader, although he criticized him for his poor political tactics. He felt that Gandhi always lost out, because he was too concerned about converting his opponent to his point of view. Bose felt that he was behaving like Buddha and Jesus and that he was unable to achieve political outcomes. He felt that every time Gandhi brought the British to their knees, he lost the initiative, because he allowed the British to play upon the diverse interests of Indians. He told Gandhi that he had twice forced the British to a round table conference, but in both cases he had lost the initiative. Bose said that power has to be taken in order to govern the country – it cannot be decided across a table. In some ways this was true, because by the end of 1947 the initiative was left with the British and the country was divided. Jinnah never fought for freedom, but he got a country.[3]

WvdH: So Bose represented an alternative that was never able to eventuate.

SB: It was a proper alternative for the future of India. But we have adopted a lot of his ideas. Under the British, the Indian Army was organized by caste; it was a communal army. Bose changed that. He also introduced planning strategies for economic development.

WvdH: Are there people in India who regard Bose's ideas as a criticism of everything that India has become.

SB: Not really. He didn't have to face the many problems that we face today. But he did have very good ideas. He was what one might call a very modern Indian, like Nehru. He could be called a cosmopolitan nationalist, because he was capable of accepting a great deal beyond the narrow confines of nationalism.

WvdH: Clearly, you're going to enjoy making this film, because you like historical re-creations, which is what many of your films are. It also seems to me that historical films are making a come-back in the broader Indian cinema.

SB: Not really. It happened with just one film, *The Legend of Bhagat Singh* [2002]. There are about four or five versions of it.[4] But there's no serious interest in historical films in India.

WvdH: What about a film like *Asoka* [2001]?

SB: *Asoka* was unfortunately not a serious historical film. It was more of a costume drama. Santosh Sivan really didn't concern himself with history or even the semblance of real history.

WvdH: What about Kamal Haasan's film, *Hey! Ram* [2000]?[5]

SB: It did attempt to deal with the issues of Partition and Hindu/Muslim conflicts.

WvdH: Then there is that film called *Indian*, directed by Shankar.

SB: I haven't seen that film. I definitely want to see it, because it has references to Bose, but simply as a militarist figure.

WvdH: It has a flashback sequence which deals with the Indian National Army. There's some documentary footage of Bose and also some doctored footage, in which the character played by Kamal Haasan shakes hands with Bose. But the film does present Bose as rejecting the nationalism of Gandhi and Nehru. The main character becomes a revenge figure. It's as if Bose's spirit had entered him and this spirit sets out to annihilate the corruption that is destroying India.[6]

SB: But that is a complete distortion of Bose, because Bose wasn't a violent figure. He felt that non-violence worked up to a point. He saw the need for diplomacy, but not Gandhi's type of diplomacy, because Gandhi always believed in complete transparency. Bose criticized him for laying his cards on the table, because people always took advantage. In terms of non-violence, I think there was only one political leader who has succeeded in using it and that was Nelson Mandela. Mandela, of course, got his inspiration from Gandhi.

WvdH: In my book on Malaysian cinema, I wrote about an Indian director, L. Krishnan, who worked in the Malaysian film industry in the 1940s and 1950s. He was born in Madras and as a young child he moved with his family to Penang. Later on he became a translator for the Japanese in Malaya, and when the British returned he was repatriated. They sent him back to Madras because he had joined the Indian National Army in 1943. He then worked in the Tamil film industry for a while and also made some Singhalese films there. In the late 1940s, Shaw Brothers recruited him and he worked for the major Malayan film studios until the early 1960s. A number of the Malayan film figures have such links to Bose.[7]

SB: The entire Indian population of Malaya and Singapore followed Bose. He was a very popular figure there. He appears in Malaysian textbooks even today. The British, on the other hand, have dealt with him very unflatteringly. He's the only nationalist leader from any of their colonies who is still regarded as a traitor. They've never forgiven him because he was an implacable foe.

WvdH: I remember reading that he went to England to study.

SB: He did very well in his studies. The British offered him a job and he would have succeeded in the Indian bureaucracy even under the British. But he resigned to join Gandhi's movement, against his father's will.

WvdH: Have you already decided on a person to play him?

SB: Yes. He's a new actor. His name is Sachin Khedekar.

WvdH: Has he acted in movies before?

SB: He's been in some films, but he's done a fair amount of theatre.

WvdH: What is your view about the changes in film distribution over the last few years, including the new technologies like DVDs and VCDs?

SB: VCDs and DVDs are actually adding to the market and that has been a good thing. Television has been both negative and positive. Television has allowed my films to reach a much larger audience, but it doesn't really add to the revenues of a film because Indian television doesn't pay very much. From the mid-1980s to the late 1990s, it became very difficult to make the kind of films I was making.

WvdH: What has happened for things to have changed since then?

SB: There's been a general crisis in the cinema: large cinema halls were no longer economical and were replaced by multiplexes, exactly as was the pattern in Europe and America. Multiplexes with their smaller seating capacities made my kind of films relevant again. So a slow improvement is taking place.

WvdH: The number of cinemas has always been very small for India considering the population, hasn't it?

SB: Yes. They are also restricted to urban areas. But then urban areas themselves are growing. In the 1980s, about 30 per cent of the country's population lived in urban areas. Today it's closer to 40–5 per cent. This means that cinema audiences are actually growing. Television has now become what it should be – an additional revenue earner and not a replacement for the cinema. We can only compare ourselves with the United States, because we have a film industry that's as large as theirs. We were beset with the same kind of problems that they were and they too have an independent cinema, which is much like the kind of films that I make. They went through a similar crisis.

WvdH: For audiences in countries outside of India it seems to me that technologies like DVD offer opportunities to see your films because they're unlikely to be shown elsewhere, apart from film festivals.

SB: Yes. For a lot of countries of the world, that is absolutely true. Now, DVDs are available from the net. Indiaplaza.com, for instance, has something like 3,000–4,000 Indian film titles.

WvdH: This is really quite a significant issue because seven or eight of your films are now available on DVD.

SB: Eight of them are available now and another four will be available in the next three or four months. Eventually all of them will be.[8]

WvdH: Do you have any active involvement in the production of the DVDs?

SB: I have nothing to do with it.

WvdH: There are a few more general issues I'd like to raise. You mentioned to me that you felt there was a change in your approach to filmmaking around the time of *Mandi*.

SB: Yes.

WvdH: How would you define that particular change?

SB: Well, I moved into different kinds of narratives, different ways of telling stories using different techniques and different structures. I also became interested in simultaneity, as in *Suraj Ka Satvan Ghoda*, or what one might call the subjective objective, simultaneous renderings of the past and the present. All these things enabled me to expand the scope of the narrative and to take on narratives which otherwise might seem unfilmable.

WvdH: These new directions don't seem to come at the expense of the political in the broader sense of the word.

SB: Never. To me the overall experience of living is very important and the overall experience of living in my country always includes politics. You cannot keep it away because it affects you.

WvdH: Who would you regard as your main audience? I suppose it's a leading question in a way, because if it is the Indian middle class, why are you so critical of it?

SB: Whether one likes it or not, the agenda of the country is being set by the urban Indian middle class. By definition, the middle class is the one that is both extremely conservative and also oriented to change. The rural communities tend to be more driven by tradition. The middle classes also fear losing their traditions. They have both an attraction as well as a revulsion towards modernity. Cinema audiences have been largely middle class in this country. We haven't been able to reach beyond the middle classes for a very long period of time, because if you look at the number of cinemas in this huge country, there are no more than between 13,000 and 14,000 cinemas. Obviously they are in urban areas. Even the audiences for television are those whose essential ambition is to be part of the middle class. So whether you like it or not your audience is bound to be the middle class.

WvdH: Are you suggesting that this is also the case for the Hindi commercial cinema?

SB: Absolutely. In fact the real problem is that the agenda for the mainstream movie is set more by the middle class than it is for my kind of film, because I want to be much more inclusive. I want to broaden the agenda and to have this very large section of the population constantly seen, not kept out.

WvdH: Even if you can't address them, they have to be incorporated in your films?

SB: That's very important to me personally.

WvdH: One of the first things you told me was that the Indian films you watched as a boy were selected from New Theatres films and Prabhat films. In a way, have you become a filmmaker in that tradition?

SB: In some ways you might say that, because the concerns of those films were about and for a much larger section of Indian society than the concerns of the mainstream cinema are today.

WvdH: Yes, I agree.

SB: One of the most successful films of recent years was *Kuch Kuch Hota Hai* [1998]. It addressed the interests and concerns of the urban affluent middle class, which is of interest to everybody, because that's where everybody wants to be. It uses a very interesting strategy of looking at tradition as not being inimical to modernity. The two are seamlessly brought together in such films. So they're great wish fulfilment dreams for the audiences.

WvdH: What would you say was your best film?

SB: I've never thought in those terms. I don't think that I would like to. But I can say that some films were not realized too well. Somehow they don't seem to have the same kind of inspirational character to them as some others do.

WvdH: The National Film Theatre in London screened a retrospective of your films in late 2002.

SB: Yes. I chose eight films, but they showed a couple more as well.

WvdH: What is the significance of such an event for you?

SB: The retrospective was part of a larger season covering the entire spectrum of Indian cinema, called *Imagine Asia*, which started in March with Satyajit Ray's films and ended with me in November. It included a lot of popular films like *Mother India*, *Awara* and *Lagaan*, Ritwik Ghatak films and Mrinal Sen films. The season covered post-independent Indian cinema and the National Film Theatre was very pleased with the response.

WvdH: You were also the guest at a discussion session, I understand.

SB: There were two events. One was a discussion with Sangeeta Datta, who has written a book on me for the British Film Institute. The next day there was the usual *Guardian* lecture at the National Film Theatre, which I'd also done in 1988, when they had a full retrospective of my films, including the documentaries and commercials.

WvdH: Why were people interested in your films? What excited them about your films?

SB: For non-Indian people, it always seems to be that the films represent India rather than Indian entertainment. For Indians who were at the screenings or for the NRIs, the non-resident Indians, it was because they like my kind of film as against the popular variety of Indian film.

Notes

1. The third commission, the Mukherjee Commission, was set up in 1999 and reported to the Indian government on 8 November 2005. The commission was charged with the task of determining whether Bose is dead or alive; if he is dead, whether he died in a plane crash or in some other circumstance; if he is alive, the location of his whereabouts. Like its predecessors, which had similar terms of reference, the commission was unable to provide irrefutable proof of Bose's fate (http://en.wikipedia.org/wiki/Mukherjee_Commission).

2. Bose was a Bengali and was repeatedly imprisoned by the British in the 1920s and 1930s for civil disobedience, eventually being exiled in 1933. On his return in 1936, he was lauded as an Indian hero on the level of Gandhi and Nehru. He became the President of the Congress Party, but his call for revolution against the British caused him to be arrested in 1940 (Ashton, 1985: 35). 'There was a big difference in outlook between him and others in the Congress executive, both in regard to foreign and internal matters, and this led to a break in early 1939. He then attacked Congress policy publicly, and early in August 1939 the Congress executive took the very unusual step of taking disciplinary action against him, who was an ex-president' (Nehru, 1960: 338-9).

3. Mohamed Ali Jinnah was a member of the Congress Party, but left it in the 1920s and retired to England. He was convinced by Muslims to return to India and became President of the Muslim League in 1934. The relationship between the League and Congress deteriorated and Jinnah argued that India represented two separate nations, Hindu and Muslim. This led him to insist upon the partition of India and a separate state for Muslims. Jinnah became Pakistan's first Governor-General, but died shortly after the creation of Pakistan (Ashton, 1985: 30-4).

4. Two films on the life and death of Sardar Bhagat Singh were released on the same day (7 June 2002): *The Legend of Bhagat Singh* and *23rd March 1931 Shaheed* (the date refers to the date he was hanged by the British), and at least two other versions were released the same year (*Shaheed-E-Azam* and *Shaheed Bhagat Singh*). Bhagat Singh was a freedom fighter and revolutionary, whose final act of throwing bombs and leaflets in the Delhi Central Assembly led to his arrest. He asked to be executed like a soldier

– a request that was denied (Kamat, 2005). *The Legend of Bhagat Singh* suggests that Gandhi was indirectly responsible for Bhagat Singh's death, due to his 'obsession' with non-violence (Gujadhur, 2005). Interestingly, Gandhi, in an article in *Young India*, praised Bhagat Singh's heroism, but opposed his recourse to violence: 'By making a dharma of violence, we shall be reaping the fruit of our own actions' (Gandhi, 1931).

5. Kamal Haasan (or Kamalahasan) has become the major star of Tamil cinema in the 1990s. Although he made his first film at the age of six in 1960, it was his role as a crime boss in the *Godfather*-derived Mani Ratnam film *Nayakan* (1987) that brought him to the attention of wider Indian film audiences. He directed and starred in *Hey! Ram* (2000), a remarkable film that deals with the events leading up to and following Partition. Saket Ram (Kamal Haasan) turns into a Hindu fundamentalist after his wife is brutally raped and killed in the communal carnage that enveloped Calcutta following Jinnah's declaration of a day of 'Direct Action'. He agrees to kill Gandhi, seen by him and his group as the cause of the division of India, but changes his mind at the very last moment as he watches another fundamentalist undertaking the deed. The film was nearly banned and was criticized for being 'pro-fundamentalist' and 'anti-Gandhi' (Lutgendorf, 2005a).

6. *Indian* (1996) is a Tamil film starring Kamal Haasan in a double role: as Chandru, a corrupt public official in contemporary Tamil Nadu, and as his father, Senapathy, who was a member of Subhash Chandra Bose's Indian National Army. Senapathy takes it upon himself to violently eradicate the endemic corruption gripping India, starting with his own son. Flashbacks show Senapathy killing British soldiers and joining Bose's army, including pseudo-documentary footage of him shaking Bose's hand. The film is seen by some critics (who reviewed the dubbed Telugu version called *Bharateeyudu*) as an attempt to 'rewrite the story of the nationalist struggle [in which] the iconic figures of Gandhi and Nehru give way to Subhash Chandra Bose ... to suggest that Gandhi and Nehru, figures popularly identified with the post-Independence nation-state, are indeed a part of the problem' (Niranjana and Srinivas, 1996: 3129, 3130).

7. This information comes from van der Heide, 2002: 133–4. Bose enlisted Indians from Southeast Asia in the Indian National Army. 'The participation of Malayan Indians in this and other Indian nationalist political organizations, all of which were strongly anti-British, made the Japanese adopt a relatively lenient stance towards the Indians in Malaya' (Andaya and Andaya 1982: 250).

8. Benegal's statement was made in January 2003. At the time of writing the following films are available on DVD: *Ankur*, *Nishant*, *Bhumika*, *Junoon*, *Kalyug*, *Mandi*, *Trikal*, *Suraj Ka Satvan Ghoda*, *Mammo*, *Sardari Begum*, *Hari-Bhari* and *Zubeidaa*. *Bose: The Forgotten Hero* is due to be released on DVD in January 2006.

Appendix 1
Filmography

The filmography lists all the feature films, but only the three documentaries and television series that are discussed in the interviews. Detailed credits are provided for the feature films and for the documentary *Satyajit Ray*. All the feature films were made in Hindi apart from *Anugraham*, which was shot in Telugu, and *The Making of the Mahatma*, which is in English, as is *Satyajit Ray*.

A more detailed list exists in Rajadhyaksha and Willemen (1999: 57–8).

ANKUR (THE SEEDLING)   1973   128 MIN.

Prod. Co.: Blaze Film Enterprises; *Dir.*: Shyam Benegal; *Ex. Prod.*: Lalit M. Bijlani; *Prod.*: Mohan J. Bijlani, Freni M. Variava; *Story/Script*: Shyam Benegal; *Dialogue*: Satyadev Dubey; *Dialect*: Aziz Qaisi; *Phot.*: Govind Nihalani; *Ed.*: Bhanudas Divkar; *Sound*: Raghunath, Jayesh Khandelwal; *Music*: Vanraj Bhatia.
Actors: Anant Nag (Surya), Shabana Azmi (Lakshmi/Laxmi), Sadhu Meher (Kishtaya), Priya Tendulkar (Saru) and Aga Mohamed Hussain (Sheikh Chand).

CHARANDAS CHOR (CHARANDAS THE THIEF)   1975   156 MIN.

Prod. Co.: Children's Film Society; *Dir.*: Shyam Benegal; *Script*: Shama Zaidi, Habib Tanvir; *Lyrics*: Nandkishore Mittal, Gangaram, Swarnakumar; *Phot.*: Govind Nihalani; *Ed.*: Anant Apte; *Music*: Nandkishore Mittal, Gangaram, Swarnakumar.
Actors: Lalu Ram, Madanlal, Bhakla Ram, Ramnath, Thakur Ram, Malabai, Fidabai, Ram Ratan, Hira Ram, Habib Tanvir, Smita Patil, Anjali Paingankar, Sadhu Meher.

NISHANT (THE NIGHT'S END)   1975   138 MIN.

Prod. Co.: Blaze Film Enterprises; *Dir.*: Shyam Benegal; *Ex. Prod.*: Lalit M. Bijlani; *Prod.*: Freni M. Variava, Mohan J. Bijlani; *Script*: Vijay Tendulkar; *Dialogue*: Satyadev Dubey; *Lyrics*: Mohammad Quli Qutb Shah (1566 AD-1612 AD); *Singer*: Priti Moti Sagar; *Art Dir.*: Shama Zaidi; *Phot.*: Govind Nihalani; *Ed.*: Bhanudas Divkar; *Sound*: Hitendra Ghosh; *Music*: Vanraj Bhatia.

Actors: Girish Karnad (the teacher), Shabana Azmi (Sushila), Anant Nag (Anjaya), Amrish Puri (Anna), Satyadev Dubey (the priest), Smita Patil (Rukmani), Mohan Agashe (Prasad), Kulbhushan Kharbanda (the policeman), Naseeruddin Shah (Vishwam), Sadhu Meher (the drunk) and the people of Pochampali.

MANTHAN (THE CHURNING)   1976   135 MIN.

Prod Co.: Sahyadri Films; *Dir.*: Shyam Benegal; *Ex. Prod.*: Radeus; *Prod.*: Shyam Benegal Sahyadri Films for Gujarat Co-operative Milk Marketing Federation Limited; *Story*: V. Kurien, Shyam Benegal; *Script*: Vijay Tendulkar; *Dialogue*: Kaifi Azmi; *Dialect*: Dina Pathak, Chandrakart Thakkar; *Lyrics*: Niti Sagar; *Singer*: Priti Sagar; *Art Dir.*: Shama Zaidi; *Phot.*: Govind Nihalani; *Ed.*: Bhanudas Divkar; *Sound*: Hitendra Ghosh; *Music*: Vanraj Bhatia.
Actors: Girish Karnad (Dr Manohar Rao), Smita Patil (Bindu), Naseeruddin Shah (Bhola), Sadhu Meher (Mahapatra), Anant Nag (Chandravarkar), Amrish Puri (Mishra), Kulbhushan Kharbanda (Sarpanch), Mohan Agashe (Deshmukh), Yashpal (Bindu's husband), Anjali Paigankar (Harijan girl), Abha Dhulia (Shanta) and the people of Sanganva.

BHUMIKA (THE ROLE)   1976   137 MIN.

Prod. Co.: Blaze Film Enterprises; *Dir.*: Shyam Benegal; *Ex. Prod.*: Silloo Fali Variava, Bhisham M. Bijlani; *Prod.*: Lalit M. Bijlani, Freni M. Variava; *Story*: inspired by Hansa Wadkar's *Sangtye Aika*; *Script*: Girish Karnad, Pandit Satyadev Dubey, Shyam Benegal; *Dialogue*: Satyadev Dubey; *Lyrics*: Majrooh Sultanpuri, Vasant Dev; *Singers*: Preeti Sagar and others; *Art Dir.*: Shama Zaidi; *Phot.*: Govind Nihalani; *Ed.*: Bhanudas Divkar; *Sound*: Hitendra Ghosh; *Music*: Vanraj Bhatia.
Actors: Smita Patil (Urvashi/Usha), Anant Nag (Rajan Kumar), Naseeruddin Shah (Sunil Verma), Amrish Puri (Vinayak Kale), Amol Palekar (Keshav Dalvi), Kulbhushan Kharbanda (Harilal), Sulabha Deshpande (Shanta), Baby Rukhsana, B. V. Karanth, Dina Pathak, Mohan Agashe (Vinayak's friend).

ANUGRAHAM/KONDURA (THE BOON/THE SAGE FROM THE SEA)   1977   137 MIN.

Prod. Co.: Raviraj Int.; *Dir.*: Shyam Benegal; *Prod.*: K. Venkatrama Reddy; *Story*: C. T. Khanolkar's novel *Kondura*; *Script*: Arudra, Girish Karnad, Shyam Benegal; *Dialogue*: Satyadev Dubey; *Lyrics*: Vasant Dev (Hindi version), Arudra (Telugu version); *Phot.*: Govind Nihalani; *Ed.*: Bhanudas Divkar; *Sound*: Hitendra Ghosh; *Music*: Vanraj Bhatia.

Actors: Anant Nag (Parashuram), Vanisri (Parashuram's wife), Amrish Puri (Kondura Swamy), Shekhar Chatterjee, Satyadev Dubey, Smita Patil (Parvati), Sulabha Despande. (This is the cast for the Hindi version; the Telugu version has a slightly different cast.)

JUNOON (OBSESSION/A FLIGHT OF PIGEONS)   1978   132 MIN.

Prod. Co.: Film Valas; *Dir.*: Shyam Benegal; *Prod.*: Shashi Kapoor; *Story*: Ruskin Bond's short story 'A Flight of Pigeons'; *Script*: Shyam Benegal; *Dialogue*: Satyadev Dubey, Ismat Chugtai; *Lyrics*: Yogesh Praveen, Jigar Muradabadi, Amir Khusro, Sant Kabir; *Phot.*: Govind Nihalani; *Ed.*: Bhanudas Divkar; *Costumes*: Shama Zaidi (Indian), Jennifer Kapoor (Western); *Sound*: Hitendra Ghosh; *Music*: Vanraj Bhatia; *Songs and background music*: Kaushik.
Actors: Shashi Kapoor (Javed Khan), Shabana Azmi (Firdus), Jennifer Kendal (Mariam Labadoor), Naseeruddin Shah (Sarfraz, Javed's brother-in-law), Kulbhushan Kharbanda (Ramjimal), Nafisa Ali (Ruth Labadoor).

KALYUG (THE MACHINE AGE)   1980   147 MIN.

Prod. Co.: Film Valas; *Dir.*: Shyam Benegal; *Prod.*: Shashi Kapoor; *Script*: Girish Karnad, Shyam Benegal; *Script Consultant*: Vinod Doshi; *Dialogue*: Satyadev Dubey; *Lyrics*: Balwant Tandon; *Singer*: Preeta Sagar, *Phot.*: Govind Nihalani; *Ed.*: Bhanudas Divkar; *Art Dir.*: Bansi Chandragupta; *Costumes*: Jennifer Kapoor; *Sound*: Hitendra Ghosh; *Music*: Vanraj Bhatia.
Actors: Shashi Kapoor (Karan Singh), Rekha (Supriya), Anant Nag (Bharat Raj), Raj Babbar (Dharam Raj), Kulbhushan Kharbanda (Bal Raj), Amrish Puri (Kishan Chand), Sushma Seth (Savitri), Victor Bannerjee (Dhan Raj), Om Puri (Bhayani Pandey), A. K. Hangal (Bhisham Chand), Vijaya Mehta (Devki), Vinod Doshi (Khubchand), Supriya Pathak (Subhadra), Rima Lagu (Kiran), Akash Khurana (Sandeep Raj), Sunil Shanbag (Sunil Raj), Ranjit Kapur (Saxena), Rajshri Sarabhai (Vibha), Urmila (Parikshit).

AAROHAN (THE ASCENT/ASCENDING SCALE)   1982   147 MIN.

Prod. Co.: Government of West Bengal; *Dir.*: Shyam Benegal; *Script*: Shama Zaidi; *Dialogue and lyrics*: Niaz Haider; *Phot.*: Govind Nihalani; *Ed.*: Bhanudas Divkar; *Music*: Purna Das Baul.
Actors: Om Puri (Hari Mondal), Victor Bannerjee, Noni Ganguly, Rajen Tarafdar, Gita Sen, Pankaj Kapoor, Srila Mazumdar, Khoka Mukherjee.

MANDI (MARKET PLACE)   1983   153 MIN.

Prod. Co.: Blaze Film Enterprises; *Dir.*: Shyam Benegal; *Prod.*: Freni M. Variava, Lalit M. Bijlani; *Script*: Shyam Benegal, Satyadev Dubey, Shama Zaidi from 'Anandi' by Ghulam Abbas; *Dialogue*: Satyadev Dubey; *Lyrics*: Mir Taqi Mir, Bahadur Shah Zafar, Insha, Makhdoom Mohiuddin, Sarwar Danda, Ila Arun; *Singers*: Asha Bhonsle, Priti Sagar; *Choreo.*: Sudarshan Deer; *Costumes*: Saba Zaidi; *Art Dir.*: Nitish Roy; *Phot.*: Ashok Mehta; *Ed.*: Bhanudas Divkar; *Sound*: Hitendra Ghosh; *Music*: Vanraj Bhatia.
Actors: Shabana Azmi (Rukmini), Smita Patil (Zeenat), Naseeruddin Shah (Tungrus), Amrish Puri (the Sufi), Kulbhushan Kharbanda (Gupta), Saeed Jaffrey (Agarwal), Om Puri (Ramgopal), Neena Gupta (Basanti), Gita Siddharth, Sunila Pradhan, Soni Razdan, Anita Kanwar, Ratna Pathak Shah, Pankaj Kapoor, K. K. Raima, Satish Kaushik, Khoka Mukherjea, Athar Nawaz, Harish Patel, Ila Arun.

NEHRU   1984   180 MIN.

SATYAJIT RAY   1984   131 MIN.

Prod. Co.: Films Division; *Dir.*: Shyam Benegal; *Prod.*: Raj Pius, Dilip Banerjee; *First Assistant Dir.*: Dev Benegal; *Phot.*: Govind Nihalani; *Ed.*: Bhanudas Divkar; *Sound*: Hitendra Ghosh.

TRIKAL (PAST, PRESENT, FUTURE)   1985   140 MIN.

Prod. Co.: Blaze Film Enterprises; *Dir.*: Shyam Benegal; *Ex. Prod.*: Silloo F. Variava, Gulshan M. Bijlani; *Prod.*: Lalit M. Bijlani, Freni M. Variava; *Story and Script*: Shyam Benegal; *Dialogue*: Shama Zaidi; *Lyrics*: Ila Arun; *Songs*: Remo Fernandes; *Art Dir.*: Nitish Roy; *Phot.*: Ashok Mehta; *Ed.*: Bhanudas Divkar; *Sound*: Hitendra Ghosh; *Music*: Vanraj Bhatia.
Actors: Leela Naidu (Donna Maria), Neena Gupta (Milagrenia), Anita Kanwar, Soni Razdan, Darlip Tahil, K. K. Raina, Kunal Kapoor, Keith Stevenson, Naseeruddin Shah (the adult Ruiz Pereira), Kulbhushan Kharbanda (Vijay Singh Rane, Kustoba Rane).

SUSMAN (THE ESSENCE)   1986   128 MIN.

Prod. Co.: Association of Co-operatives and Apex Society of Handloom, Sahyadri Films; *Dir.*: Shyam Benegal; *Ex. Prod.*: S. K. Mishra, V. K. Agnihotri, P. P. Williams,

A. S. Narayana Swamy, A. Didar Singh; *Prod*.: Shyam Benegal/Sahyadri Films; *Script*: Shama Zaidi; *Lyrics*: Sant Kabir; *Singers*: K. V. Kuruvilla, Ila Arun; Sangeet Martand Pandit Jasraj sings poems of Kabir composed by Sharang Dev; *Art Dir*.: Nitish Roy; *Phot*.: Ashok Mehta; *Ed*.: Bhanudas Divkar; *Sound*: S. W. Deshpande, Hitendra Ghosh; *Music*: Sharang Dev, Vanraj Bhatia.

Actors: Shabana Azmi (Gauramma), Om Puri (Ramulu), Kulbhushan Kharbanda (Narasimha), Neena Gupta (Mandira Rai), Mohan Agashe (Co-op President), Pallavi Joshi (Chinna), K. K. Raina, Annu Kapoor, Harish Patel, Ila Arun (Janaki).

BHARAT EK KHOJ (THE DISCOVERY OF INDIA)   1988
APPROX. 53 HRS

ANTARNAAD (INNER VOICE)   1992   166 MIN.

Prod. Co.: Suhetu Films; *Dir*.: Shyam Benegal; *Prod*.: Raj Pius, Anil Mani; *Script*: Shama Zaidi, Sunil Shanbag, inspired by the work of Pandurang Shastri Athavale; *Lyrics*: Vasant Dev, Ila Arun; *Art Dir*.: Samir Chanda; *Costumes*: Pia Benegal; *Phot*.: V. K. Murthy; *Ed*.: Sutanu Gupta; Sound: Ashwyn Balsaver; *Music*: Vanraj Bhatia.
Actors: Shabana Azmi, Kulbhushan Kharbanda, Om Puri, K. K. Raina, Ravi Jhankal, Ila Arun.

SURAJ KA SATVAN GHODA (THE SEVENTH HORSE OF
THE SUN)   1992   129 MIN.

Prod. Co.: National Film Development Corporation, Doordarshan; *Dir*.: Shyam Benegal; *Script*: Shama Zaidi from Dharmvir Bharati's novel; *Lyrics*: Vasant Dev; *Singers*: Udit Narayan, Kavita Krishnamurthy, Shubha Joshi; *Art Dir*.: Nitish Roy; *Paintings*: Gulam Mohammed Sheikh; *Costumes*: Pia Benegal; *Phot*.: Piyush Shah; *Ed*.: Bhanudas Divkar; *Sound*: Ashwyn Balsaver, Hitendra Ghosh; *Music*: Vanraj Bhatia.
Actors: Amrish Puri (Mahesar Dalal), Neena Gupta (Satti), Ila Arun (Lily's mother), K. K. Raina (Manek's brother), Pallavi Joshi (Lily), Rajeshwari Sachdev (Jamuna), Ravi Jhankal (Ramdhan), Lalit Tiwari (Chaman Thakur), Raghuvir Yadav (Shyam), Riju Bajaj (Tanna), Rajit Kapur (Manek Mulla).

MAMMO   1994   119 MIN.

Prod. Co.: Doordarshan, National Film Development Corporation; *Dir*.: Shyam Benegal; *Ex. Prod*.: Raj Pius; *Story*: Khalid Mohamed; *Script*: Kalid Mohamed, Shama Zaidi, Javed Siddiqui; *Lyrics*: Gulzar; *Singer*: Jagjit Singh; *Art Dir*.: Samir

Chanda; *Costumes*: Pia Benegal; *Phot.*: Prasann Jain; *Ed.*: Aseem Sinha; *Sound*: Ashwyn Balsaver, Hitendra Ghosh; *Music*: Vanraj Bhatia.

Actors: Farida Jalal (Mammo/Mahmooda Begum), Surekha Sikri Rege (Fayyazi), Amit Phalke (Young Riyaz), Himani Shivpuri (Anwari), Srivallabh Vyas (Sabir), Rajit Kapur (Adult Riyaz), Lalit Tiwari (Riyaz's father), Rajeshwari Sachdev (Riyaz's mother).

THE MAKING OF THE MAHATMA   1996   145 MIN.

Prod. Co.: National Film Development Corporation, South African Broadcasting Corporation; *Dir.*: Shyam Benegal; *Ex. Prod.*: Ravi Gupta, Anant Singh; *Story*: Fatima Meer's book *The Apprenticeship of a Mahatma*; *Script*: Fatima Meer in collaboration with Shyam Benegal and Shama Zaidi; *Costumes*: Pia Benegal, Diana Chilliers; *Phot.*: Ashok Mehta; *Ed.*: Avril Beukes; *Music*: Vanraj Bhatia.

Actors: Rajit Kapur (Gandhi), Pallavi Joshi (Kasturba), Keith Stevenson (Rustomjee), Paul Slabolepszy (Smuts), Himal Devnarain (Cachalla), Strini Pillai (Dada Abdullah), Charles Pillai (Thambi Naidoo), Siraj Khan (Adult Harilal), Prean Naidoo (Vincent Lawrence), John Whiteley (Harry Escombe), Dale Cutts (Rev. Baker).

SARDARI BEGUM   1996   117 MIN.

Prod. Co.: Plus Channel (India); *Dir.*: Shyam Benegal; *Prod.*: Amit Khanna, Mahesh Bhatt; *Story and Screenplay*: Khalid Mohamed; *Additional Screenplay and Dialogue*: Shama Zaidi; *Lyrics*: Javed Akhtar; *Singers*: Asha Bhosle, Subha Joshi, Aarti Ankalikar-Tikekar, Poorva Joshi; *Choreo.*: Roshan Kumari; *Costumes*: Pia Benegal; *Art Dir.*: Samir Chanda; *Phot.*: Sanjay Dharankar; *Ed.*: Aseem Sinha; *Audio*: Ashwyn Balsaver; *Music*: Vanraj Bhatia.

Actors: Amrish Puri (Hemraj), Kiron Kher (Sardari Begum), Smriti Mishra (Younger Sardari), Shrivallabh Vyas (Jabbar Abbasi), Syed Khurshid (Young Jabbar), Rajit Kapur (Sadiq Moosvi), Rajeshwari Sachdev (Sakina), Salim Ghouse (Manik Sen), Surekha Sikri Rege (Iddan Bai), S. M. Zaheer (Fateh Khan), Uttara Baokar (Hemraj's wife), Ahmed Khan (Mehmood Abbasi), Ashok Lath (Mark d'Cruz), Kumud Mishra (Amode Bajaj), Ravi Jhankal (Police Inspector), Javed Khan (Maulvi), Seema Bhargava (Kulsum's mother), Rajina Rai Bisaria (Tehzeeb Abbasi).

SAMAR (CONFLICT)   1999   121 MIN.

Prod. Co.: National Film Development Corporation/Ministry of Welfare; *Dir.*: Shyam Benegal; *Prod.*: Raj Pius; *Script and Dialogue*: Ashok Mishra, based on case studies by Harsh Mandar; *Costumes*: Pia Benegal; *Art Dir*.: Samvi Chanda; *Phot*.: Rajen Kothari; *Ed*.: Aseem Sinha; *Audio*: Ashwyn Balsaver; *Re-recording*: Hitendra Ghosh; *Music*: Vanraj Bhatia.

Actors: Rajeshwari Sachdev (Uma and Dulari), Seema Biswas (Real Dulari), Kishore Kadam (Kishore and Nathu), Raghuvir Yadav (Real Nathu), Ravi Jhankal (Murali Singh and Chamak Singh), Rajit Kapur (Kartik, the film director), Ashok Mishra (Ashok Mishra, the scriptwriter), Divya Dutta (Divya and Chuniya), Yashpal Sharma (Real Ramesh Singh), Ruby Bhatt (Ramesh Singh's wife), Neelesh Malaviya (Actor Ramesh Singh), Saroj Sharma (Saroj and Leekavati), Rajkamal Nayak (Actor Babba), Ravilal Sangre (Real Babba), Rakesh Sahu (Actor Santuram), Sandeep Shrivastava (Real Santuram), Satosh Pandey (Actor Ramlal), Copal Dubey (Real Ramlal), Sadashiv Amrapurkar (DIG Hiralal).

HARI-BHARI (FERTILITY)   2000   134 MIN.

Prod. Co.: National Film Development Corporation/Ministry of Health; *Dir*.: Shyam Benegal; *Ex. Prod*.: Raj Pius, Anil Pandit (for NFDC); *Script*: Shama Zaidi, Priya Chandrasekar; *Dialogue*: Shama Zaidi; *Lyrics*: Maya Govind; *Singers*: Richa Sharma, Nusrat Wasim, Saira Khan, Rajeshwari Sachdev, Raghuvir Yadav, Ritika Sahni; *Costumes*: Pia Benegal; *Art Dir*.: Samir Chanda; *Phot*.: Rajen Kothari; *Ed*.: Aseem Sinha; *Sound*: Ashwyn Balsaver; *Re-mixing*: Hitendra Ghosh; *Music*: Vanraj Bhatia.

Actors: Shabana Azmi (Ghazala), Rajit Kapur (Khurshid), Rajeshwari Sachdev (Salma), Surekha Sikri Rege (Hasina), Nandita Das (Afsana), Alka Tridevi (Najma), Meghna Kothari (Young Hasina), Seema Bhargava (Rampyari), Lalit Tiwari (Khaleel), Srivallabh Vyas (Munir).

ZUBEIDAA   2000   150 MIN.

Prod. Co.: FKR Productions; *Dir*.: Shyam Benegal; *Ex. Prod*.: Raj Pius; *Prod*.: Farouq Rattonsey; *Story and Script*: Khalid Mohamed; *Dialogue*: Javed Siddique; *Creative Consultant/Associate Dir*.: Shama Zaidi; *Lyrics*: Javed Akhtar; *Singers*: Lata Mangeshkar, Kavita Krishnamurthy, Alka Yagnik, Udit Narain, Richa Sharma, Sukhwinder Singh; *Choreo*.: Bhushan Lakhandari, Ewa Maria Cherukuru; *Costumes*: Pia Benegal; *Art Dir*.: Samir Chanda; *Phot*.: Rajen Kothari; *Ed*.: Aseem Sinha; *Sound*: Ashwyn Balsaver; *Re-mixing*: Hitendra Ghosh; *Music*: A. R. Rahman.

Actors: Karisma Kapoor (Zubeidaa), Rekha (Mandiri Devi), Manoj Bajpai (Raja Vijandra Singh/Victor), Rajit Kapur (Riyaz Masud), Surekha Sikri Rege (Fayyazi), Amrish Puri (Suleiman Seth), Farida Jalal (Mammo), Shakti Kapoor (Dance Master Hiralal), Lillete Dubey (Rose Davenport), Ravi Jhankal (Girivar Singh),

Smriti Mishra (Sardari Begum), S. M. Zaheer (Sajid Masud), Seema Bhargava, Parzaan Dastur (Young Riyaz), Devendra Malhotra (Old Maharaja), Kiran Rathore (Maid), Raj Dedhia (Young Rohan), Raahul Maharya (Uday Singh), Vinod Sharawat (Mehboob Alam).

BOSE: THE FORGOTTEN HERO   2005   228 MIN.

Prod. Co.: Sahara India Media Communication Ltd, Shyam Benegal Sahyadri Films; *Dir.*: Shyam Benegal; *Ex. Prod.*: Raj Pius; *Prod.*: Barbara von Wrangell; *Script*: Atul Tiwari, Shama Zaidi; *Costumes*: Pia Benegal; *Art Dir.*: Samir Chanda; *Phot.*: Rajen Kothari; *Sound*: Ashwyn Balsaver; *Music*: A. R. Rahman.
Actors: Sachin Khedekar (Subhash Chandra Bose), Surendra Rajan (Gandhi), Jishu Sengupt (Sisir Bose), Divya Dutta (Ila Bose), Pankaj Berry (Abid Khan), Rajpal Yadav (Bhagatram Talwar), Lalit Tiwari (Checkpost policeman), Christian Willis (Jail superintendent), Arindam Sil (Jail warden), Ahahahmed Khan (Mian Akbar), Howard Lee (Governor of Bengal), Kulbhushan Kharbanda (Uttamchand Malhotra), Rajeshwari Sachdev (Captain Lakshmi Seghal), Rajit Kapur (Abid Hasan), Pratap Sharm (Nehru), Udo Schenk (Adolf Hitler).

Appendix 2
Films Cited in the Text

This list only mentions Indian films and television series, excluding those of Shyam Benegal.

23rd March 1931 Shaheed (23rd March 1931: Martyr), Guddu Dhanoa, 2002
36 Chowringhee Lane, Aparna Sen, 1981
Aag (Fire), Raj Kapoor, 1948
Aakrosh (Cry of the Wounded), Govind Nihalani, 1980
Aanken (Eyes), Vipul Shah, 2002
Agantuk (The Stranger), Satyajit Ray, 1991
Agneepath (Path of Fire), Mukul S. Anand, 1990
Ajooba, Shashi Kapoor, 1991
Akaler Sandhaney (In Search of Famine), Mrinal Sen, 1980
Alam Ara (World-Adorning), Ardeshir Irani, 1931
Amar Akbar Anthony, Manmohan Desai, 1977
Andaz (A Matter of Style), Mehboob Khan, 1949
Aparajito (The Unvanquished), Satyajit Ray, 1956
Apur Sansar (The World of Apu), Satyajit Ray, 1959
Aranyer Din Ratri (Days and Nights in the Forest), Satyajit Ray, 1969
Ardh Satya (The Half-Truth), Govind Nihalani, 1983
Asoka, Santosh Sivan, 2001
Aurat (Woman), Mehboob Khan, 1940
Awara (The Vagabond), Raj Kapoor, 1951
Baazi (The Wager), Guru Dutt, 1951
Balanagamma, C. Pullaiah, 1942
Bandini (The Caged), Bimal Roy, 1963
Bandit Queen, Shekhar Kapur, 1994
Barsaat (Rain), Raj Kapoor, 1949
Bhavni Bhavai (A Folk Tale), Ketan Mehta, 1980
Bhuvan Shome, Mrinal Sen, 1969
Bombay, Mani Ratnam, 1995
Charulata, Satyajit Ray, 1964
Chaudhvin Ka Chand (Full Moon), M. Sadiq/Guru Dutt, 1960
China Gate, Rajkumar Santoshi, 1998

Coolie, Manmohan Desai, 1983

Coolie No. 1, David Dhawan, 1995

Damini, Rajkumar Santoshi, 1993

Deedar (Vision), Nitin Bose, 1951

Deewar (The Wall), Yash Chopra, 1975

Desher Mati (The Motherland), Nitin Bose, 1938

Devdas, Naresh Chandra Mitra, 1928

Devdas, P. C. Barua, 1935

Devdas, Bimal Roy, 1955

Devdas, Chashi Nazrul Islam, 1982

Devdas, Sanjay Leela Bhansali, 2002

Dharti Ke Lal (Children of the Earth), K. A. Abbas, 1946

Dil Se (From the Heart), Mani Ratnam, 1998

Dilwale Dulhania Le Jayange (The Brave-Hearted Will Take the Bride), Aditya Chopra, 1995

Do Bigha Zameen (Two Acres of Land), Bimal Roy, 1953

Duvidha (In Two Minds), Mani Kaul, 1973

Earth, Deepa Mehta, 1998

Ek Din Achanak (Suddenly One Day), Mrinal Sen, 1988

Elippathayam (The Rat Trap), Adoor Gopalakrishnan, 1981

Fire, Deepa Mehta, 1996

Fiza, Khalid Mohamed, 2001

Gaja Gamini, M. F. Husain, 2000

Garam Hawa (Hot Winds), M. S. Sathyu, 1973

Genesis, Mrinal Sen, 1986

Ghare Baire (The Home and the World), Satyajit Ray, 1984

Ghulami (Slavery), J. P. Dutta, 1985

Guddi (Darling Child), Hrishikesh Mukherjee, 1971

Hey! Ram, Kamal Haasan, 2000

Hum Paanch (We Five), Bapu, 1980

Hu Tu Tu, Gulzar, 1999

In Custody, Ismail Merchant, 1993

Indian, Shankar, 1996

Inner Eye, The, Satyajit Ray, 1972

Jalsaghar (The Music Room), Satyajit Ray, 1958

Jukti Takko Aar Gappo (Reason, Debate and a Story), Ritwik Ghatak, 1974

Junglee (The Savage), Subodh Mukherjee, 1961

Kaagaz Ke Phool (Pale Flowers), Guru Dutt, 1959

Kabhi Kabhie (Sometimes), Yash Chopra, 1976

Kabhi Khushi Kabhie Gham (Sometimes Happiness, Sometimes Sorrow), Karan Johar, 2001

Kalpana (Imagination), Uday Shankar, 1948

Kannathil Muthamitta (A Peck on the Cheek), Mani Ratnam, 2002
Karan Arjun (Karan and Arjun), Rakesh Roshan, 1995
Kharij (The Case is Closed), Mrinal Sen, 1982
Khayal Gatha (Khayal Saga), Kumar Shahani, 1988
Kuch Kuch Hota Hai (Something is Happening), Karan Johar, 1998
Lagaan (Once Upon a Time in India/The Tax), Ashutosh Gowariker, 2001
Lakhrani, Vishram Bedekar, 1945
Legend of Bhagat Singh, The, Rajkumar Santoshi, 2002
Lokshahir Ramjoshi, Baburao Painter and V. Shantaram, 1947
Maachis (Matches), Gulzar, 1996
Mahabharata, B. R. Chopra, 1988–90
Masoom (Innocent), Shekhar Kapur, 1982
Maya Darpan (Mirror of Illusion), Kumar Shahani, 1972
Maya Memsaab (The Enchanting Illusion), Ketan Mehta, 1992
Meghe Dhaka Tara (The Cloud-Capped Star), Ritwik Ghatak, 1960
Mirch Masala (A Touch of Spice), Ketan Mehta, 1985
Moksha (Salvation), Ashok Mehta, 2001
Monsoon Wedding, Mira Nair, 2001
Mother India, Mehboob Khan, 1957
Mr and Mrs Iyer, Aparna Sen, 2002
Mr India, Shekhar Kapur, 1987
Mughal-E-Azam (The Great Mughal), K. Asif, 1960
Muqaddar Ka Sikandar (Blessed by Destiny), Prakash Mehra, 1978
Naseeb (Destiny), Manmohan Desai, 1982
Nayak (The Hero), Satyajit Ray, 1966
Nayakan (The Hero), Mani Ratnam, 1987
Other Story, The, Anand Patwardhan, 1994
Pakeezah (Pure Heart), Kamal Amrohi, 1971
Parama, Aparna Sen, 1985
Parash Pathar (The Philosopher's Stone), Satyajit Ray, 1957
Pardes (Foreign Land), Subhash Ghai, 1997
Pather Panchali (Song of the Road), Satyajit Ray, 1955
Pitru Putra Aur Dharamyudh (Father, Son and Holy War), Anand Patwardhan, 1994
Pyaasa (Eternal Thirst), Guru Dutt, 1957
Rabindranath Tagore, Satyajit Ray, 1961
Raja Harischandra, D. G. Phalke, 1917
Raja Hindustani, Dharmesh Darshan, 1996
Ramayana, Ramanand Sagar, 1986–8
Ram Ke Naam (In the Name of God), Anand Patwardhan, 1992
Rangeela (Colourful), Ramgopal Verma, 1995
Roja (The Rose), Mani Ratnam, 1992

Roti (Bread), Mehboob Khan, 1942

Rudaali (The Mourner), Kalpana Lajmi, 1992

Saathiya (Companion), Shaad Ali, 2002

Sadgati (Deliverance), Satyajit Ray, 1981

Sahib Bibi Aur Ghulam (King, Queen, Knave), Abrar Alvi/Guru Dutt, 1962

Salaam Bombay!, Mira Nair, 1988

Sant Tukaram, V. Damle and S. Fattelal, 1936

Sardar, Ketan Mehta, 1993

Satya (The Other Side of Truth), Ramgopal Verma, 2000

Shaheed Bhagat Singh (The Martyr Bhagat Singh), Tarun Wadhwaa, 2002

Shaheed-E-Azam (The Great Martyr), Sukumar Nair, 2002

Shakti (The Strength), Ramesh Sippy, 1982

Shatranj Ke Khiladi (The Chess Players), Satyajit Ray, 1977

Sholay (Flames of the Sun), Ramesh Sippy, 1975

Silsila (The Affair), Yash Chopra, 1981

Sujata (The Well-Born), Bimal Roy, 1959

Tamas (The Darkness), Govind Nihalani, 1986

Tarang (Wages and Profit), Kumar Shahani, 1984

Teesri Kasam (The Third Vow), Basu Bhattacharya, 1966

Thampu (The Circus Tent), G. Aravindan, 1978

Trishul (Trident), Yash Chopra, 1978

Umrao Jaan, Muzaffar Ali, 1981

Uski Roti (A Day's Bread), Mani Kaul, 1969

Utsav (The Festival), Girish Karnad, 1984

Vamsha Vriksha (The Genealogical Tree), Girish Karnad and B. V. Karanth, 1971

Vanaprastham (The Last Dance), Shaji Karun, 1999

Vijeta (Victory), Govind Nihalani, 1982

War and Peace, Anand Patwardhan, 2001

Zanjeer (The Chain), Prakash Mehra, 1973

Bibliography

Andaya, Barbara Watson and Leonard Y. Andaya (1982), *A History of Malaysia*, London: Macmillan.

Arora, Poonam (1994), 'The Production of Third World Subjects for First World Consumption: *Salaam Bombay* and *Parama*', in Diane Carson, Linda Dittmar and Janice R. Welsch (eds), *Multiple Voices in Feminist Film Criticism*, Minneapolis: University of Minnesota Press, 293-304.

Ashton, Stephen (1985), *Indian Independence*, London: Batsford.

Banerji, Bibhutibhushan (1987), *Pather Panchali* (translated by T. W. Clark and Tarapada Mukherji), London: Lokamaya Press.

Benegal, Shyam (1998), *Satyajit Ray: A Film by Shyam Benegal*, Calcutta: Seagull Books (script reconstructed by Alaknanda Datta and Samik Bandyopadhyay).

—— (2002), *Bharat Ek Khoj*, http://www.shyambenegal.com/bharatekkhoj.html (accessed 10 February 2002).

Bharucha, Rustom (1989), 'Haraam Bombay!', *Economic and Political Weekly*, 10 June, 1275-9.

—— (1991), 'A View From India', in David Williams (ed.), *Peter Brook and the Mahabharata: Critical Perspectives*, London: Routledge, 228-52.

Bond, Ruskin (2002), *A Flight of Pigeons*, New Delhi: Viking.

Brandon, James R. (ed.) (1993), *The Cambridge Guide to Asian Theatre*, Cambridge: Cambridge University Press.

Chakravarty, Sumita S. (1993), *National Identity in Indian Popular Cinema, 1947-1987*, Austin: University of Texas Press.

Chatterjee, Partha (1993), *The Nation and its Fragments: Colonial and Postcolonial Histories*, Princeton: Princeton University Press.

Cooper, Darius (2000), *The Cinema of Satyajit Ray: Between Tradition and Modernity*, Cambridge: Cambridge University Press.

Das Gupta, Chidananda (1980), 'New Directions in Indian Cinema', *Film Quarterly*, 34: 1, 32-42.

—— (1991), *The Painted Face: Studies in India's Popular Cinema*, New Delhi: Roli Books.

Datta, Sangeeta (2002), *Shyam Benegal*, London: British Film Institute.

de Bary, William Theodore (1958), *Sources of Indian Tradition*, New York: Columbia University Press.

Dirks, Nicholas B. (1995), '*The Home and the World*: The Invention of Modernity in Colonial India', in Robert A. Rosenstone (ed.), *Revisioning History:*

Film and the Construction of a New Past, Princeton: Princeton University Press, 44–63.

Dwyer, Rachel (2002), *Yash Chopra*, London: British Film Institute.

—— and Divia Patel (2002), *Cinema India: The Visual Culture of Hindi Film*, New Brunswick: Rutger University Press.

Eisenstein, Sergei (1951), *Film Form: Essays in Film Theory* (edited and translated by Jay Leyda), London: Dennis Dobson.

Etem, Faria (2002), 'No Borders for *Devdas*', *Cinemaya*, 56–7, 92–6.

Gandhi, M. K. (1931) 'Gandhi on Singh', in *Kamat's Potpourri*, http://www.kamat.com/mmgandhi/onbhagatsing.htm (accessed 21 October 2005).

—— (1982), *An Autobiography, or The Story of My Experiments with Truth*, London: Penguin.

Gandhy, Behroze and Rosie Thomas (1991), 'Three Indian Film Stars', in Christine Gledhill (ed.), *Stardom: Industry of Desire*, London: Routledge, 107–31.

Garga, Bhagwan Das (1996), *So Many Cinemas: The Motion Picture in India*, Mumbai: Eminent Designs.

Gillett, John (1976), '*Ankur*', *Sight and Sound*, 45: 2, 123.

Greenough, Paul (1995), 'Nation, Economy, and Tradition Displayed: The Indian Crafts Museum, New Delhi', in Carol A. Breckenridge (ed.), *Consuming Modernity: Public Culture in a South Asian World*, Minneapolis: University of Minnesota Press, 216–48.

Gujadhur, Ashley (2005), '*The Legend of Bhagat Singh*', *Planet Bollywood*, http://www.planetbollywood.com/Film/LegendofBhagatSingh/index.html (accessed 21 October 2005).

Hood, John W. (2000), *The Essential Mystery: Major Filmmakers of Indian Art Cinema*, Hyderabad: Orient Longman.

Horton, Andrew (1997), '"What Do Our Souls Seek?": An Interview With Theo Angelopoulos', in Andrew Horton (ed.), *The Last Modernist: The Films of Theo Angelopoulos*, Trowbridge, Wiltshire: Flicks Books, 96–110.

Irwin, Robert (1995), *The Arabian Nights: A Companion*, London: Penguin.

Jairazbhoy, N. A. (1975), 'Music', in A. L. Basham (ed.), *A Cultural History of India*, Delhi: Oxford University Press, 212–42.

Jasraj, Pandit (1993), *Pandit Jasraj, vocal* (Compact disc), Monument Records, MRCD 1009.

Jha, Suman K. (2003), 'Gujarati Primer', *The Times of India*, 2 January, 12.

Jordens, J. T. F. (1975), 'Medieval Hindu Devotionalism', in A. L. Basham (ed.), *A Cultural History of India*, Delhi: Oxford University Press, 266–80.

Kaali, Sundar (2000), 'Narrating Seduction: Vicissitudes of the Sexed Subject in Tamil Nativity Film', in Ravi S. Vasudevan (ed.), *Making Meaning in Indian Cinema*, New Delhi: Oxford University Press, 168–90.

Kabir, Nasreen Munni (1996), *Guru Dutt: A Life in Cinema*, Delhi: Oxford University Press.

—— (2001), *Bollywood: The Indian Cinema Story*, London: Channel 4 Books.

Kakar, Sudhir (1989), *Intimate Relations: Exploring Indian Sexuality*, New Delhi: Penguin.

Kamat, Jyotsna (2005), 'Martyrdom of Sardar Bhagat Singh', in *Kamat's Potpourri*, http://www.kamat.com/karlanga/itihas/sbsingh.htm (accessed 21 October 2005).

Kapur, Anuradha (1990), *Actors, Pilgrims, Kings and Gods: The Ramlila at Ramnagar*, Calcutta: Seagull Books.

Kazmi, Nikhat (1999), 'Mr India's Virgin Queen', *The Times of India*, 15 January, 20.

Khandpur, K. L. (1985), 'Compulsory Screening of Documentaries in India', in T. M. Ramachandran (ed.), *70 Years of Indian Cinema (1913-1983)*, Bombay: Cinema India-International, 505-11.

Lannoy, Richard (1971), *The Speaking Tree: A Study of Indian Culture and Society*, London: Oxford University Press.

Lutgendorf, Philip (2005a), '*Hey! Ram*', in *Philip's Fil-ums: Notes on Indian Popular Cinema*, http://uiowa.edu/~incinema/HEYRAM.html (accessed 21 October 2005).

—— (2005b), '*Kalyug*', in *Philip's Fil-ums: Notes on Indian Popular Cinema*, http://uiowa.edu/~incinema/Kalyug.html (accessed 21 October 2005).

Malcolm, Derek (1986), 'India's Middle Cinema', *Sight and Sound*, 55: 3, 172-4.

Mansfield, Peter (1992), *The Arabs*, London: Penguin.

Masselos, Jim (1993), *Indian Nationalism: An History* (Third revised edition), New Delhi: Sterling Publishers.

Masud, Iqbal (1985), 'The Cinema of Shyam Benegal', in T. M. Ramachandran (ed.), *70 Years of Indian Cinema*, Bombay: Cinema India-International, 177-86.

—— (1995), 'The Great Four of the Golden Fifties', in Aruna Vasudev (ed.), *Frames of Mind: Reflections on Indian Cinema*, New Delhi: UBS Publishers' Distributors, 29-41.

—— and Bikram Singh (1989), 'Growing-up Pains? Critics on the Not-so-New-Cinema', *Cinema in India*, 3: 1, 22-6.

Mazumdar, Ranjani (1991), 'Dialectic of Public and Private: Representation of Women in *Bhoomika* and *Mirch Masala*', *Economic and Political Weekly*, 26 October, WS-81-4.

Milne, Tom (1977), 'Indian Gambits', *Sight and Sound*, 46: 2, 94-9.

Mishra, Vijay (1992), 'Decentering History: Some Versions of Bombay Cinema', *East-West Film Journal*, 6: 1, 111-55.

—— (2002), *Bollywood Cinema: Temples of Desire*, New York: Routledge.

Mukherjee, Meenakshi (1994), *Realism and Reality: The Novel and Society in India*, New Delhi: Oxford University Press.

Nair, Suresh (1999), 'God, Women, Power!', *The Times of India*, Matinee Section, 22 January, 6.

Nandy, Ashis (1994), *The Illegitimacy of Nationalism*, Delhi: Oxford University Press.

—— (1995), 'An Intelligent Critic's Guide to Indian Cinema', in *The Savage Freud and Other Essays on Possible and Retrievable Selves*, Delhi: Oxford University Press, 196–236.

—— (ed.) (1998), *The Secret Politics of Our Desires: Innocence, Culpability and Indian Popular Cinema*, Delhi: Oxford University Press.

—— (2001), 'Invitation to an Antique Death: The Journey of Pramathesh Barua as the Origin of the Terribly Effeminate, Maudlin, Self-destructive Heroes of Indian Cinema', in Rachel Dwyer and Christopher Pinney (eds), *Pleasure and the Nation: The History, Politics and Consumption of Public Culture in India*, New Delhi: Oxford University Press, 139–60.

—— Shikha Trivedy, Shail Mayaram and Achyut Yagnik (1995), *Creating a Nationality: The Ramjanmabhumi Movement and Fear of the Self*, Delhi: Oxford University Press.

Nehru, Jawaharlal (1960), *The Discovery of India* (edited by Robert I. Crane), New York: Anchor Books.

Nichols, Bill (1991), *Representing Reality: Issues and Concepts in Documentary*, Bloomington: Indian University Press.

Niranjana, Tejaswini and S.V. Srinivas (1996), 'Managing the Crisis: *Bharateeyudu* and the Ambivalence of Being "Indian"', *Economic and Political Weekly*, 30 November, 3129–34.

O'Flaherty, Wendy Doniger (ed.) (1981), *The Rig Veda*, London: Penguin.

Prasad, M. Madhava (1998), *Ideology of the Hindi Film: A Historical Construction*, New Delhi: Oxford University Press.

Pudovkin, V. I. (1949), *Film Technique and Film Acting* (translated by Ivor Montagu), New York: Bonanza Books.

Rajadhyaksha, Ashish (1984), 'Filmotsav '84', *Framework*, 25, 104–8.

—— (1996), 'India: Filming the Nation', in Geoffrey Nowell-Smith (ed.), *The Oxford History of World Cinema*, Oxford: Oxford University Press, 678–89.

—— (1998), 'Indian Cinema', in John Hill and Pamela Church Gibson (eds), *The Oxford Guide to Film Studies*, Oxford: Oxford University Press, 535–40.

—— (2000), 'Viewership and Democracy in the Cinema', in Ravi S. Vasudevan (ed.), *Making Meaning in Indian Cinema*, New Delhi: Oxford University Press, 267–96.

—— and Paul Willemen (1999), *Encyclopaedia of Indian Cinema* (Revised edition), London: British Film Institute/New Delhi: Oxford University Press.

Rao, Nityanand (1996), 'So, Who Are These Konkanis?', *Press Trust of India*, http://www.culture.konkani.com/Historical/77 (accessed 6 August 1999).

Ray, Satyajit (1976), 'Four and a Quarter', in *Our Films, Their Films*, Hyderabad: Orient Longman, 100–7.

—— (1982), 'Under Western Eyes', *Sight and Sound*, 51: 4, 268–74.

Reisz, Karel and Gavin Millar (1968), *The Technique of Film Editing* (Enlarged edition), London: Focal Press.

Richman, Paula (ed.) (1991), *Many Ramayanas: The Diversity of a Narrative Tradition in South India*, Berkeley: University of California Press.

Robinson, Andrew (1989), *Satyajit Ray: The Inner Eye*, London: André Deutsch.

Rushdie, Salman (1981), *Midnight's Children*, London: Jonathan Cape.

—— (1995), *The Moor's Last Sigh*, London: Jonathan Cape.

—— (2002), *Step Across This Line: Collected Non-Fiction 1992-2002*, London: Jonathan Cape.

Sathe, Vasant (1999), 'Reform Hindu Society to Stop Conversion', *The Times of India*, 22 January, 6.

Sheikh, Gulam Mohammed (1983), 'Mobile Vision: Some Synoptic Comments', *Journal of Arts and Ideas*, 5, 43-52.

—— (1993), 'The Viewer's View: Looking at Pictures', in Tejaswini Niranjana, P. Sudhir and Vivek Dhareshwar (eds), *Interrogating Modernity: Culture and Colonialism in India*, Calcutta: Seagull Books, 143-54.

—— (1997), 'The Making of a Visual Language', *Journal of Arts and Ideas*, 30-1, 7-32.

Stam, Robert (2000), *Film Theory: An Introduction*, Malden, Mass.: Blackwell.

Tagore, Rabindranath (1936), '*Karna and Kunti*', in *Collected Poems and Plays of Rabindranath Tagore*, Macmillan: London, 561-5.

Thomas, Rosie (1987), 'India: Mythologies and Modern India', in William Luhr (ed.), *World Cinema since 1945*, New York: Ungar, 301-29.

Thoraval, Yves (2000), *The Cinemas of India*, New Delhi: Macmillan.

Times Foundation (2004), 'Shyam Benegal Receives Indira Gandhi Award', http://www.timesfoundation.indiatimes.com/articleshow/907761.cms (accessed 6 June 2005).

Times of India, The (1999) 'The Play Goes On' (Editorial), 22 January, 10.

Times of India, The (2001), '*Bharat Ek Khoj* on DD-1', 30 April, http://www. bharatvani.org/general_inbox/pramod/bharatekkhoj.html (accessed 29 March 2003).

Upadhye, A. N. (1975), 'Jainism', in A. L. Basham (ed.), *A Cultural History of India*, Delhi: Oxford University Press, 100-10.

van der Heide, Bill (1996), 'Experiencing India: A Personal History', *Media International Australia*, 80, 53-9.

van der Heide, William (2002), *Malaysian Cinema, Asian Film: Border Crossings and National Cultures*, Amsterdam: Amsterdam University Press.

Vasudev, Aruna (1978), *Liberty and Licence in the Indian Cinema*, New Delhi: Vikas Publishing House.

—— (1986), *The New Indian Cinema*, New Delhi: Macmillan India.

Warder, A. K. (1975), 'Classical Literature', in A. L. Basham (ed.), *A Cultural History of India*, Delhi: Oxford University Press, 170-96.

Index